A sophisticated and engaging ethnographic account of the Palestinian citizens of Israel, the first to be published since the 1970s, *Overlooking Nazareth* examines specific situations of friction, conflict and cooperation in Natzerat Illit. This Israeli new town is built on formerly Palestinian land, just outside the biblical town of Nazareth, and has a population of 25,000 (Jewish) Israelis and 3,500 Palestinians. Dr Rabinowitz, who has written widely on the current political situation in Israel and has conducted extensive fieldwork in the Galilee, describes his study as a guided walk along a border, a sketch of interfaces, 'where the complex, often paradoxical aspects of the border situation are negotiated and acted out most vividly'. He highlights the extent to which anti-Palestinian sentiments for which the town is known actually reflect widespread views of most Israelis. Selected case studies investigate the real-estate market in the town, the ways in which both Israelis and Palestinians view issues of territory and territorial control, segregated education, hospitality and more. There are detailed biographical accounts of three Palestinian residents – a medical doctor, a basketball coach and a local politician.

This is a major contribution to our understanding of the confrontation between Israelis and Palestinians, in which the grand causes and effects have been transposed to a more intimate as well as pragmatic level. On a wider theoretical level, *Overlooking Nazareth* offers a powerful, reflexive critique of liberalism, leading to fresh insights into notions of ethnicity, nationalism and anthropological traditions.

Cambridge Studies in Social and Cultural Anthropology

105

OVERLOOKING NAZARETH

Cambridge Studies in Social and Cultural Anthropology

The monograph series Cambridge Studies in Social and Cultural Anthropology publishes analytical ethnographies, comparative works and contributions to theory. All combine an expert and critical command of ethnography and a sophisticated engagement with current theoretical debates.

A list of books in the series will be found at the end of the volume.

Founding Editor
Jack Goody, University of Cambridge

OVERLOOKING NAZARETH

The ethnography of exclusion in Galilee

DAN RABINOWITZ

Hebrew University, Jerusalem

CAMBRIDGE
UNIVERSITY PRESS

Published by the Press Syndicate of the University of Cambridge
The Pitt Building, Trumpington Street, Cambridge CB2 1RP
40 West 20th Street, New York, NY 10011-4211, USA
10 Stamford Road, Oakleigh, Melbourne 3166, Australia

First published 1997

Printed in Great Britain at the University Press, Cambridge

A catalogue record for this book is available from the British Library

Library of Congress cataloguing in publication data
Rabinowitz, Dan, 1954–
    Overlooking Nazareth: the ethnography of exclusion in Galilee/
by Dan Rabinowitz
        p.   cm. – (Cambridge studies in social and cultural anthropology; 105)
    Includes bibliographical references
    ISBN 0 521 56361 5 – ISBN 0 521 56495 6 (pbk)
    1. Natzerat Illit (Israel) – Politics and government
2. Palestinian Arabs – Israel – Natzerat Illit – Politics and government
I. Title II. Series
DS110.N28R33   1996
956.94′5–dc20   96–11922
                                                        CIP

SE

To Iros

Contents

Maps

Tables

Preface

Research for this book depended on and benefited from the hospitality and cooperation of many Palestinian and Israeli residents of Natzerat Illit. It is a pleasant duty to thank Pnina and Gadi Liebreider, Salim and Odet Khūri, Benny and Ra'aya Halevi, Samiḥ and 'Alya Riziq, Edna and Eli Rodrig, Nasif and Nūha Bader, Lutfi and Vida Mash'ūr, 'Atallah Mansūr and many others who opened their hearts and homes to me and to my family during our sojourn in Natzerat Illit and after.

Most of the people mentioned and quoted in the book appear under pseudonyms. The two exceptions are Ra'id Riziq and Salim Khūri, who feature centrally in chapters 8 and 9 respectively. Both found the time to have me translate and read the relevant chapters to them in early 1995, then agreed to appear in the book under their real names. I am grateful to them for this, as well as for the insights and intuitions I gained through being with and talking to them since 1988.

During the various stages of the project I was fortunate to have the intellectual support and encouragement of many friends and colleagues. My initial writing-up period in Cambridge in 1989 and 1990 was enriched by comments and support from Declan Quigley, Paul Sant-Cassia, Barbara Bodenhorn, Tanya Luhrman, and Vinay Shrivastava. Humphrey Hinton was of valuable assistance with computers and other equipment.

Special thanks are due to Ernest Gellner. Fully cognizant that some of the perspectives contained herein contrast with his view of ethnography, I remain grateful to him for his steadfast support, keen interest and penetrating commentary in the early stages of this project.

Subsequent stages of writing, which took place in Israel since 1990, benefited enormously from insights and comments by Henry Rosenfeld, Michael Shalev, Eyal Ben-Ari, Aharon Ben-Avot, Tal Kokhavi, Zali

Gurevitch, Don Handelman, the late Makram Kūpti, Michael Herzfeld, Barukh Kimmerling and Eric Cohen. Yuval Portugali from Tel-Aviv University and Danny Trutch from Tel-Aviv Books extended valuable assistance with the maps. I thank them all for their contributions, and remain solely responsible for mistakes and misrepresentations which may have persisted.

This project would not have materialized without the generous financial support of the William Wyse Fund at Trinity College Cambridge, The Merchant Taylor Fund at Pembroke College Cambridge, The Avi Hayeshuv Foundation in Geneva, Mr Maurice Rabb of Capetown, and a New York-based organization the directors of which prefer it to remain unnamed. I am most grateful to all of these for their assistance.

Earlier versions of chapters 3, 4, 8 and 9 appeared as articles in *American Ethnologist, Urban Anthropology, Man* and *Journal of Anthropological Research* respectively. Their permission to print is thankfully acknowledged.

My father, Lennie Rabinowitz, who died when I was about half-way through this project, was, and in many ways still is, a constant source of confidence and faith. His spirit is a part of this particular project in more than one way.

Finally, my spouse Iros, whose belief, endurance and, above all, sensitivity and insight were my anchors in the field as well as during writing. I dedicate this book to her with love and gratitude.

Note on transliteration
The Arabic words appearing in the text are transliterated according to the standards of the *International Journal of Middle Eastern Studies*.

PART 1

BIGOTED LIBERALS

1

The Ḥaj, the mayor, and the deputy prime minister

A journey with the Ḥaj

The Ḥaj walks slowly up the hill overlooking the highway which leads into the Israeli new town of Natzerat Illit.[1] Constructed in the 1960s, the modern road and the near-by motor factory lie in a flat section of a little valley, an uncharacteristic feature in this otherwise uneven terrain. It is spring and the rolling hills abound with bloom.

A resident of the adjacent Palestinian town of Nazareth, (al-Naṣira in Arabic) the Ḥaj has not set foot here since his land was seized by the Israeli government in the 1950s, to be annexed to the municipal territory of Natzerat Illit. 'This bit of level ground', he tells us, pointing at the factory yard, with rows of brand new military vehicles fresh off the production line, 'was known as Karm Ṭabariya.[2] Good land. My uncle, who leased it by a *Ḍaman* arrangement from Yūsūf al-Fahūm's family, used to grow there barley, sesame and wheat.'[3]

Palestinians have individual names for landscape features and agricul-tural plots. Hill tops, slopes and valley sections, threshing rings and water holes, trees and seasonal puddles carry specific epithets. A map of Nazareth and its environs, surveyed and published by the British in 1930, specifies some of the features which the Ḥaj remembers (see map 1).[4]

Most of the sites, however, have since been transformed. Founded in 1957, the new town of Natzerat Illit now hides the natural shapes and land marks beneath residential compounds, commercial centres, industry. The past existence of Palestinians can hardly be inferred by anybody unfamil-iar with the recent history of the terrain.

The Ḥaj remembers ploughing in winter, the long anticipation during spring, the summer harvest. Like the fateful one of 1948:

3

1. The ridges east of Nazareth, ca. 1940

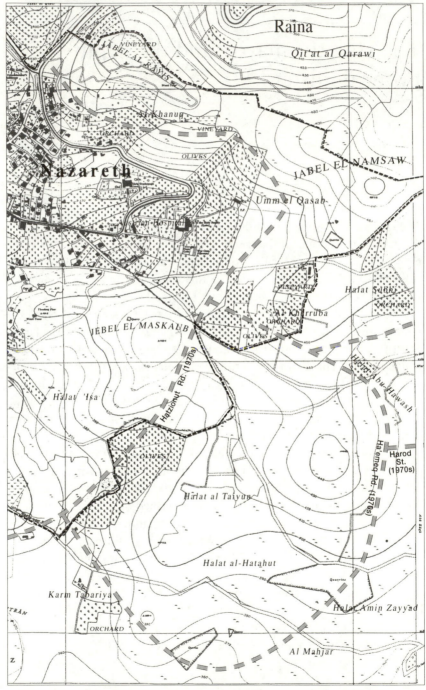

*superimposed: main roads, Natzerat Illit (built 1970s) ▬ ▬ ▬

We had a good crop that year. The 31 *dūnams* my family cultivated here produced seventy *Kells* of wheat and seventy of barley.[5] We were lucky to have managed to transport the grain back home to Nazareth before the town was seized by the advancing Israeli army. Our camels worked particularly hard that summer. . . . now, with everything covered by those apartments and the roads, the days of Karm Ṭabariya appear so distant.

The hill we stand on has ruined walls, scattered rubble and the shrivelled remnants of an old orchard. 'This was Salim Mūṣṭafa 'Abd al-Khaliq's house', says the Ḥaj. 'He bought it from the Fahūms a long time back, and lived here until he was finally evicted like the rest of us in the 1950s.'

The Ḥaj, his son and I pack ourselves into the car and drive along the road into the southern section of the Israeli town. The old man, erect in the front seat, looks out intently, as though determined to rediscover further clues of his geography. The signposts, street names and billboards neither help nor confuse him: they are in Hebrew, very few in English. Not a letter in his native Arabic, one of the two official languages of the state: it took a court order in 1993 for the all-Israeli municipal council of Natzerat Illit to lift a ban it had imposed on Arabic script in signs and billboards.

The Ḥaj points left towards a sizeable block of flats. ''Abd-allah al-Hataḥūt owned an olive orchard along this ridge', he says. I slow down, but even at 20 kilometres per hour the pace seems indecently fast. The past rushes by us like a smoke screen.

We go by a plot which once belonged to Amin Zayad, father of Nazareth's Tawfiq Zayad.[6] The Ḥaj identifies a large apartment house at the intersection of Harod street and Yizrael Boulevard and tells us it is built on Ni'emeh al- Qassim's land. The car then glides towards a school named after Moshe Sharet, once prime minister of Israel. From his mental map the Ḥaj retrieves the original name of the plot: Ḥalat Abū Hawash. 'Used to belong to my grandfather' he says wryly. 'Hawash means strong, ferocious man.'

A compound of red-roofed houses, erected recently for new immigrants, forces another sigh of recognition. 'Ḥalat al-Mathūma', the old man utters, dream-like. 'A fair maiden lived here generations back. Legend has it she was once accused of promiscuity, and slain by kin.'

Our tour of the new Israeli town finally brings us to the Jewish cemetery, situated on a hill overlooking mount Tabor and Marj 'ibn 'amer – the Plain of Yizra'el – to the east. 'There used to stand here a pile of stones – a *rūjūm*' the Ḥaj tells us. 'We called it Rūjūm al-'Ajami. Folks believed the stones were holy, and whoever stole one would come to harm at night.'

We waste no time searching, knowing the *Rūjūm* is long gone. Has anybody ever paid the awful price?

Later that afternoon, in the Ḥaj's home in downtown Nazareth, the old Ḥaja – a blood relation of her husband – says:

Oh yes, I know these places well. Our family always lived here, in downtown al-Naṣira, and cultivated plots up on the mountain. It's only half an hour's walk away. In summer we used to set off at dawn, riding the empty camels to the fields. We would spend the morning harvesting in Karm Ṭabariya, then haul the crop to the *bayader* (threshing ring) in Al Baiyyada. We would return at dusk, the camels carrying big piles of straw. The grain remained on the mountain, where merchants would come to purchase it directly from the ring. We kept the camels at a shed behind the house as late as 1970, then sold them off. It really made no sense any longer, with the mountain quickly disappearing under the *Shikūn*. All we have left are memories. But these are fading quickly too now.

The use of *shikūn* – Hebrew for housing estate – as a name for Natzerat Illit is widespread among the Palestinian residents of adjacent Nazareth.[7] Dismissive of the new town's name, *shikūn* tends to lump it with a country-wide architectural phenomenon, dislodging it from local specificity. This misrecognition on the part of Palestinians is one manifestation of their resentment against what they see as an unlawful invasion of their territory and an abuse of their primordial rights.

Natzerat Illit was established as part of the third stage in Israel's drive to 'Judaize Galilee',[8] a policy initially endorsed by the Israeli cabinet in March 1949 (Kipnis 1983:723–4). The Palestinian population, while deci-mated during the 1948 war which brought Israel its independence, still formed an overwhelming majority in Lower Galilee. Not surprisingly, the hills of Nazareth became a prime target for the state's Judaization policy.

Oren Yiftachel's analysis of this policy (1994) indicates that it is by no means unique to Israel. Multi-ethnic states elsewhere, he demonstrates, tend 'either to disperse the minority throughout the state or penetrate minority regions with settlement of other ethnic groups' (Yiftachel 1994:43, after Gurr 1993 and Sibley 1987). The Ḥaj's memories suggest however that no matter how efficient the implementation of such policies, the heritage of those invaded or dispersed dies hard.

Israeli Residents of Natzerat Illit often refer to David Ben-Gurion, Israel's first prime minister, as the figure whose ideological legacy deter-mined the town's future role in the quest for Israeli dominance in Galilee. A letter written by Ben Gurion in 1957, proudly reproduced in an official publication issued for Natzerat Illit's thirtieth anniversary states that:

...the new settlement must be a Jewish town that will assert a Jewish presence in the area. Not a suburb of Arab Nazareth, but a separate town in its vicinity.

(Natzerat Illit 1987)

The nature of this project, whereby the minority or ethnic borderland (Anzaldua 1987, Rosaldo 1988) becomes the dominant group's own frontier, has been successfully disguised in Israel by the concept of 'development town' (*'Ir Pitūaḥ*). A non-problematic view of the matter,[9] sees 'development towns' as part and parcel of the inevitable and historically moral process of settling the old–new Jewish homeland. A more critical view has been suggested by a number of researchers, including Shlomo Swirski (1985, 1989), and, in a less emphatic tone, Tom Segev (1984). Their analyses highlight this type of settlement as a eurocentric project which mobilized immigrants – mostly oriental Jews – to settle less-attractive peripherial tracts, including borderlands.

Natzerat Illit, where immigrants from Eastern Europe were and still are the majority, is not the prototypical case of Israeli new town. The fact remains however that most immigrants who settled in the town had limited effective choice in the matter.[10] Many of them were brought to Galilee upon arrival in Israel, often directly from the harbour or the airport. The concept of being drafted by the core to settle the periphery, while not necessarily supporting the view of European domination over oriental Jews (see Shohat 1988), is certainly as valid in Natzerat Illit as it is elsewhere in Israel.

Natzerat Illit was thus designed by the hegemonic forces of Israel; carried out primarily by immigrants; and came at the expense of Palestinians.

Counter penetration
The Israeli vision for Natzerat Illit – a purely Jewish new town amidst the Palestinian heartland in Galilee – was eroded in the 1970s and 1980s with the gradual arrival of immigrants of another variety. Circumstances specified in chapter 2 encouraged Palestinian residents of Nazareth, typically newlyweds and families in the earlier stages of their developmental cycle, to rent, buy, or build properties in the Israeli town. By 1988, when I embarked upon this study, Natzerat Illit had approximately 3,500 Palestinian residents – almost an eighth of the town's population. Ironically, the town established to effectively exclude Palestinians from their ancestral agricultural land was now re-entered by their urban middle-class compatriots.

Israel has a number of long-established mixed towns, where Palestinians and Israelis have lived side by side for decades, sometimes longer. These include Haifa (Ḥeifa in Hebrew; Ḥaifa in Arabic), Acre ('Acco; 'Acca), Jaffa (Yafo; Yafa), Ramla (Ramla; al-Ramla) and Lidda (Lod; Lidd).[11]

Since the advent of Zionism, and most powerfully after 1948, these mixed towns saw Jewish newcomers penetrating predominantly Palestinian turf. The arrivals either replaced the Palestinians altogether or settled side by side with them. Following 1948 and well into the 1970s this process of replacement spread to rural areas too, through the establishment of Israeli settlements on land expropriated from its Palestinian owners. The residual Palestinian community – a subdued, reluctant and largely helpless group – was reduced to a shadow of its pre-1948 past.

Natzerat Illit, however, is quite irregular in this respect. While its early stages did see Israeli settlers taking hold of Palestinian land – largely unpopulated, though more productive than many Israeli residents now like to recognize – its recent history sees large-scale penetration of Palestinians into an essentially Israeli community.

Most Israeli residents of Natzerat Illit see the Palestinian presence in the town at best as an unfortunate hiccup in an otherwise healthy master plan to Judaize Galilee; at worst as a dreaded and highly orchestrated Palestinian onslaught – a conspiracy by Palestinian nationalists to take over the town, merge it into adjacent Nazareth and, by extension, incorporate it into a distant, threatening Arab entity. A widespread sentiment amongst Israeli residents throughout the 1980s was that the Palestinian presence is the single most demeaning aspect of Natzerat Illit, and that it alone accounts for the consistent failure of the town to attract desirable immigration from more prestigious parts of Israel. Large-scale immigration from the crumbling Soviet Union in the early 1990s, which signalled a substantial addition to the Israeli population of Natzerat Illit, somewhat modified the sense of Palestinian threat. The basic sentiment, however, has not disappeared.

The geo-political history of Natzerat Illit in Lower Galilee is somewhat analogous to that of Israel in the Middle East. An Israeli island in an Arab ocean, reluctantly hosting a Palestinian contingent it perceives as a potentially disloyal, even dangerous fifth column.

The conflict built into the relationship between Israelis and Palestinians in Natzerat Illit is not something I stumbled on once I settled in the town for ethnographic fieldwork. It was, in many ways, the reason why I chose Natzerat Illit in the first place. Consequently, this book, complete with its selective choices, may diverge from what some might expect of a first ethnographic monograph about a community.

I see this work primarily as a guided walk along a border, a sketch of interfaces, a non-random selection of friction situations, conflictual relations and cooperation. Eight scenes have been selected for detailed representation: conflicting narratives of local history; the split real-estate market; notions of boundaries and territorial continuity; the split education system; the paradox of Palestinian hospitality in Natzerat Illit; the trials and tribulations of a senior Palestinian involved in a local sports club; a Palestinian general practitioner; and the campaign by Palestinians in Natzerat Illit to gain initial access to local level politics.

Some of these scenes, or others generically similar, would have been chosen probably by any ethnographer doing fieldwork anywhere. My choice in this rather problem-oriented work, however, was also to deliberately seek arenas where the complex, often paradoxic aspects of the border situation are negotiated and acted out most vividly.

The outcome, as in most ethnographies, is nothing but a sample guided by my tropes, my biases and opportunities. In some respects, it goes against the grain of ethnographic inquiry, the strength of which I always saw in its capacity to start with comprehensive, barely qualified grasps of 'culture' and 'society', then work towards some insight into undercurrents. My rather linear curiosity about the Israeli–Palestinian urban interface must be the key to both the scopes and limitations of this work.

The claim of rationality by the Western state

One theoretical preoccupation of this study is with the claims of western statism to rational and even-handed treatment of all its citizens, including ethnic and national minorities.

The state of Israel models itself on formulae of western liberal democracies. The declaration of independence, signed by a national assembly of deputies in May 1948, pledges the state's resolve to protect the rights of every individual regardless of gender, religious denomination, colour or creed. The declaration, while never legally recognized as a formal constitution, was subsequently supplemented by a complex code of legislation which defines all state affairs and guides the behaviour of individuals. The declaration and Israel's more formal legislation share a basic commitment to universalistic values and, ostensibly, to their operational directives.

David Kretzmer's work on the legal status of the Palestinian citizens of Israel (1990) convincingly exposes loopholes, intentional omissions and provisions designed to maintain Jewish Israeli control over land, water, the right of entry, citizenship, allocation of welfare benefits and more, all under a deceptively coherent legal guise. The result, he asserts, is a state system which bars Palestinian citizens from equal access to vital resources.

Kretzmer's task would not have been necessary in the first place had it not been for the claim of Israel, in line with liberal western political philosophy, that the state acts as a faithful guardian of rights and privileges of all its citizens and institutions.

The first part of this book, which draws its insights mainly from a study of the agency and rhetoric of Israelis in Natzerat Illit, focuses on the capacity of liberals to engage in marginalizing and racializing practices. It argues that the failure of mainstream liberalism to engender fair and rational action to match its noble principles does not stop at indifference and does not only breed inaction. It can easily produce predatory discrimination. In Israel, I argue, this happens mainly through the application of a double standard: Palestinian *individuals* are often treated leniently, in accord with the ethos of personal equality and meritocracy; when it comes to *The Palestinians* as collective, the application of these values is arrested, thus intensifying discrimination and abuse.

Israelis, not uniquely, tend to rationalize – and thence present *post factum* as inherently rational – what are in fact contingent, politically and ideologically motivated choices. This is related to the imperfections of rationality and its claims at large, as alluded to for example by Tambiah (1990:117–20). Specifically to inter-ethnic contexts, it is reminiscent of Bruce Kapferer's argument that ideologies ostensibly designed to benefit a given population are not immune from deployment in support of much less benign causes (Kapferer 1988). Kapferer's analysis of inter-ethnic strife in Sri Lanka rests on a description of the seemingly harmless belief that the state embodies hierarchies enshrined within Buddhism. In certain political circumstances, however, this framework pushes peace-loving Buddhist clergymen to perpetrate indiscriminate violence against the Tamils, all in the name of fighting earthly incarnations of metaphysical evil (Kapferer 1988:86–7). Similarly, his discussion of Australian 'ANZAC Nationalism' suggests that while the self image and underlying claims of Australian popular Nationalism are linked to egalitarianism, its undercurrents are essentially exclusivist and even racist. This, he argues, is demonstrated in the treatment of non-anglo immigrants into Australia since the 1950s and in the lot of urban aboriginals (Kapferer 1988:142).

Michael Herzfeld (1993) generalizes the point further in his exploration of the role of 'Western Bureaucracy in the production and perpetuation of indifference – the rejection of common humanity' (Herzfeld 1993:1). Using his own observations of Greece, alongside studies of communities in Portugal (Brogger nd), France (Zonabend 1993) and others, Herzfeld argues that once up against indifference – a self-generating side effect of modern superstructures – benevolent institutions and ideologies fail to follow their convictions with constructive action. Israel, so often represented as a 'western' bulwark against 'oriental' savagery, thus becomes a vivid case of the limitations and contradictions inherent in the complacent self-representation of that very 'West'.

This book seeks to further the debate by demonstrating that a similar process takes place beyond the bureaucratic superstructure and its institutions, as part of routine agency of 'ordinary' individuals. The case of Israelis in Natzerat Illit and their views and agency towards Palestinian residents is characteristic of many western and westernizing states, where actors are engaged in an attempt to modernize.

Individuals who find themselves in situations which force decisions on inclusion and exclusion are often unencumbered by conscious inclinations to deal with 'heavy' issues on an abstract, let alone moral or theoretical level. Life in Natzerat Illit is particularly rich in such occasions. Israelis coming into contact with Palestinians are suddenly faced with dilemmas typical of members of the euro-centre preoccupied with keeping others out; the Palestinians, for their part, are forced to devise *ad hoc* strategies to deal with their exclusion.

Studying everyday exclusionism in a place like Israel is doubly suggestive given the unique history of the Jewish people. Israelis see their collectivity as the physical and moral progeny of a group consistently discriminated against, marginalized and racialized, the holocaust being the most horrific, though by no means isolated case. This notwithstanding, Israel and Israelis score no better – and often substantially worse – than other nations when it comes to humane treatment of minorities. A critique of the rational and liberal 'western' state is all the more poignant in such circumstances.

My first visits to Tel-Aviv in spring 1988, having moved to Natzerat Illit to begin fieldwork that January, had me and my spouse telling friends and relatives about the obstinate refusals on the part of Israelis in Natzerat Illit to tolerate the Palestinian presence in their midst. Our listeners, typical of middle-class north Tel-Aviv, could hardly stomach the descriptions of exclusivism and inegaliterianism on the part of fellow Israelis. Not surprisingly, they were soon equating Natzerat Illit with prejudice and backwardness. This was in line with the media image of the town as a peripheral pocket of bigoted intransigence – an effigy owing primarily to television coverage of local Israeli provocation against Palestinian residents in the early 1980s.

Chapters 3, 4 and 5 do depict Israelis in Natzerat Illit as harbouring intolerance and downright racist attitudes towards their Palestinian townsfolk. My argument, however, is that Israelis in Natzerat Illit are not a freak phenomenon. They are by no means an exceptional and problematic group that somehow fails to live up to the moral standards represented by the state and adhered to by the majority of citizens. On the contrary, they represent an average selection of essentially liberal values and the agency which such values tend to produce within the Israeli context. The difference between Israelis in Natzerat Illit and those who live in other parts is not so much in varying levels of sophistication, height of brow or moral standards, as in diverging circumstances. It is, I argue, the trying life near the political frontier between communities that pushes liberalism to its limits, exposing its failure to prescribe behavioural patterns to match its lofty rhetoric. This can be seen as part of a wider contradiction within the dominant ideology – how to hold on to power while at the same time espousing universalism.

The second part of the book, mainly chapters 7, 8 and 9, highlights the agency and discourse of Palestinians who find themselves at interfaces with Israeli individuals and institutions in Natzerat Illit. Focusing on Palestinians who upset the 'normal' order by claiming positions of power, responsibility and authority *vis-à-vis* their Israeli counterparts, my theoretical emphasis is on the concept of resistance and its recent development in anthropology. Palestinians generally avoid linkage between individual breakthroughs and the notion of productive overthrow of the hegemony. This in turn encourages a temptation to analyze their behaviour in terms of Gramsci's model (1971) of subconscious subaltern resistance – his predecessor of the higher state of consciousness so badly needed for revolt.

I wish to avoid this rather cheerful angle on the agency and destiny of Palestinian citizens of Israel. Reading Gramsci more critically, and working from the premises developed by Kaplan and Kelly (1994), Comaroff and Comaroff (1991) and Abu-Lughod (1989), I analyze the capability of Palestinians to occasionally come up with temporary upsets of the going order as something which enables them to carry on with Israel's hegemony, thus suppressing any urge to fundamentally upset it.

A place in history

The term 'Palestinian citizens of Israel' is preferred throughout this work to the more frequently used terms 'Israel's Arabs', 'Israeli Arabs' 'Arabs in Israel' or 'Israel's Arab citizens'. All of these labels, to be sure, refer to one and the same group – those Palestinians who either remained in Israel throughout the 1948 hostilities, returned there or were born there since, thus procuring Israeli citizenship. Likewise, members of the dominant group in Israel are referred to in this study as simply 'Israelis', or sometimes 'Jewish Israelis'.

Elsewhere (Rabinowitz 1992a, 1993) I present a more comprehensive argument explaining this choice of idiom. In brief, the use of the term 'Palestinians' for those members of the Palestinian people who happened to become citizens of Israel carries meaning not only as a signifier and pre-server of cultural specificity, but as a marker of political and national identity. The routine choice on the part of the majority of Israelis to use 'Arabs' as the chief component of the label denoting Palestinian citizens of Israel is neither neutral nor innocent. It projects a preference to see the Palestinians as members of a culture – a legitimate component of 'Israeli society', which the majority of Israelis perceive unproblematically as 'plu-ralistic'. Most Israelis conveniently overlook the fact that the term 'Arabs' silences the link which Palestinians have to the disputed homeland, whose name in Arabic is Falastin.

The ambiguity regarding labelling the Palestinian citizens of Israel is symptomatic of the indeterminacy associated with their status inside Israel and in the Middle East at large. The Palestinian citizens of Israel are marginal twice over, living in a double bind. Citizens of Israel, they are members of a racialized minority perceived by many Israelis as potentially disloyal and subversive – an adequate excuse for Israel and Israelis to keep them at bay for almost fifty years. Currently representing one-eighth of the entire Palestinian people, the Palestinian citizens of Israel are implicated by their residence, acculturation, and citizenship in Israel, and find them-selves marginalized by their parent ethnos too. Shaped between the mid-1960s and the early 1990s primarily outside Israel, Palestinian nationalism has yet to designate a proper place for them. The size and economic strength of their community in relation to other segments of the Palestinian people notwithstanding, their ambiguity within the Palestinian fold is obvious. A recent manifestation of this marginality was their exclu-sion, as a collective entity, from the peace negotiations conducted and tem-porarily concluded in 1993 and 1994 between their state of citizenship (Israel) and their people (The Palestinians).

A segment of a transnational group existing as an isolated minority within a state dominated by others, the Palestinian citizens of Israel are 'Arabs' for Israelis, and 'Israelis' for Arabs elsewhere. They are, as it were, trapped between their host state and their absent, scattered nation.[12]

A trapped minority, they are by definition non-assimilating – a combi-nation of their own choice, a dictum from the dominant group and pres-sure from their mother nation. Significantly, their non-assimilating nature is perceived as permanent, acculturation notwithstanding. While consis-tently acquiring more of the values and the symbols of Jewish Israel and incessantly attempting to gain more access to its political arena, they neither want to nor are invited to assimilate.

The marginality of Palestinians in Israel is clearly manifest in narratives of history. The hegemonic narrative in Israel regarding new towns and settlement in general, invokes hitherto 'uninhabited' and 'empty' tracts of land as miraculously 'discovered' by Zionist settlers laboriously redeeming territory from historical oblivion, reclaiming it from geographical, ecological and social void. The result is an assertion of Jewish presence, based on the right of an ancient people to return to its homeland after a long absence.

A booklet issued in 1987 to celebrate Natzerat Illit's thirtieth anniversary features a brief article by the mayor, with the following summary of local history:

Here within our settlement were uncovered the ruins of Ksūlot, from the time of Joshua's conquering of the land. Later, Second Temple priests lived and created here, while in our time 'a town now stands where once there was a military post, perhaps thanks to those days'.[13]   (*Natzerat Illit 1987:1*)

Another contributor to the booklet is Labour's leader at the time Shimon Peres, then deputy prime minister for Labour to right-wing Likud's Yitzhak Shamir. His message reads:

The thirtieth anniversary of Natzerat Illit celebrates three decades since a geographical breakthrough, the fulfilment of a great vision, a social transformation. . .

Natzerat Illit is a real pearl of Galilee. Even the historian Josephus Flavius[14] recognized the Galileeans as original, fearless people, folk who love their land no end – a love which does not come at the expense of creativity and action.

You, present day residents of Natzerat Illit, are like the ancient Galileeans: enthusiastic, caring, industrious, creative. It is your duty to remember: Natzerat Illit is a key town, a key to the gates of action Zionism.

The realization of values which are so Zionist, so humane, will ensure that Natzerat Illit will flourish and succeed for thirty more years.

Blessings,
Shimon Peres (ibid)

Official publications issued by the municipal council of Natzerat Illit are consistent with these two examples in as much as they include no hint of human presence in the area between the first century AD and 1957. A similar image emerges from accounts by Israeli residents, who generally consider the place to have been an empty wasteland before 1957 – a notion which has since become an integral part of the local myth of origin. The Israeli view that space had been redeemed directly from the elements, consistently misrecognizing narratives such as the Ḥaj's, is at the base of legitimizing Natzerat Illit as an exclusively Israeli community, with no place for Palestinians. Part of my project here is to challenge this assertion, and question the validity of the social and political implications it had and still has for many Israelis in Natzerat Illit and beyond.

The Israeli folk-version of the modern history of the land is directly informed by the dominant historical narrative underwriting Zionism. First, this version goes, were the Jews – the ancient Israelites, living in a land proclaimed for them by God. Then came the unfortunate disapora, a time in which some 'Arab' peasants came to live poorly in the ancient land, failing to cherish and develop it, blissfully unaware of being Palestinian or otherwise belonging to a wider entity. Then enter Zionism: the very same 'people' which left almost two thousand years before, has finally returned. Cohesive, dynamic, progressive, modernizing and indubitably righteous by virtue of biblical prerogatives and continuous suffering, the Jewish people came to claim its share again. Since then, according to this prevalent view, the country has undergone transformations along two indivisible, pre-destined courses. The Jewish immigrants, who see themselves as having no alternative, reclaim the land, develop it, incessantly expanding territorial bases and maximizing national cohesiveness; the Palestinians keep losing land, growing exceedingly alienated from their commonwealth within the state of Israel and beyond.

This version of the past begot a vision of the future, originally conceived by Labour Zionism but still much in demand by the populist right. According to this vision, given time and good fortune the Palestinians will somehow fade away to join their kind in distant Arab countries. Those who choose to stay in Israel will harbour deep gratitude for the gift of life, progress and modernity endowed by Israel.

Natzerat Illit is thus a recent construction not only in terms of its physical presence on the ground. It is, essentially, a discursive object created by Israelis as part of turning Israel and Galilee into particular socio-political spaces. Eyal (1993:41) applies Foucault's notion of object construction (1972) to the way Israeli orientalists have come to 'talk of one thing and the same' in reference to the 'Arab village' inside Israel. A particular discourse with certain sets of rules, institutions and power relations enabled the lumping together of certain phenomena relating to 'Arab life' in Israel, in turn producing a conceptual framework allowing these details to be interpreted according to a specific political perspective. A new space was thus conceived, in which hitherto unrelated pieces of data could be explained and understood, in turn injecting more validity and authority to the new category.

Natzerat Illit, and for that matter Israel at large, are not specific, pre-existing Palestinian spaces simply conquered and renamed by Zionism. Initially, the mountains east of Nazareth were no more than a medley of random plots and scattered fields – certainly not an earlier version of the object known today as Natzerat Illit. Those who made the town material-ize by using the physical environment as an unproblematic, dehistoricized substrate, are also those who have invented the very discourse which acknowledges it, refers to it, believes it.

Environmental transformation thus surfaces as central to the process of re-objectifying place, not less and often more significantly than military conquest and sovereignty. This point becomes doubly important in the case of trapped minorities, whose potential to produce competing repre-sentations of the past, the present and the future, threatens dominant majorities even when the latters hold a total hold on power.

The importance of memory and its role in shaping national identities, often through shattering competing discourses of minorities and other groups with counter-claims to territory, has been alluded to by Renato Rosaldo (1988) and Michael Taussig (1990). Ted Swedenburg explores similar issues with specific reference to the Palestinians (1990, 1991).

Zionism has been as diligent as any colonizing movement in this project, relentlessly producing a narrative which has no place for Palestinians. Environmental transformation of the borderzones and its representation in the canon have always formed an indispensable part of this process. Azmi Bishara writes that:

... the (Palestinian) villages which no longer exist were squeezed out of the public space, erased from the signposts of memory. They received new names, those of Hebraic settlements, but left their marks: cactus bushes, stones from disintegrating walls, bricks from ruined houses.

... The Israeli public space knows only one collective memory, a castrated memory the sole purpose of which is to push away the sense of exile and alien-ation. The Jewish Other exorcised the wholly Other, the native, the Other of the place. . . . History itself will prove . . . that if the victim is to forgive he must be acknowledged as the victim. This is the difference between a historic compromise and a cease fire.   *(Bishara 1992:6).*

Jonathan Boyarin recognizes two types of victimization of Palestinian space in Israel – one *in situ*, a second *in memoriam*. His essay (1992) tells how he prepared a conference paper on Israeli aspects of the culture of ruins. Rather than confine himself to a discussion of the Western Wall and of Masada, as was presumably expected of him by the conveners, he chose to speak of Palestinian ruins: the village of Lifta and the relics of agricul-tural terraces in Bab al-Wad between Jerusalem and Tel-Aviv. In his words:

The existence of physical ruins in an *Israeli* landscape is at least potential evidence of a collective struggle over control of space. Enabling this evidence to be heard, to become a counter-balance to the accepted Zionist myth that the Jewish state was re-established in an empty land, is a different matter . . . Precisely since the Palestinians are stateless, their attempts to renew their hold on the public space of memory are futile. These attempts are repelled with anger, accused of being murderous, well disguised efforts to drive away the Israeli presence. At the same time, the Israeli silencing of the heritage of Palestinian loss effectively blocks all efforts for a sympathetic understanding of the roots of hatred and resistance to Israeli rule.   *(Boyarin 1992:11, my translation).*

The amnesic silence displayed by Israeli informants in Natzerat Illit regarding the Palestinian presence in the hills they now inhabit indeed silences the Palestinian heritage of loss. It puts the Palestinians in a hopeless situation whereby the dominant majority which took away their land, imposing on them its alien sovereignty, also denies their right to bury, lament, and commemorate the meaning of the land they lost.

The two competing narratives pertaining to the history of Natzerat Illit reflect deep-seated strategies of reasoning. Both Israelis and Palestinians have their genuine reasons for attachment to the place. The Israelis have an ideology/theology of an ancient covenant with god, and a solid notion of the land as a haven from the mortal dangers of life in the diaspora. The Palestinians, for their part, have made centuries-long existence in the land, familial and personal memories of dispossession, discrimination and marginalization into the central pivots of their identity.

Ethnography, anthropology and the place of Palestinians in the social science of Israel

Anthropology has so far failed to make a significant mark on the debate of Israel's treatment of its Palestinian citizens or, for that matter, on the debate of the Palestinian predicament at large (see Peteet 1991:4–8). This is related to the almost chronic meagreness of anthropological theory in studies of the Palestinians (*ibid*). Much of the research into the Palestinian community in Israel tends to be based on quantified overviews of the macro system,[15] with ethnographic monographs pitifully few and far between.[16]

This is paradoxic, especially in view of current preoccupation within anthropology with the increasingly complex aspects of the post-modern world.[17] The fact remains, however, that the theoretical agenda of the study of Palestinians inside Israel is determined primarily by other branches of the social sciences, primarily sociology and political science.

The Palestinian sociologist Elia Zureik (1979:2) highlights the silence which shrouded the Palestinian citizens of Israel within social science research carried out by Israelis before the 1970s – a theme reiterated recently by sociologists Baruch Kimmerling (1992) and Ahmad Sa'adi (1992). The phenomenon is partly explained by sociologist Aziz Haidar's notion (1987) of the division of labour in Israeli academic life between sociologists – researching Jewish Israel – and orientalists – researching Palestinians.

Zureik (1979) suggests that analyses based on the Israeli orientalist tradition, so heavily dependent on classic modernization theories, breed an unsophisticated concept of 'Arab culture' and lead to gross misrepresentations of the psycho-social characteristics of the Palestinians.[18] The outcomes, he asserts, tend to overlook the political heart of the problem, namely the Palestinian tragedy of losing land, honour and cohesion in 1948 and of becoming second-class citizens on their own ancestral land.

Subsequent social science research, considerably less committed to the Zionist agenda or altogether dismissive of it, concentrated on more contextualized studies of the Palestinian citizens of Israel and their subordinate position within Israeli economy, society and politics.[19] Focused more energetically on power relations, this body of knowledge is, essentially, about what Israelis do to Palestinians.

More recent works on Israel demonstrate a willingness to use the status and treatment of the Palestinian citizens of Israel as a prism through which to analyze the nature of the Israeli state and its society. Such an approach offers greater theoretical depth to a field of knowledge hitherto relatively poor in opportunities for meaningful generalization.

Gershon Shafir's analysis (1989) of the treatment of land and labour within Zionism stresses the specific circumstances of the Jewish national movement. This allows him to somewhat modify Zureik's (1979) rigid definition of Israel as a settler colonial state, and dwell on differences between the Israeli situation and, for example, imperial extensions in European planters and farmers colonies. Shafir's most significant contribution is his assertion that the Zionist zeal to control the budding labour and land markets in Palestine, and the collective apparatus devised to do so, are not what Zionist ideology habitually purported them to be. Rather than founded in the universalistic ethos of east european socialism, with which early Zionism so fondly wanted to identify itself, attempts to control labour and land were primarily designed to keep the Palestinians out, or, minimally, at bay.

Michael Shalev's work on Israel's split labour force (1992), Lev Grinberg's complimenting project on the Labour Movement (1991), Yoav

Peled's and Yagil Levy's work on the place of the 1967 war in Israeli historiography and social science (1993), Ilan Pappe's revisionist historiographic accounts of the colonial context of the establishment of Israel (1988, 1994), Benny Morris's critical review of the birth of the problem of the Palestinian refugees (1987, 1994) and Avi Shlaim's accounts of geopolitical processes in the Middle East (1990) likewise offer critical approaches to dominant Israeli ideologies pertaining to the Palestinians and their place in Israel. These studies highlight the Zionist political agenda of excluding Palestinians as a self-perpetuating mechanism structuring central episodes and processes in Israeli public life.

This study follows in the same critical direction. I treat the political, social, cultural and economic subordination of Palestinians in Israel as a lamentable, self-evident reality. Appreciation of this reality is this book's point of departure, not its goal. Rather, my theoretical project is to show that the Palestinian presence in Israel has significant consequences on individual and collective agency by Israelis and by Palestinians in most aspects of daily life.

Writers have conceptualized the Israeli contradiction between having a Jewish state and at the same time calling it a democratic one. Smooha, fully cognizant of the problem, tries to explain away the paradox by labelling Israel 'ethnic democracy'. Working from the distinction between majoritarian and consociational democracies (Lijphardt 1977), he suggests the adjective 'ethnic' to denote the dominance of one *ethnos* over the other (Smooha 1990:391). The democratic nature of the state, he argues, is manifest in the rights granted to Palestinians as individual citizens.

Yoav Peled (1992) critically labels Israel 'ethnic republic'. He contrasts the virtually exclusive access of Jewish Israelis to the 'republican core' of political life with the nominal and weak citizenship offered to the Palestinian citizens. Peled shows that while careful – though not always successful – not to violate the legal rights of Palestinians, the state effectively keeps them away from the debate of, influence on and benefits of the 'common good' of the republic.

Rather than the state or 'society' – the two collective idioms which form the substrate of the 'Jewish versus Democracy' debate regarding the political reality of Israel – my focus here is individual agency. The situation at the borderzone, I argue, forces out some fundamental, personal dilemmas which often lead to fascinating contradictions. On the one hand, many Israelis in Natzerat Illit subscribe to the beliefs that all persons are created equal, that citizenship amounts not only to equity in access to resources but also to universal natural rights, and that the liberties associated with them apply across the board. On the other hand, when the choice is at their own front door, another set of forces takes over, often producing an essentially racist code of action. The ethnography of Natzerat Illit will demonstrate that the liberal ethos, while prevalent and deep, is easily suspended when it comes to action.

Zemach (1980) surveyed the views of Israelis regarding Palestinians and the amount of democratic rights that Israel should grant them. One result is that many Israelis consistently subscribe to basic tenets of democracy, but easily defer them when it comes to Palestinians. This is similar to what I found in Natzerat Illit with Israelis who faced the need to back belief with action.

Much of the debate regarding the nature of the Israeli state focuses on the extent to which a writer is willing to acknowledge positive change in the condition of the Palestinian citizens. Those who see no progress tend to support a rigid view of Israel as a controlling, colonial settler state complete with durable mechanisms designed to block its native Palestinians from influence and power. Writers more willing to recognize progress are likely to have a more charitable view of Zionism and the Israeli state. My observations of Natzerat Illit have been interpreted by Sami Smooha as lending some support to his argument that Israel is in fact becoming more accessible to its Palestinian citizens (Smooha 1992, chapter 22). At the same time, the local emphasis of my work, coupled with my refusal to interpret individual progress as tantamount to growing equality between collectives, bolsters Zureik's claims that Palestinian advent in Israel is too local and peripheral to justify a lenient reappraisal of the state. My distinction between the treatment of Palestinians and *the Palestinians* goes along with Peled's (1992) critical appraisal of Israel as an ethnic republic.

The debate regarding progress made (or not) by Palestinian citizens of Israel is rightly centred on the state, its mechanisms of control and its willingness to allow Palestinians full participation. The application of ethnographic methods and anthropological theory may show how personal, local and national issues come to converge. Using these methods, this book will hopefully be a reminder of how an important dimension of life in Israel can benefit from ethnographic inquiry, and how the ethnography of Palestinians inside Israel can be of use in the pursuit of theoretical modifications of minority situations generally.

The anthropologist as comrade, secret agent, interlocutor
In 1987 my spouse and I, both native Israelis of Ashkenazi middle-class backgrounds, began to make inquiries regarding moving to Natzerat Illit,

where we eventually lived between January 1988 and May 1989 for my main period of fieldwork. We soon realized that as prospective settlers of an area officially designated 'development zone 'b',[20] we were entitled to a number of bureaucratic perks. One was a substantial reduction in income tax payments and partial exemption from local rates. Another was entitlement to a 'relocation bonus' of 500 Israeli shekels (approximately 250 US dollars at the time). There was also a handsome government guaranteed mortgage available to us should we decide to buy an apartment or a house in Natzerat Illit, and other, smaller fringe advantages.

This institutional support was compatible with a consistent, though not always explicit message which our fellow Israelis in Natzerat Illit conveyed, namely that they saw us as comrades in the pioneering struggle of settling Galilee. Our promise as Israeli-born, well educated, presumably ideologically sound, was only slightly tainted by my vague vocation and suspected transience. People often expressed their confidence that we would return to Natzerat Illit once my writing-up period in Britain was up. Our suspicion that a return was quite unlikely made us uneasy with these expectations, especially as they were often complemented with genuine, warm hospitality and a sincere and flattering eagerness to befriend us. Perhaps we were meant to fall prey to the old Jewish trick of attraction by guilt.

Whether we liked it or not, however, we were temporarily sucked into the master plan designed to turn the demographic tide in Galilee against the Palestinians. As Israelis moving out from Tel-Aviv to Natzerat Illit, we were, statistically and technically speaking, agents of the Judaizing plan. The bureaucracy treated us as such, as did our new Israeli friends and neighbours. This unintended agency on my part was impossible to reconcile with the sympathy I had for the Palestinian residents, who rightly see themselves as those who pay the personal and collective price for Israel's penetration of their homeland.

My relationship with the Israeli residents of Natzerat Illit was based on an ideological mismatch I was not quite ready to take on board at the time. Although we hardly took advantage of the benefits the system offered us, the conceptual dilemma was there. Initially I tended to solve the problem by separating the benefits of being on the right side of the bureaucracy from the 'bigger', more 'political' aspects of Israeli–Palestinian relations. Manifestations on the ground of state policies regarding territory and its control, could thus be left conveniently outside 'politics'. Like many Israelis I could innocuously count them as part of the perpetual negotiation of the individual with the bureaucracy, an arena where ideology and principles carry little weight. This enabled me to sterilize the problem of my own agency, ticking it off the list of 'big', 'important' issues. The assumptions underwriting such policies and practices were kept apart from my daily life.

A sentiment which haunted me throughout my fieldwork and to some extent to date is related to the reactions of Israelis in Natzerat Illit to my research project. Those of them who became aware of it often made me feel as though it somehow threatened to rupture a long-standing bond of silence which all were struggling to keep. Their uneasiness regarding the Palestinian presence in the town became clear to me even before I moved to Natzerat Illit. And while cases of people who actively withheld information or did not want to cooperate were few and far between,[21] I still had the distinct impression that my inquiry pursued subjects and themes my Israeli neighbours, friends, informants – like Israelis generally – were ill prepared to grapple with just yet.

My place amongst the Palestinian residents of Natzerat Illit and their ability to trust me oscillated between my two attributes: being a young Israeli male; and being an anthropologist inclined to write a version of 'their story'. An Israeli of my background, age and gender could easily be an agent of the internal security service Shabak – a thought which, Palestinian mates have told me, inevitably crossed their minds during my initial period in the field. Things I heard subsequently, particularly public introductions made on my behalf by Palestinian friends, revealed some of the mitigating features that clearly helped my entry. These included my commentary and features articles in the week-end editions of *Haaretz* and *Hadashot* – two nationwide dailies in Hebrew which some of my Palestinian friends read and all of them knew; my enrolment with a British university rather than an Israeli one; and introductions through my father, a veteran Rotarian, to Palestinian members of the Rotary Club of Nazareth.

Above all, however, was the constant feeling which Palestinian citizens of Israel have, that their story is undertold, and the promise which I embodied to tell a version of it. I often think that anyone prepared to spare the time and genuinely listen to Palestinians is automatically elevated to the supreme status of being 'objective' – a cherished quality they tend to attribute to persons willing to represent their angle with little or no commitment to mainstream narratives of Zionism and the state.

This book is neither an attempt at a 'correct' representation of the Palestinians and their version of their strained existence in Natzerat Illit, nor an effort to regain the trust and sympathy of Israelis. It is, I like to think, first and foremost the account of someone caught in the thick of a lively, frightening and fascinating frontier. Almost five years since I have left the place, I know my life will always be affected by the crossfire.

2

Tale of two cities

Galilee: a geo-political frontier

Galilee (Hagalil in Hebrew, al-Jalil in Arabic), is a series of limestone ridges stretching generally from east to west. Running south from the Israeli–Lebanese border in the north, the terrain of Upper Galilee rises to an altitude of over 1,200 metres (4,000 ft) at Jabal al-Jarmak (Mount Meron in Hebrew). Further to the south the hills grow gentler, edging down into the softer landscapes of Lower Galilee, where they are often separated by broad, fertile valleys.

Some of these valleys have been inhabited for as long as 200,000 years.[1] Replete with archaeological sites representing most periods from the Late Bronze to the present (see Shmueli, Sofer and Keliot 1983, chapter 2), Lower Galilee was a Palestinian rural heartland at the eve of the Zionist settlement of Palestine. Its Palestinian population grew considerably at or about the turn of the twentieth century (Ben-Arieh and Oren 1983:350).

Compared with other parts of the country, the Palestinian population of Lower Galilee experienced relatively little change following the 1948 war and the establishment of Israel.[2] A motorist travelling on the network of modern roads constructed in the 1980s is exposed to a jigsaw puzzle of hitherto isolated Palestinian hill-top villages with scattered, individually cultivated plots.

Palestinian villagers in Lower Galilee as well as elsewhere in Israel now mostly work in the lower sections of the Israeli labour market.[3] Those who persist with agriculture grow vegetables and cereals in the flatter parts, deciduous fruit trees in more elevated areas.

The ridge lying furthest to the south of Lower Galilee is The Nazareth Hills – a structure rising between 350 and 550 metres above sea level. Rounder to the north, its southern edge is an escarpment plunging steeply

Table 1. *The Population of Nazareth 1800–1992*

Year	Population
1800	1,500
1852	3,000
1881	5,939
1904	6,458
1912	7,988
1914	8,584
1922	7,424
1945	14,200
1948	18,000
1949	30,000
1961	
1983	49,000
1989	55,000
1992	60,000

Sources: Palestinian Encyclopedia:439; Ben-Arieh and Oren (1983:340); State of Israel (1993); Stendel 1982

almost a thousand feet to the plain of Yizra'el (Marj ʿibn 'amar in Arabic). The urban core of old Nazareth lies in a valley approximately 3 kilometres north of this escarpment. Natzerat Illit, occupying the higher hills towering over Nazareth to the east, has its southern houses within a 100 metres of the escarpment. There is more to this location, I sometimes think, than mere topography. The tight proximity to the abyss is metaphoric of the precarious, turbulent life which the new Israeli town has carved for itself on the national divide.

Harshness is featured also in the town's mountainous climate. It seldom snows in Natzerat Illit, but the exposed terrain, the biting, hurling winds and steady supply of clouds which sweep through streets and corridors in winter often create an air of alienated isolation.

Centre piece of Lower Galilee since the early nineteenth century, the Palestinian town of Nazareth is now approximately 60,000 strong. Table 1 indicates the growth of Nazareth over two centuries to date.

The town which saw prophets, kings and emperors along its chequered history was little more than an overgrown village at the turn of the nineteenth century. Its population, then numbering between 1,000 and 2,000, was mostly Muslim (Stendel 1982, Ben-Arieh and Oren 1983:340). The nineteenth century however saw a growing Ottoman interest in keeping good relations with western powers, a tendency which brought about an institutional resurgence of Christianity throughout the Middle East. Religious orders from western and central Europe, Greece, Tsarist Russia and the United States became part of the Palestinian landscape. Jerusalem, Bethlehem and Nazareth, the three most holy places for Christianity, grew rapidly.

The growth of Nazareth in the nineteenth century is accounted for primarily by incoming Christian Palestinian immigrants, whose proportion in the population rocketed by 1880 to 68 per cent (Ben-Arieh and Oren 1983:340). Nazareth is still the most important centre of Palestinian Christians in Israel. The fact that most Palestinian immigrants to adjacent Natzerat Illit are Christians merits a brief historical account of this community.

Christian continuity in a predominantly Muslim Palestine since the seventh century was based on a mixture of religious tenets and political pragmatism. Christian Arab communities, which tend to be relics of pre-Islamic Byzantine Orthodoxy, were defined in the Kor'an, together with the Jews, as *Ahl al-kitab* (people of the Book) and were granted protection in return for the payment of the *Jizya* tax. This enabled Christians and Jews to survive throughout the early Arab empire.

Middle Eastern Christian communities such as the Nestorians, Syrian Jacobites, Copts and early Maronites represent old schisms with Byzantine orthodoxy on theological as well as ethnic grounds. The Christians of Palestine, however, (like those of coastal Egypt and Syria) tended to remain faithful to imperial Orthodoxy. Greek Orthodoxy is in fact the largest Christian denomination in their midst to date.

It was only as late as the Ottoman period that heterodoxic religious tenets were introduced into the Christian Palestinian community. First, the introduction of the concept of separate rites for Eastern Christian communities in the eighteenth century opened the Catholic option. Many who had been reluctant to make a wholesale theological conversion to Catholicism, were now willing to accept Rome's supremacy and tangible assistance (Bets 1979). The result in Palestine was the Greek Catholic denomination. The subsequent advent of missionary efforts by French, Italian, American and British clergy prompted other Palestinian Christians to convert to Roman Catholicism and Protestantism.

The official British estimate of the Palestinian Christian population in 1944 was 135,500, including the West Bank (Betts 1979:69). Of the Palestinians who fled Palestine in 1948, whose total number is estimated between 500,000 and 800,000, between 55,000 and 60,000 were Christian (*ibid*). The 1961 figure for Christian Palestinians in Israel was 50,500 (*ibid*), growing to 117,000 by 1988 (State of Israel 1988).

The relative importance of Christians in the political and public life of the Palestinian citizens of Israel (see Tsimhoni 1989) was and still is analogous to the central role of Christians in the Arab world at large. George Antonious of Arab nationalism fame and, more recently, George Habbash of the Democratic Front for the Liberation of Palestine are only two outstanding figures in a long list of Christian activists who left their marks on Middle Eastern politics.

Nazareth represents a typical breakdown of Palestinian Christians. There are some 27,000 Christians in the town, of whom approximately half are Greek Orthodox. Second largest is the Greek Catholic denomination, third the Roman Catholic, fourth the Maronite, a small offshoot from Lebanon. The Protestant, Anglican, Baptist and Copt communities are considerably smaller, each no more than a few hundred strong.

Nazareth's economy is based on the hinterland of Lower Galilee. Commerce, light industry and tourism have been the major occupations for over a century. In 1875, the Templars – a German lay order which established a number of agricultural colonies in Palestine since the 1850s – completed a carriageway from the port of Haifa to Tiberias via Nazareth. This accelerated the town's development, securing its place as the main commercial centre in Galilee. 1875 also saw the appointment of Nazareth's first municipal council (Palestinian Encyclopaedia 1980:439).

The 1920s and 1930s saw most of the mountain towns of Palestine – Nazareth no exception – gradually overtaken by the booming coastal plane (Kimmerling and Migdal 1993). This notwithstanding, by 1948 the town had almost 18,000 inhabitants, a thriving economy, an elaborate religious life, a good education system, a strong medical community and a relatively high quality of life.

One of the very few Palestinian towns whose inhabitants stayed put during the war of 1948 (Morris 1987:201–3), Nazareth absorbed considerable numbers of 'internal refugees' in 1948 and 1949.[4] Thousands of Palestinian villagers from Saffuriya, Mjaydal, 'Ain-Dūr, Ma'alūl and other rural communities in Galilee destroyed by the Israeli forces during or immediately after the war took refuge in the town. Following initial periods in church facilities, make-shift shelters or with relatives, many families found housing and employment in Nazareth and settled down. Residents of pre-1948 villages tended to stick together in their new urban locations, sometimes naming new neighbourhoods in Nazareth after their ruined villages.

Thus, ironically, the loss of Palestinian rural communities in Galilee became a source of strength for Nazareth. The heart of a 150,000 strong urban sprawl – the town itself plus seven villages around it – Nazareth now makes the largest and most important Palestinian urban centre in Israel.

One result of the influx of internal refugees after 1948 has been the steady growth of the proportion of Muslims in the population. By the late 1980s the Muslim community made up approximately 55 per cent of the town's population.

Between the mid-1960s and the 1990s, a time in which the communist party and its parliamentary coalitions are the chief political outlets for the Palestinian citizens of Israel, Nazareth was by far the political and social capital of the Palestinian community countrywide. In 1975 the town became the first urban municipality in Israel ever to be controlled by a communist-led coalition. Twenty years on, the coalition is in power still.

The demographic and economic growth of Nazareth was coupled with an increasing shortage of land available for housing, commerce and industry. The town is situated in a closed-in valley. The steep slopes which tower to its south and west, an old cemetery to the north and a flooding *wadi* to the east have always limited its urban expansion. The problem was exacerbated, however, when in the 1950s the Israeli government seized over 15,000 *dunams* (3,750 acres) to the east of Nazareth, to serve the newly established town of Natzerat Illit.

A close examination of the municipal boundaries as delineated on pre-1948 British maps indicate that only approximately 8 per cent of the land assigned to Natzerat Illit – some 1,200 dunams, 300 acres – had formerly belonged officially to the municipality of Nazareth.[5] This notwithstanding, the annexation to Natzerat Illit of the only mass of land reserve available for Nazareth's future expansion had dire consequences for the Palestinian town and its prospects. As it happened, the new delineations of the 1950s left Nazareth with a municipal territory of only 12,500 *dunams* – approximately 3,000 acres (Khamaisi 1989:4). The amount of land expropriated from individual Nazarenes, regardless of municipal jurisdiction, was naturally larger, though difficult to ascertain.

The growing scarcity of land in Nazareth was coupled with a severe financial crisis at the municipal level, stemming partly from unequal allocation of state resources to local Palestinian authorities (see Palestinian Encyclopaedia 1980:439; al-Haj and Rosenfeld 1990:105). With virtually no industrial or other productive development, and with slow initiative and low expenditure by central government on public housing, the town, now swollen with internal refugees, has little to offer in the way of housing. Most construction projects happen when people decide to build on their own land. With many plots measuring approximately one *dunam* (a quarter of an acre), houses normally consist of three or four apartments, and are primarily designed to house a patriarchal couple and a number of their married sons – a far cry from an economical urban land-use pattern.

Apartment blocks or other versions of 'saturated construction'[6] are rare in Nazareth, where less than 1,000 apartments were built in the four decades following 1948. Properties for sale or rent are particularly few and far between. By the late 1970s the substantial disparity between heavy demand and poor supply turned Nazareth into one of the most expensive real-estate markets in northern Israel. Housing problems became particularly pressing for young couples. With employment opportunities and kinship networks focused in Nazareth, many young families were finding accommodation exceedingly difficult to finance.

In late 1957 some 300 Jewish Israeli settlers took residence in newly constructed houses near the top of Jabil Siḥ – the first instalment of what would become Natzerat Illit. Many of them were new immigrants, most of them employed in one way or another by the government. The early operation was designed and managed by an inter-departmental committee dominated by Ministry of Defence personnel.

The site selected for the first houses of the new town was a high spot commanding a good view of Palestinian Nazareth, notably the easiest to defend in the event of military conflict. The place, now covered by a pine copse, was even more exposed in those early days than it is now, the rugged terrain pushing the inclement weather to its worst. The site of first construction in 1957 thus emerges as a direct continuation of the military conquest of the ridge by Israel in July 1948.

Most of the individuals who settled on the summit in 1957 subsequently left the town – many in its early days. While Mordechay Alon, who served as chief of the establishing committee in the 1950s, did become head of the local council and later mayor of the town before he moved on in the late 1970s, there is no sense in Natzerat Illit today of the pioneering group as having had a lasting impact on the community and culture of the town. This may partly explain the fact that the local mythology of origin is relatively poor. Beyond 1957 as the formative date and the magic number of 300 founders, the local archives offer only scant detail of those early days or of the individuals who had been present.

Table 2. *Israelis in Natzerat Illit*
1961–1989

Year	Population	Basis
1961	4,291	Census
1972	14,400	Census
1983	21,248	Census
1985	22,600	Extrapolated
1986	22,300	Extrapolated
1987	21,900	Extrapolated
1988	21,600	Extrapolated
1989	21,800	Extrapolated

Sources: State of Israel 1988, State of Israel
1990:69

The new settlement was not initially called Natzerat Illit. Newspaper articles, for example, often referred to it as Kiryat Natzeret[7] or Vered Hagalil ('Rose of Galilee'). Only in the early 1960s, when the new settlement was formally recognized and had a local council appointed, did the name Natzerat Illit become official.

The ambiguity regarding its name, however, lingered on for decades. By the late 1980s very few Israeli residents were habitually referring to their town by its official name Natzerat Illit – literally Upper Nazareth. Instead, most Israeli residents used either Natzeret or Natzerat, omitting Illit altogether. For a community united behind the notion that their town is permanently separate from Palestinian Nazareth and must always remain so, this incongruence is significant. For me it symbolizes the ambiguity regarding the place of the community – and for that matter, of Israelis generally – in the Palestinian heartland of the Nazareth Hills.

The first twenty-five years of Natzerat Illit were marked by steady growth. Its expansion from 1957 to 1985, while not uniform, was continuous (see table 2).

The majority of Israelis in Natzerat Illit are first generation immigrants from Central Europe, North Africa, South America and the Soviet Union (see table 3). As in other new towns in Israel (see Matras 1973; Weintraub and Kraus 1982), population growth corresponded to the major waves of immigration into Israel.[8] Immigrants from Rumania and Hungary in the late 1950s, from Morocco, Tunisia and Algeria in the 1960s, and from the Soviet Union in the 1970s and in the 1990s have left their particular respective marks on the town.

Table 3. *Israelis in Natzerat Illit by country of origin, 1983*

Origin	Persons	Percentage of total
Israeli born	1,424	(6.7)
Asian origin	1,210	(5.6)
North African origin	4,911	(23.0)
Europe-American origin	13,703	(64.5)
Total	21,248	(99.8)

Source: State of Israel 1988

Each wave of immigrants directed at Natzerat Illit was complimented with a package of housing development initiated, financed and carried out by central government and the Jewish agency. Consequently, the bulk of the town is made of bounded housing compounds – *shekhūnot* in Hebrew – each planned and executed in one coordinated pulse.

Many residential compounds are named after labour party leaders of the 1950s and 1960s, including prime ministers Ben-Gurion and Eshkol, finance minister Sapir and defence minister Lavon. Others bear the names of government agencies which carried out development, notably Rasko and Amidar. Most apartments have two bedrooms, a living room, a tiny kitchen, a bathroom and a toilet. Blocks have anything from eight to 120 apartments, and a compound may include from five large blocks to forty smaller ones.

The general outcome is by no means more inspiring than towns established in the 1950s and 1960s elsewhere in Israel. Whereas in Natzerat Illit few of the estates would qualify as slums, the gloomy signs of the period are nevertheless there: monotonous edifices made of cheap materials, narrow corridors, constricted stairways, unimaginative and badly lit interiors.

The most significant period of development in Natzerat Illit occurred following the 1967 war. The early 1970s saw large-scale immigration from the Soviet Union, in turn triggering accelerated construction and further industrial development. It was then that the town expanded from the northern ridge of Jabal Siḥ, where construction had begun two decades earlier, to the town's southern and by now larger section, near the cliff which towers over Jezrael. This expansion had the original industrial zone, once outlying the town to its south, overtaken by new compounds to the south, to become trapped between the older and the newer sections of the town.[9]

The early housing projects in the 1950s and 1960s were supplemented by the introduction to Natzerat Illit of industry. First came *Ze-De*, a chocolate factory owned by a Jewish industrialist from Central Europe; then *Kitan*, a textile factory owned by the *Histadrut*, Israel's trade union federation, and the *Natzerat Illit Motorcar Works*, established in the early 1960s. The 1970s saw the transfer to Natzerat Illit of a medium-sized state-owned munitions factory, a branch of *Ta'as*, Israel's Military Industries.

Such factories, either owned by the government or heavily subsidized by it (as was *Ze-De* before it was bought out by *Elite*, Israel's largest sweets conglomerate) are a standard feature of new towns in Israel. While offering a steady supply of jobs for semi-skilled and unskilled labourers, this mass and centralized industrialization often arrests long-term economic growth. Handling the local community as a virtually endless reservoir of cheap labour, it does little in the way of re-investing profits in the community. Bolstering the power of local union leaders and the Histadrut, such plants tend to draw massive subsidies from central government or the highly politicized Histadrut, often regardless of real economic performance. In Natzerat Illit these works still make a significant segment of the economy. Small-scale industry and commerce were thus underdeveloped in the 1980s, with a substantial proportion of the local work force – particularly the better qualified – commuting to factories and offices in other towns.

Compared to other new towns, the Israeli population of Natzerat Illit is relatively solid economically, with a generally even distribution of wealth. Levels of education are above average for Israel, although young persons born and raised in Natzerat Illit tend not to return after their university years or once they have qualified in their professions. There are a number of prosperous families, though none outrageously rich. Poorer Israeli folk tend to be of North African origin, but also elderly people of East European origin, mainly those who live by themselves.

With less than 30,000 inhabitants at the time of fieldwork, Natzerat Illit is by no means a big town. Its physical environment however spreads out to the point of losing a sense of closeness and personal warmth often found in smaller towns. Residential compounds are not only well bounded, but also removed from one another, compelling people to use cars and buses rather than walk between them.

While generally speaking a workers' town, Natzerat Illit does not often seem to be hard at work. The spread-out nature of its residential compounds, the scattered distribution of the factories in various corners of the town, the quietness of the little rows of neighbourhood shops and the general absence of people from the streets create a somewhat drowsy atmosphere. In the absence of a central mall prior to 1992, shopping was limited to a number of humble establishments in old commercial centres tucked within residential compounds.[10] With no cinema or other venues to offer entertainment at the time, streets and public spaces were often deserted after hours of commerce. The town often felt empty – a sense which seemed particularly poignant on autumn and on winter evenings, as the light turns.

Natzerat Illit is the only Israeli town (not counting those in the territories occupied by Israel since 1967) cut off from other Israeli settlements by a belt of Palestinian villages and towns. Every journey in or out of Natzerat Illit must in fact be negotiated through Nazareth, its urban sprawl or its rural hinterland.[11] One result is that community ties with neighbouring Israeli towns such as Migdal Haemek (6 km south-west), 'Afula (15 km south) and Tiberias (25 km north) are scarce. This reinforces in Natzerat Illit an aura of isolation and seclusion disproportionate to actual geographic distances. (See map 2.)

The most dynamic commercial scene throughout the 1980s, while not necessarily representing the most significant monetary turnover, was the Tuesday open-air market, located in a field near the western entrance to the town. The affair, which has since been moved to an alternative site slightly to the south, is attended by peddlers and vendors from across the north of Israel and the northern section of the West Bank. Customers arrive from Natzerat Illit, Migdal Haemek, but also from Nazareth and the Palestinian villages around it. With prices considerably lower than those found in food and clothing sections of department stores and supermarkets, the market offers cheaper shopping for essential items and for small consumer goods. It is also a significant venue for interaction between Israelis and Palestinians, both vendors and shoppers. As in shops and other commercial establishments in Nazareth routinely frequented by Israeli residents of Natzerat Illit, this interaction hardly leads to personal relations beyond the fleeting nature of the individual deal.

When the municipal boundaries of Natzerat Illit were about to be finalized in the 1970s, the ministry of the interior was persuaded by the municipality to include within the town a number of tracts hitherto outside the town's jurisdiction. One such area is the north-western slope of the northern ridge, which carries the Arabic name of Kūrūm Raina – orchards of Raina – or simply al-Kūrūm – the orchards. (See map 3.)

Plots on al-Kūrūm were owned by Palestinian residents of the neighbouring village Raina and of Nazareth. Unlike the move of 1957, this time land designated to be incorporated to Natzerat Illit was not expropriated

2. Road map of the Nazareth area

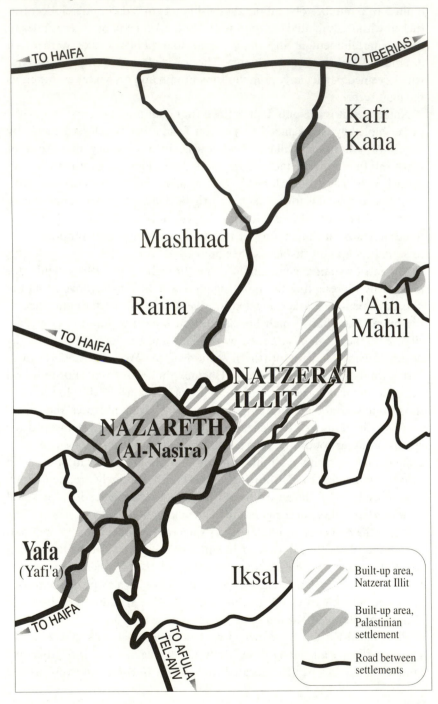

3. The western section of the municipal boundaries of Natzerat Illit

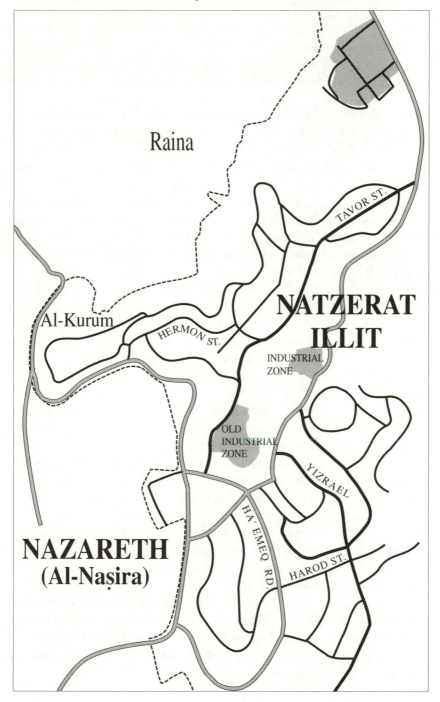

from its Palestinian holders, so the transfer of jurisdiction over to Natzerat Illit involved no change of ownership. [12]

The transfer of al-Kūrūm into the jurisdiction of Natzerat Illit triggered a change of land-use status from agricultural to urban. This in turn facilitated considerable simplifications of planning procedure for residential purposes, and Palestinian owners immediately began to build on or to sell their land to other Palestinians who were inclined to build.

The 1980s thus saw the gradual growth of a well-rooted Palestinian neighbourhood in al-Kūrūm – a spontaneous development which took the Israeli leaders of Natzerat Illit rather by surprise. By 1989, between 200 and 250 Palestinian families (up to 1,200 persons) were living in private houses and small apartment blocks on the slope.

Al-Kūrūm, which has no Israeli residents, now represents approximately one-third of the Palestinian population of the town, and a true Palestinian stronghold within Natzerat Illit (see map 4.)

The economic growth which characterized Natzerat Illit during the period following the 1967 war came to an end with the economic crisis following the 1973 war and the ensuing energy crisis. Immigration into Israel was scarce, construction at a lull. The economic slump, which intensified in the early 1980s, had a more severe effect on Israel's periphery than on the coastal plain. A substantial proportion of residents left Natzerat Illit for other places in Israel and abroad. While precise numbers are virtually impossible to ascertain, it is clear that growth declined considerably and, by the mid-1980s, became negative[13].

This notwithstanding, decisions taken at the height of growth in the early 1970s came to fruition on the ground by the mid- and late-1970s. New residential compounds, with higher building standards, were completed in the rapidly developing new southern section of the town, encouraging veteran residents to leave their older flats in the northern section and move to new ones in the south (*Haaretz* 1978; *Haaretz* 1981).

However, with no additional immigration to settle older properties in the north, the real-estate market suddenly absorbed a large number of superfluous apartments, many of them older and less attractive. Since demand even for new apartments in the southern section was limited, real-estate prices plunged throughout.

The contrast with neighbouring Nazareth, where rise in real-estate prices was steady, became dramatic. Yisrael Zangvil's famous statement of 1894 could now be turned on its head: the Palestinians of Nazareth, a town with no houses, were being tempted to settle in Natzerat Illit, many in houses which had no people.

4. The distribution of Palestinian households in Natzerat Illit, 1988

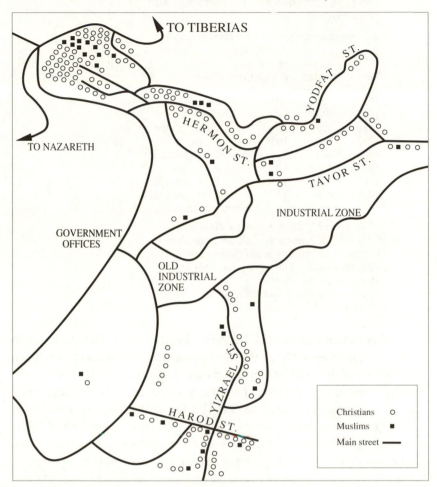

Arrival of the Palestinian tenants

Unable to afford to build or buy apartments and homes in their community, Nazarene couples began in the 1970s to rent and buy in Natzerat Illit. Their presence in the new town, starting as a trickle in the late 1960 (*Al Hamishmar* 1984), became substantial in the late 1970s, intensifying further in the early 1980s (Bar-Gal 1986). Table 4 gives an idea of the growth of the Palestinian population between 1963 and 1987. The 1988 Knesset elections voters roll and my own survey of early 1989 indicate that by early 1989 the Palestinian community in the town included some 800 households.

Table 4. *Palestinians in Natzerat Illit 1963–1987*

Year	Number	Percentage of town's population	Basis
1963	0	0.0	Census
1972	600	4.0	Census
1980	1,600	9.0	Extrapolated
1983	2,366	10.0	Census
1985	3,000	11.7	Extrapolated
1987	3,200	12.7	Extrapolated
1988	3,300	13.2	Extrapolated
1989	3,400	13.5	Extrapolated

Note: the 1972 figure refers to 'Non-Jews'.
This category probably includes a number of
Christian spouses of Jewish immigrants from
Central Europe. The actual number of
Palestinians was smaller.
Sources: State of Israel 1988, State of Israel
1990:69

The Palestinian residents of Natzerat Illit tend to be Christians, most adults being natives of Nazareth.[14] The proportion of Muslims went down from one-third in 1983 to approximately a quarter by the end of the decade.[15] Families tend to be at the early stages of their developmental cycle, typically having moved to Natzerat Illit within the first three years following marriage, often after the birth of the first or second child.[16] It is a generally young community, with very few persons living by themselves. Young families tend to get support from kinsmen and kinswomen in Nazareth, typically mothers and maternal aunts assisting daughters and nieces with child care, thus enabling younger women to go out to work.

Palestinians living in Natzerat Illit are mainly waged employees,[17] typically skilled industrial or professional workers. Al-Kūrūm, where people live in private homes, has self-employed lawyers, accountants, doctors, welfare officers, bankers and other professionals. Palestinians living in apartments in humbler parts of town include teachers, clerks, construction workers but also waged professionals. In 1983 over half of the Palestinian residents of Natzerat Illit who were employed were in industry and public services, including teaching (see tables 5–9). In 1989 about three-quarters of the Palestinian residents of Natzerat Illit were owner-occupiers of their apartments.[18] Income per capita was more or less balanced with that of local Israeli residents.[19] The majority of households owned cars, tele-

Table 5. *Palestinians and Israelis in Natzerat Illit and Nazareth by age groups (1983)*

Age grp.	Natzerat Illit Palestinians		Nazareth (Palestinians)		Natzerat Illit Israelis	
	Persons	%	Persons	%	Persons	%
0–9	763	32.0	12,318	27.5	5,240	20.6
10–14	201	8.4	5,754	12.8	2,163	9.3
15–19	153	6.4	5,504	12.3	1,597	8.2
20–24	174	7.3	4,442	9.9	1,491	7.7
25–29	272	11.4	3,382	7.5	1,863	7.8
30–34	249	10.5	2,557	5.7	2,018	8.0
35–39	175	7.4	2,332	5.2	1,597	6.5
40–44	105	4.4	1,989	4.4	1,050	4.4
45–49	72	3.0	1,795	4.0	1,078	4.5
50–54	72	3.0	1,421	3.1	1,043	4.4
55–59	56	2.3	983	2.1	1,161	4.4
60–64	23	0.9	667	1.4	975	4.1
65–69	11	0.5	465	1.0	812	3.4
Over 70	42	1.7	1,169	2.6	1,532	6.8
Total	2368	100.0	44,779	100.0	23,620	100.0

Note: ND: no data
Sources: For 1983 – State of Israel (1985:246–7, 251–2)
        1989 – My own sample, 247 questionnaires, 243 valid cases

Table 6. *Palestinians in Natzerat Illit by children per household with children (1983 and 1989)*

No. of children	1983		1989	
	No. of households	Percentage of households	No. of households	Percentage of households
1	108	25.3	27	12.5
2	127	29.8	57	26.4
3	100	23.4	49	22.7
4	51	12.0	49	22.7
5	26	6.1	23	10.6
6–7	13	3.0	9	4.1
8–9	1	0.2	1	0.4
10	0	0.0	1	0.4
Total	426	100.0	216	100.0
Mean	2.54 children		2.74 children	

Sources: For 1983: State of Israel (1986, vol. 8:246–7). (Comprehensive data)
        For 1989: My survey of 247 households; (216 valid cases non-comprehensive data)

Table 7. *Palestinians in Natzerat Illit by occupation (1983 and 1989)*

Occupation	Percentage 1983	Percentage 1989
Industry	26.0	15.1
Public services (incl. teachers)	25.0	15.6
Construction	19.5	23.5
Transport	6.9	13.8
Commerce	6.5	8.0
Finance	5.5	2.7
Personal services	5.0	4.4
Total	100.0	100.0

Sources: For 1983: State of Israel (1985, vol. 13) (Total number in survey: 745 adults)
For 1989 – My survey of 247 adults (200 valid cases)

Table 8. *Palestinians in Natzerat Illit by position in the employment structure (1983 and 1989)*

Employed as	Percentage (1983)	Percentage (1989)
Skilled Industry and professional workers	38.0	34.2
Technical workers	15.4	24.9
Unskilled	10.0	3.3
Clerical workers	8.7	12.1
Service workers	8.7	7.1
Sales workers	6.7	5.5
Academic, engineers and high school teachers	6.0	16.0
Total	100.0	100.0

Sources: For 1983: State of Israel (1985, vol. 13:276–7)
For 1989: My survey of 247 adults (181 valid cases)

phones and washing machines. In 1983 approximately 10 per cent of Palestinian families in Natzerat Illit belonged to Israel's top socio-economic decile. Two-thirds, however, belonged to the lowest four deciles.[20]

Economically, the community is representative of the more wealthy sections of the Palestinian community in Israel. Unemployment is low, a marked contrast with Nazareth, where unemployment ratios in the 1980s were never under 10 per cent, often nearer 20 per cent. This relative economic robustness is not surprising given the high proportion of Christians – a community which lost less land, invested more in education and social

Table 9. *Christian Palestinians and Israelis above age 15 in Natzerat Illit by years of schooling (1983 and 1989)*

| | 1983 | | 1989 | |
| | Natzerat Illit | | Natzerat Illit | |
Years of Schooling	Christian Palestinians	Israelis	Christian Palestinians	Israelis
0–4	5.5	12.3	9.3	3.1
5–8	26.1	20.8	29.7	23.7
9–12	50.5	48.9	48.1	43.8
13 plus	17.4	18.0	13.0	28.2
Median number of years of schooling:				
Men	10.9	11.2	10.3	—
Women	11.3	10.8	10.2	—
General	10.9	11.2	10.2	11.29

Sources: For 1983: State of Israel (1985, vol. 5:254–7)
For 1989: my survey of 247 adults (226 valid cases)

mobility, and is generally more affluent than any other segment of the Palestinian community inside Israel. My survey of 1989 indicates that nearly one in three Palestinian residents of Natzerat Illit had completed more than thirteen years of education. In 1983 a third of the Christian women living in Natzerat Illit were employed outside their domicile – almost double the proportion in Nazareth, though lower than the 45 per cent figure for Israeli women in Natzerat Illit (State of Israel 1985).

Comparisons between the economic situation of Palestinians and Israelis in Natzerat Illit can be done on two levels. Conventional measurements of income per capita and per family and the complimentary figures for expenditure and ownership of consumer goods – suggests a slightly wealthier Israeli community, with a more even distribution of wealth. There are more rich Palestinians in Natzerat Illit than rich Israelis, and more poor Palestinians than poor Israelis.

The second level of comparison is rather more telling. Economically and culturally, Israelis in Natzerat Illit are peripheral to the Israeli centre in the coastal plain. The Palestinian residents, in contrast, are part of metropolitan Nazareth, thus at the core of the most dynamic economic centre in the Palestinian sector of the state. They work in Nazareth, own businesses there, invest and reinvest in the Palestinian town. The fact their fortunes lie outside Natzerat Illit makes them more independent, enterprising and economically dynamic than their Israeli townsfolk, most of whom lack external contacts, scope or income.

The limited place of Natzerat Illit in the economic lives of its Palestinian residents undoubtedly contributes to their perception of the town as a suburban offshoot of metropolitan Nazareth. This is compounded by their kinship reality, as well as by the fact that they send their children to schools, clubs and youth activities in the Palestinian town. They shop in Nazareth, obtain medical and other welfare services, worship and are buried there. Politically, Nazareth remains their centre of gravity and identification.

Residence in Natzerat Illit, it must be noted, is attractive for newly-wed Palestinians not only due to the reasonable real-estate prices in the Israeli town. Apartment blocks in predominantly Israeli Natzerat Illit also offer them a convenient escape from the pressures and tensions associated with living in an extended patriarchal household in neighbourhoods which are often dense with kin – a syndrome recently labelled 'the tyranny of kinship'.[21]

A Palestinian resident of Natzerat Illit once explained his choice of residence in the predominantly Israeli town, contrasting the anonymity he enjoys living in a housing estate in Natzerat Illit with the situation in a similar estate in Nazareth:

I would never live in a housing estate in Nazareth. Why, do you think it's fun, every time you go down to your car and start it, to know that twenty pairs of eyes are watching you from twenty windows? And really, there is nothing you can do about it. Arabs are like that. They always want to know.

Young professionals, who make up a substantial proportion of Palestinian residents of Natzerat Illit, are keenly aware of other irksome aspects of living amongst kin in their communities of origin. A young doctor who has lived in Natzerat Illit since he married in the 1970s once told me that:

People think because you are their father's cousin's nephew and you live next door, they can knock at your door at midnight to ask for help with their child who cannot fall asleep. Or with their VAT report, if you are an accountant. And of course there is no way you can turn away a relative in such a situation. You end up feeling you lose control over your own time.

The Palestinian presence in Natzerat Illit is thus linked primarily to the real-estate market in the Nazareth area since the 1970s, as well as to the desire of educated younger Palestinians to have privacy and to escape the pressures associated with living in an extended family household.

An understanding of the reasons which push Palestinians to rent and buy in Natzerat Illit is essential if we are to comprehend the social reality of the town. It is doubly significant given the preoccupation on the part of Israeli residents with the purpose and characteristics of this immigration. To anticipate a later theme: the tendency of Israeli residents to overlook the economic and individual nature of the Palestinian presence encourages them to visualize it as a premeditated, coordinated and malicious onslaught on them and, by extension, on the state of Israel. This, I argue, is a central factor in the social and political relationship between the two communities in Natzerat Illit. For Israeli residents, the issue of Palestinians' motives is indeed emotive.

Residential mix

In the late 1980s approximately two-thirds of Natzerat Illit's Palestinian residents – some 500 households – lived in apartment buildings in predominantly Israeli compounds across the town. More than half occupied buildings where Israeli households were either in the majority or equalled the number of Palestinian households.[22]

With the balance of presence either symmetric or in favour of Israelis, Palestinians living in such buildings tend to maintain a low collective profile. They are inclined to cultivate the image of good, friendly, almost timid neighbours. Some take part in informal gatherings attended by Israeli residents on benches, concrete fences or in other semi-public spaces such as patios and mini-plazas in and around their buildings of residence. Palestinian women often strike up friendships with Israeli women, many older than themselves. They spend time together in their respective apartments, in staircases and lawns, having coffee, doing household chores, talking. Babies and toddlers often become a focus of attention and mutual support, with elderly Israeli women helping younger Palestinian mothers with child minding.

A Palestinian man I met, a carpenter by trade, habitually constructed the Tabernacles *sukah* in the court-yard of the apartment block where he and his wife live with seven Israeli families. The childless couple, both in their forties, take an active part in neighbourly routines, including helping other households with child care. They have, over the years, amassed an impressive command of local information and have a central place in the social life of the building.

Palestinian residents of buildings where Israeli families are in the majority tend to circumvent political controversy. They tend not to take part in debates of current affairs, knowing how often such discussions deteriorate into heated arguments. If and when they do make comments they tend to palliate and qualify their utterances in an attempt to minimize unnecessary tension.

Palestinians living in apartments in Natzerat Illit tend to see themselves as temporary residents of the town even when they are owner–occupiers. Many plan to stay in Natzerat Illit only as long as it may take them to afford buying or building a home elsewhere – either in Nazareth or in their native village.[23] This partly explains their reluctance to become involved in political debates, as well as in long-term formal neighbourhood affairs such as residents committees (*va'ad bayit*).[24] The assertion of self as the prototypical good neighbour, and the removal from interactions with Israeli neighbours of all manifestations of a collective, politicized identity as Palestinians, is self-conscious and intentional. I often felt as though the Palestinian residents, grateful for merely being allowed to buy or rent in a predominantly Israeli neighbourhood in Natzerat Illit, go to great pains in their perennial effort to keep the boat from rocking.

A second residential pattern in Natzerat Illit has Palestinian residents living in buildings where the majority of apartments are occupied by Palestinians.[25] Some buildings have small clusters of kinspersons, typically two or three siblings or cousins with their respective nuclear households. Most cases, however, have Palestinian neighbours with no family connections between them whatsoever.

Compared to Palestinians living in predominantly Israeli apartment buildings, residents of these Palestinian 'islands' tend to be less tentative in asserting their identity. For example, they are less inhibited regarding the use of Arabic in semi-public spaces such as staircases and parking lots. Parents tend to leave windows open and communicate in Arabic with children playing outdoors. Front doors are often kept ajar to allow women to wander freely into neighbouring apartments. People often open doors and windows for brief surveillance of staircases, entrance halls and courtyards if a stranger is approaching. Residents' committees in the three all-Palestinian buildings situated in the southern part of town tend to be especially active and dynamic. Throughout the late 1980s these buildings in fact enjoyed superior maintenance and care compared to neighbouring blocks of similar design and age.

And yet these elements, while clearly influencing people's sense of space, do not quite redefine these blocks as Palestinian turf. An important factor here is size. Unlike residential clusters in Palestinian communities elsewhere, the Palestinian islands in Natzerat Illit's mixed compounds are limited in geographic and demographic scale, and hence in their capacity to cater for every social need. All Palestinian families in Natzerat Illit are, after all, displaced components of larger kinship units,[26] with the majority of households leaning on Nazareth-based kin as foci for familial gravity. Much like Palestinian families in buildings dominated by Israelis, these larger Palestinian clusters too prefer not to stand out as distinctly separate (and obviously 'Arab') in a predominantly Israeli neighbourhood.

This highlights the unique nature of al-Kūrūm, the all-Palestinian residential area which developed at the north-western corner of Natzerat Illit since the 1970s. Al-Kūrūm gradually became a significant, well-bounded Palestinian space and one of the most cohesive residential groups in town. Its success and desirability triggered more expansion, with Palestinian families buying houses in an adjoining, previously all-Israeli suburb. This enlarged the territorial continuum of Palestinian presence and ownership in this area of Natzerat Illit, which now hosts approximately a third of the total Palestinian community.

A key idiom used by the prosperous suburban Palestinian residents of al-Kūrūm to refer to other parts of Natzerat Illit is the in-out metaphor. Palestinians living in the mixed areas are described by residents of al-Kūrūm as living *dakhil* – Arabic for inside. This usage is by no means unique to Natzerat Illit. West Bank Palestinians, for example, use *dakhil* to denote Israel proper (within the 1967 borders). The Palestinian citizens of Israel are thus often labelled by their brethren outside Israel as '*Arab al-dakhil* – the Arabs of the inside.[27]

The in-out metaphor is present also in Israeli military jargon, where *ḥadira* (penetration) and *knissa lashetaḥ* (entrance to an operational zone) denote presence and action beyond enemy lines. In all three examples, the other's territory, linked to insecurity and discomfort, is described as 'within'; the speakers, in contrast, see themselves safely outside that territory or on its margin.

Residents of al-Kūrūm thus see the main bulk of Natzerat Illit as space to which they – just like residents of Nazareth or neighbouring Palestinian villagers – are quite external. For them their neighbourhood, while formally within the jurisdiction of Natzerat Illit, is by no means space turned Israeli. Al-Kūrūm remains distinct from Israeli territories of the 'inside', persisting in an ambiguous spatial limbo. Marginal, it is at the same time also more secure.

The insecurity associated with the 'inside' of Natzerat Illit surfaced in January 1989. At that time, activists in service of the newly established, exclusively Palestinian independent list of candidates for the local council, were looking for a place to house their office and headquarters for the approaching campaign. A basement flat in al-Kūrūm was considered. Its location, at the bottom of a steep and slippery slope, was not ideal. Most activists were young men and women who lived in the mixed neighbourhoods 'inside', some distance away. Most of them did not own private cars. There is no bus service to al-Kūrūm, and street lighting is poor and restricted. Since sessions that winter were inevitably going to be scheduled at night, when people had returned from work, the basement flat had obvious drawbacks. These notwithstanding, it was hired anyway. Pragmatic considerations such as access and convenience obviously came second to the advantages of hiring a place within a space perceived as safe. The fact that most public meetings of the campaign took place in adjacent Nazareth rather than Natzerat Illit (chapter 9) points in the same direction.

But externality is not the only idiom which establishes al-Kūrūm as Palestinian space. Another idiom is infrastructural discrimination and municipal neglect. Water supply, the sewage system, the presence and maintenance of roads, street lights, nursery schools and other municipal amenities are all wanting in the neighbourhood. All in Israel are aware of the distinction between the cityscape in Palestinian communities and that of Israeli settlements. There are gross inequalities in central government budgeting, variations in tax collection, differences in budgetary priorities, and considerable informal restrictions on access of Palestinians to the planning process. These parities invariably result in public spaces in Palestinian towns and villages being considerably less tended than those of Israeli settlements of similar size, a reality apparent also in the existence and size of industrial parks, public amenities and regional roads. A Palestinian friend once pointed at the rickety surface we were using on our way to his village in the hills of Galilee, exclaiming: 'this is an Arab road. Compare it to that smooth, safe road leading to the new cluster of Jewish settlements over there, and you feel as though you are comparing these rugged mountains to the plains of Florida.'

Not surprisingly, the issue of municipal services and environmental neglect became a major point of friction between the residents of al-Kūrūm and the municipality of Natzerat Illit. The council's justification of the indisputably inferior infrastructure in the neighbourhood tends to play up the difficult topography, the dispersed nature of development, the low number of households per unit area (which pushes costs per capita higher) and the rapid and unplanned development in the area. The residents, for their part, perceive such explanations as excuses, adamantly attributing the situation to discrimination against them as Palestinians.

The politics of environmental neglect and of restricted services in

Palestinian communities is paramount in the way Palestinians citizens of Israel establish spatial meaning. In the case of al-Kūrūm it became a major factor in the politicization of Palestinian space, which eventually led to a concerted move towards political organization (see chapter 9).

Exclusion and inclusion: the *matnas* as fable

There are spaces in Natzerat Illit which Palestinians and Israelis alike view as out of bounds for Palestinians. One case is the Ministry of Defence industrial plant (Ta'as) east of the town. There, most people say, Palestinians can neither be employed nor visit, as every person wishing to gain entry is subject to a thorough security check ahead of time. Clearly, the medium ensuring the establishment of this particular space as exclusively Israeli is state security and secrecy – domains which Israelis as well as Palestinians see as exclusively Israeli (see Rabinowitz 1992b:9 and chapter 4).

But space need not be associated with state security for Palestinians to be excluded from it. It can equally be a bastion of Israeli high culture. One such case is the local community centre (*matnas*). Conceived in the 1970s and materialized since in virtually every Israeli town in Israel and in a growing number of Palestinian towns as well, matnas – an acronym for *Merkaz Tarbut No'ar Vesport* (a centre for culture, youth and sports), denotes a space which would ideally be run by the community and for it, an outlet for local cultural traits and interests. Since its inception, however, it has also had the task of proliferating high culture to Israel's periphery. Naturally, it pushes a version of high culture as seen by the dominant, often paternalistic Ashkenazi establishment (see Dominguez 1989 chapter 4).

A not-for-profit association, *Haḥevra Lematnasim* (the Society for matnas), with its headquarters in Jerusalem, was set up primarily to fund and help establish new centres. It is also involved in the preliminary stages of the operation, including supervision of programming and cultural content. Once a building is complete and routine operation is under way, the project is handed over to a local executive committee, with ongoing involvement of national headquarters assuming a more advisory role.

The newest of the three venues that *Haḥevra Lematnasim* operates in Natzerat Illit, in cooperation with the local council, is the Berkowitz centre. Named after the donors who gave some of the funds towards it in the 1980s, it has a large auditorium, a good public library, and a number of rooms and smaller lecture halls for afternoon and evening classes and activities. There is also a sports centre, with a gym and an indoors swimming pool.

Ostensibly open for all, the Berkowitz matnas employs no active gate-keeping. This notwithstanding, few Palestinian residents of the town ever set foot in the centre. Those who have visited mostly attended evening performances of cinema or theatre, though none make a habit of it. A Palestinian doctor once told me of the experience of attending a theatre show in the matnas with his wife:

It was all right, in the sense that no one bothered us. But we still felt that it was not our place. We were outsiders, and felt uncomfortable. No one, as far as we could judge, actually detected we were Arabs. Of course we did not quite advertise it openly, and kept our conversation hushed as we normally do on such occasions. But the whole thing was awkward, as if we were about to be found out as trespassers or something.

A limited number of Palestinian children enrol for afternoon activities in the matnas in music, dance, marshal arts or sports. I once asked one of the administrators if I could look through the lists of participants, making clear my purpose was to ascertain whether any Palestinians actually participated in activities, and if so how many. The administrator, whom I had met socially on a number of occasions, was clearly uneasy with my request. She proceeded to manipulate the situation so as to allow me only a quick browse through the records. Photocopying the lists was out of the question, though the glimpse I had was long enough to recognize only three or four Palestinian names on a dozen lists or so, each list averaging about twenty young participants.

Somehow, what lingers of the episode is not the actual result, which was by no means surprising, but the administrator's coyness. I find it difficult to say whether her self-consciousness stemmed from having too many Palestinian participants – thus jeopardizing the cultural meaning of the matnas as a bulwark of Israeli culture – or from having too few – thus questioning the reach and relevance of the centre to all segments of the local population.

On another occasion, a Palestinian woman tried to stress the extent to which she and her relatives were integrated in the social and community life of Natzerat Illit. The woman, herself a graduate of an Italian school for Palestinian girls in Haifa, obviously considered western acculturation as a primary marker for such integration. Enthralled, she spoke of her grand niece, who took piano lessons in the matnas:

They had that end of year public concert in the auditorium the other day, and I came along with the girl's parents. It was such a beautiful occasion. Imagine, the teacher calling each pupil by their name to come up on stage and perform. My grand niece was the only Arab girl there, but it really did not matter: what does it matter if one is Arab, Jewish, or whatever? She was there, dressed like anybody else, doing the same thing. Now surely that is the main thing, isn't it?

The 1980s saw a total absence in the area of Nazareth of permanent venues for live music, theatre and the cinema. The advents of television and later of video home systems and cable television had forced the only cinema houses in the area – Diana in Nazareth and Nurit in Natzerat Illit – to convert the premises to other purposes.[28] This shortage, combined with the high level of education amongst Palestinians in Natzerat Illit, who otherwise could have been potential clients for the performing arts and for children's activities, makes their absence from the matnas even more suggestive.

One exception to the generally scant presence of Palestinians in the matnas is the centre's swimming pool – one of two in the town, and the only one indoors. A dozen or so Palestinian early morning swimmers, all of them men, used to attend the pool on a regular basis throughout the late 1980s, sharing the water with local Israeli men.[29] Significantly, there were hardly any Palestinian residents of Natzerat Illit amongst the Palestinian swimmers, virtually all being residents of Nazareth.

This gave the management of the sports division at the matnas an opportunity to curb the number of Palestinian swimmers. First, the Palestinian swimmers were asked to pay a higher admission fee. Second, management periodically spread rumours to the effect that the entry of Palestinians would be banned altogether. Both stipulations, it must be noted, were not expressed in terms of keeping Palestinians out. Rather, they were presented as differentiated treatment of residents versus non-residents. Conveniently, all non-resident swimmers were Palestinians, and virtually all Palestinian swimmers were non-residents. Thus, the higher admission fee and potential ban became a standing reminder of the marginal and disenfranchised status these men and Palestinians generally held in the centre. That same sports division also consistently turned down requests by the three basketball clubs operating in Nazareth, all of which wanted to practise in the matnas gym – the only indoor basketball facility in Natzerat Illit and Nazareth at the time.

The scant use of the matnas by individual Palestinians was matched by the failure of any organized attempts by Palestinians to use the venue for public affairs. Palestinian entrepreneurs who attempted to hire the place for cultural events were repeatedly turned down by the centre's all-Israeli board of trustees. A member of the board once illustrated to me the dynamics of such refusals:

We [the board] were approached by some Arab impresario who wanted to have an Arab beauty queen contest in the auditorium. He had no other option for a venue in Arab communities in the area, as Arabs would have ostracised him for even thinking of such an event, which they see as immoral. He applied for a booking, and we found ourselves in a tricky situation. On the one hand, there was no reason to reject his offer on administrative grounds. Probably the contrary, as he was willing to pay the full rate and to schedule the event for any vacancies we had, and let me tell you – we had quite a few. On the other hand, we certainly do not want Arabs to start staging events in the matnas.

To solve the problem the board was convened in its capacity as supreme programme committee of the matnas and simply said the event was not in line with the goals and purposes of the institution. We let that Arab know of our decision, and never heard from him again. I think the event was finally staged in some hall in Haifa.

We did the same on another occasion, with an Arab agent who wanted to stage one of Emil Habibi's plays in Arabic. We refused, of course. We had a play of his in Hebrew once. But Arabic? No way.

It could be argued that it is the idiom of Western Ashkenazi high culture – as remote and irrelevant for most Palestinian citizens of Israel as it is for Israeli *Mizrahim* – which engenders the matnas as out of bounds for Palestinians. The issue, however, goes further and deeper than cultural preferences. The matnas – in Natzerat Illit as elsewhere in Israel – is a reflection of a particular version of Israeliness, one in which Israeli nationality is fused with a specific brand of culture.

The linkage between, on the one hand, a cultural menu which is deliberately devoid of Middle Eastern music and which systematically silences the Arabic language (see Regev 1993:47–60), and, on the other hand, what many Israelis have been socialized to accept as 'truly' Israeli, cannot be overstated. It gains unique impetus in the borderlands of Lower Galilee, where Israelis, including matnas board members, perceive themselves as under siege: a powerful enemy across the boundary is menacingly poised to swamp them with a culture they see as not only degrading, vulgar and primitive, but also undermining a wholesome Israeliness they want so badly to identify with.

The matnas and the way it is manipulated to represent a stronghold of 'Israeli' culture, is allegorical to Natzerat Illit and to the state of Palestinian citizens of Israel at large. While a central component of the matnas's charter promotes universal admission, such universality can never truly happen. Admission will always be restricted to persons and events which suit those aspects of the mission perceived as preordained by the dominant culture and its emissaries, in this case the state and *Hahevra Lematnasim*. Board members of the matnas, otherwise perfectly liberal in their attitudes to art and culture, cannot bring themselves to have a play performed in Arabic. Palestinians find themselves invited and kept at arms length at one and the same time. Formally, the turf is no exclusion zone. In reality, a good proportion of entitled citizens experience their sojourn as gaol within the homeland.

3

To sell or not to sell

The Palestinian residents of Natzerat Illit treat the town primarily as a satellite of Nazareth, a convenient suburb to commute from to the Palestinian town. Few of them are employed in Natzerat Illit, hardly any at all own businesses in it or participate in its social and cultural life. Their involvement in economic transactions is almost exclusively restricted to renting and purchasing homes. Their visibility is mainly connected with their residency.

The real-estate realm thus emerges as the main arena where relations between Israelis and Palestinians are acted out. It is an arena which most readily transliterates issues of space, territoriality, control and domination into personal decisions which actors must take, then live with the consequences. Palestinians occupying mixed residential compounds in Natzerat Illit pose especially powerful dilemmas for themselves and for their Israeli townsfolk. Their case, with its particular sociological meanings naturally became a focus of my attention.

Palestinians' choice of residence in Natzerat Illit, while obviously related to the economic reality, is also, fundamentally, a decision to live with Israelis. Whatever the rationale behind it, it is a choice which Israeli residents find hard to stomach. For many Israelis, the Palestinian presence in the town is commandeered from the realm of individual choice into the menacing domain of collective Palestinian intent. This tendency is partly fuelled by media coverage of Palestinian discourses of land, the *patria*, right of return and the importance of extended presence on the ground. These images, replete with symbols and conceptualizations so similar to those invented and used by Zionism decades earlier, strike a sensitive cord among Israeli onlookers.[1]

This concern on the part of Israelis with Palestinian collective will is inevitably exacerbated by the particular circumstances of Natzerat Illit. The borderlands, whereby Israelis face a considerable Palestinian constituency, push Israelis to see most aspects of Palestinian agency as dangerously analogous to the mythologized conduct of bygone Zionist pioneers. This analogy and its sociological consequences are the main analytical project of this chapter.

The split real-estate market
Israeli housing authorities and agencies have always done their utmost to check the Palestinian inflow to Natzerat Illit. Two measures have been particularly effective: selective approval of government-backed mortgages, and selective sale of publicly owned properties.

Until the late 1980s Israel had an underdeveloped market for commercial building credit. Working within the law of mortgages, the Ministry of Housing grants the right for one mortgage per family, normally defined as a married couple and their dependent children. Ostensibly extended on a non-commercial basis, such mortgages are underwritten by the state. Between the 1950s and the 1980s banks, insurance companies and other financing outfits, were restricted by legislation and supporting regulations and barred from entering the market. Thus the state sustained what amounted to a virtual monopoly over the middle and lower sections of the building credit market. While the market has since been opened and diversified, government-backed mortgages still play a major role in helping young couples, immigrants, the handicapped and others to obtain long-term housing credit.

A certain procedure exists for obtaining a government-backed mortgage. Once the applicant identifies a property he wants to buy or land he wants to build on, and has a signed agreement for the sale, he files a mortgage application with the local branch of the Ministry of Housing. The ministry studies the application and the auxiliary paperwork attesting to the sale, the property in question, the applicant's income and other personal details, then issues a mortgage clearance document (*Teudat Zakaut*). Equipped with this document, the applicant approaches a mortgage bank for a loan. Complicated tables of entitlement are issued periodically, with factors such as the location of the desired property, the applicant's financial status, medical and family circumstances and so on, determining the final offer and the terms of repayment.

The law of mortgages, like every other state law, has no explicit preference of ethnic groups. In principal, Palestinian citizens of Israel are entitled to a government-backed mortgage just like other citizens. In actual fact, however, the mortgages they get are lower, and their terms of repayment are less attractive than those offered to Israelis. This is achieved mainly by using service in the security forces, which Palestinians do not do, as a decisive factor in the final calculation.

But rights of Palestinians are also curbed by other administrative means. In the early 1980s Palestinians applying for mortgages in northern Israel began noticing that their clearance document had a line added near its lower margin: 'not to be materialized in development Zones 'a' and 'b''.[2] With most Israeli new towns included precisely in such zones, and with most Palestinian communities excluded from them, the intention on the part of the ministry was obvious: to outmanoeuvre Palestinian applicants, restricting them to buy and build in their native communities.

This stipulation, while obviously contradictory to the spirit of the law, has never been challenged in court, where it would probably have proven indefensible. The Palestinians' acquiescence in fact allows officials ample opportunity to manipulate exceptions. Treating service in Israel's police as service in the security forces, for example, makes a good number of Palestinian citizens, mostly Christians, eligible for government-backed mortgages regardless of location – a privilege which rubs off on first-order relatives. Not surprisingly, many Palestinians living in Natzerat Illit have immediate kin who serve or used to serve in the police. Given the real-estate prices in Nazareth, the combination of a relatively cheap apartment in Natzerat Illit and the opportunity to have up to 95 per cent of its cost financed by a government-backed mortgage was tempting for many Nazarenes.

A second institutional check on Palestinians seeking residence in Natzerat Illit is the refusal by government-owned property agencies, notably Amidar, to sell apartments – new as well as second hand – to Palestinians.

Amidar is a property conglomerate controlled and operated by the Ministry of Housing. Literally meaning 'my people dwells', it was established in the 1950s to provide housing for incoming Jewish immigrants, who upon arrival automatically assume the formal status of *Oleh Hadash* (new immigrant). This entitles the immigrant a number of privileges, including highly subsidized housing. Financed by the Jewish agency, apartments for new immigrants were built almost entirely by public sector companies, including Amidar. The occupant paid a small monthly sum as mortgage repayment, and could become, with time, owner–occupier. Many did, especially in the 1980s, when government policy encouraged occupiers to become owners. Others, however, had left before assuming ownership, or stopped paying their monthly dues, thus losing rights. This way or the other, Amidar and similar publicly owned outfits gradually found themselves managing vast amounts of property.

While Amidar's main line has always been construction, it sometimes also managed Palestinian properties whose owners had been forced to leave the country during the 1948 hostilities or shortly after.[3] Forty years on, Amidar still owns substantial amounts of property in various parts of Israel. Having been a major builder in Natzerat Illit since the 1950s, it is probably the largest local property owner.

Tabor street in Natzerat Illit's northern section had a dozen blocks or so which had been constructed by Amidar in the 1960s. By the late 1980s these blocks were dilapidated and half empty. Many of the flats had been given up by previous dwellers, who preferred newer premises in the southern section of Natzerat Illit or had emigrated out of town altogether. Some units had been standing empty for at least a decade. Many others had broken windows, shattered woodwork, disconnected electricity and faulty water piping.[4] When I once inquired of a veteran Palestinian resident of Natzerat Illit why Palestinians never bought or rented property in these half-empty blocks, she smiled wryly and explained:

Oh Arabs could never be allowed there. Why, don't you know? It is all Amidar. And everybody knows that Amidar simply do not let or, god forbid, sell properties to Arabs. They have this guy in charge here in their branch in Natzerat Illit, who knows exactly how do deal with us Arabs. I know because my young cousin, who is desperately looking for a place here for her family, has made inquiries with him. She sat at his desk and opened her mouth, and he immediately came back at her, asking, as though politely: 'have you been in the army? the police?' She knew then and there that they don't stand a chance, and went away humiliated.

Amidar's consistent refusal to sell to Palestinians, which spans at least the period of right-wing Likud control of the Ministry of Housing and of Amidar (1977–1992), meant that publicly owned properties in Natzerat Illit were effectively out of bounds for Palestinians.

Barred from purchase or rental of publicly owned properties, Palestinians wishing to take up residence in Natzerat Illit can only buy or rent from Israeli individuals. Israelis, typically seeking to sell apartments they had been given upon their first arrival in Natzerat Illit, look to maximize sale revenue and use the money for new housing, locally or elsewhere. Unable to afford suitable accommodation in expensive Nazareth, Palestinian newcomers in the 1970s and 1980s were ready to purchase or rent properties for prices in excess of their otherwise depressed market values. Even so the prices they were asked in Natzerat Illit were considerably lower than what they would have had to pay for similar properties in Nazareth. A split real-estate market thus developed, with Israeli sellers facing the simple choice of selling to a Palestinian or selling short. I shall return to the notion of the split market, suggesting a modification, later in this chapter.

Most people preferred profit to conviction. Contradictory to the general antagonism to the Palestinian presence as this pattern may have been, it soon became a norm. A conservative estimate of the number of apartments purchased by Palestinians in Natzerat Illit during the 1980s is 500.

The notion of collective Palestinian intent

Natzerat Illit is cut off from all other Israeli communities by the Palestinian belt of metropolitan Nazareth and the villages around it. This sense of seclusion adds uncertainty to a community already unsure about its place in contemporary Israel. The material, political and cultural life of Israel is often described as taking place *Bein Hadera le Gedera* (between Hadera and Gedera) – the 80 kilometre long-strip of urban sprawl along the coastal plain, north and south of Tel-Aviv. It is there that the identity of modern Israel is engendered, often rendering those living in other areas irrelevant and marginal (Ben-Zadok and Goldberg 1984). Natzerat Illit, with its overwhelming majority of first and second generation immigrants, its jittery economy and its high level of dependence on central government, is certainly a place whose incorporation into mainstream Israel is slow and problematic (see Swirski 1985; Ben-Ari and Bilu 1987:249).

The fact that Israelis are a majority in most parts of Israel renders minority–majority issues fairly meaningless for them most of the time. This is not the case in Lower Galilee, where Israelis are a minority – a fact which inevitably colours their perspective (see Sofer 1989:98 for an outstanding illustration).

David Shipler quotes a young Israeli resident of Natzerat Illit who expressed typical disenchantment with the notion of sharing a community with Palestinians:

I was born in Jerusalem, and have been here [in Natzerat Illit,] seven years. We came from Petaḥ Tiqva [a town in the Tel-Aviv metropolis,] and they told us Natzerat Illit was a Jewish settlement. If we had thought for a moment, even in a million dreams, it would turn even into 10 per cent Arab . . .

(Shipler 1987:286)

Such views are not unique to Natzerat Illit. They represent a widespread view amongst Israelis of Palestinians and their accommodation by the state. Tolerated as nominal but marginal citizens, Palestinians are regarded by some Israelis as residents-by-mercy whose ambiguous status could make them subject to expulsion at (Israeli) will. While positions on this point naturally span a range of interim views, my impression is that most Israelis subscribe to the necessity of spatial segregation.

Preoccupation on the part of Israeli residents of Natzerat Illit with the extent to which the Palestinian presence is an orchestrated effort was reflected as early as 1976 in the infamous Koenig report (Koenig 1976:193). The report, authored by the then director of the northern region of Israel's Ministry of the Interior – himself a resident of Natzerat Illit – spells out official misgivings on 'the Arab threat' to Israeli dominance in Galilee, and makes suggestions as to how to combat the situation. Significantly, the mayor of Natzerat Illit may have been involved in drafting the Koenig report. In a newspaper interview on 3 December 1982 he twice declines to comment on the suggestion that he had been a contributor to the report, then proceeds to comment positively on its content (*Hotam* 1982:20–1).

Koenig seems to have been on the mark of popular sentiment. Statements made by Israeli residents and office holders in Natzerat Illit in the early 1980s project a virtually universal belief that the rising number of Palestinian residents is a result of a scheme devised and funded from abroad (see *Hotam* 1982, *Maariv* 1983). A young Israeli told *Al Hamishmar* (1983) that, 'The hand of the PLO is strong. They have funds as well as arms. We must stop them from taking over Natzerat Illit.' Similar sentiments appear in Atallah Mansour's interview with a leading activist of the local Jewish vigilant group MENA (Hebrew acronym for *Maginey Natzerat Illit*, 'Defenders of Natzerat Illit'), who spoke openly of oil money and PLO involvement in what he portrayed as a take-over bid of the Jewish town (*Haaretz* 1983). Leaflets published by MENA in the summer of 1983 urging Israeli residents not to sell to Palestinians were worded in terms of national duty. One of them reads:

Citizens of Natzerat Illit!!!

A phenomenon has spread in our town lately, whereby apartments are let and sold to non-Jews. As a response to this worrying phenomenon a voluntary body has been founded, consisting of citizens who care. Our organization is non-political, and consists of people of all walks of life, every part of town and all political persuasions. Our aim is guided by nationalism and Zionism. It is to raise the consciousness of the residents of Natzerat Illit to the problem and to remind them that our town was founded to be a Jewish town, a centre for the entire Galilee.

Natzerat Illit was established for Jews.

The state of Israel invested phenomenal amounts of funds in the construction of our town as a Hebraic town (*Ir Ivrit*), as part of Judaizing Galilee. Let us not sell our Jewish independence for money. Our blood is at stake. Letting or selling your apartments to non-Jews is a sin and a national bankruptcy.

These notions were echoed in 1989 when an Israeli resident of about thirty, a native of Natzerat Illit, told me that:

You have to understand how they [the Palestinians] operate. It is not random. They begin in a given neighbourhood, and suddenly all of them go there. Slowly they annex (*mesaphim*) the whole area. For instance lower Yizrael street is now 'hot'. So they all go there to settle (*leakhless*). It is really a settlement operation (*mivtsa ikhluss*), with a guiding hand (*yad mekhavenet*).

They say they go to live in areas where other Arabs are already living because these are the only parts of town where they are accepted. But when I see, as in block 450, how they first move in to ground floors, then gradually take over the whole block, this is what makes me think that the whole thing is directed (*megamati*).

At this point the man took a piece of paper, drew a schematic map of the town, and used it as an illustration:

You see? They take over (*mishtaltim 'al*) the town's main arteries. They slowly encircle it (*maqifim*). They come from all directions... They began with ground floor flats in Rasko, and then used it as a base to penetrate from. Now they are everywhere... They are even eyeing the Ventura housing complex, where people once vowed they will never let Arabs in.

For me there are three things which could explain this progression. Either a mentality of sticking together at all times; or a fear of living amongst Jews; or, that there is a guiding hand which tells them where to buy and where to take over (*lehishtalet*). Maybe it isn't all PLO (*Ashaf*). But in some blocks there is a clear direction.

Similar views, in various degrees of crudeness, were put forward to me by Israeli residents of Natzerat Illit on several occasions. One version came from a man of European origin, commanding a solid social and material standing in the community, whose general political outlook could be described as rational and liberal. When it came to the presence of Palestinians in the town he had the following to say:

When I first arrived here almost thirty years ago, all the surrounding Arab villages were tiny. A dot over there, some houses further. Now look around here. The villages of 'Iksal, 'Ain-Mahil, Yafi'a, Raina, not to mention Nazareth itself, are all bursting and bubbling with development. Look at their size, and at the way they cover ground. I am in no position to comment on whether it is an orchestrated effort (*ma'amatz mekhuvan*); but I can certainly say that this encircling development all around us effectively chokes Natzerat Illit and can seriously arrest its development.

These accounts, while differing in sophistication and explicitness, revolve around one theme. The speakers invariably perceive the string of moves by Palestinian individuals as leading to inevitable territorial gains at the expense of Israel and Israelis. They attribute the Palestinians with the will and the ability to orchestrate the movement of people across territory in a task-oriented, essentially malicious progression. The subjects, (repeatedly referred to as the nondescript 'they'), collectively 'eye', 'encircle', 'move', 'penetrate', 'progress', 'occupy', 'choke' and 'take-over'. The narrative is clearly of 'them' doing things to 'us' through the medium of territory (see Elliot 1986, GAP 1987).

These metaphors are highly suggestive of the way the Israeli residents of Natzerat Illit view their Palestinian townsfolk and Arabs at large. It is in military battles that armies get hold of 'main arteries' and 'advance along' them; that 'bases' are 'consolidated' as stepping stones for 'further penetration'.

The military experience is probably the most lucid example of idealized and ideologized Israeliness. The Israeli army is not construed by Israelis as merely a large organization fulfilling instrumental roles. It is perceived primarily as a tool serving the innermost objectives of Zionism – the seizure of land, its protection, the safeguard of the property and persons of Israelis and, by implication, of Jews worldwide.[5] Several writers have alluded to the fact that military episodes and roles form the single most important framework engendering affiliation with mainstream Israeli society.[6]

What gains particular significance in this case is the expressive statement of attribution of military characteristics to Palestinians. Not only does it assign efficiency and pluck to the Palestinians, it also constructs a Palestinian effigy which is the mirror image of the Israeli warrior: displaying an unquestionable congruence between ideology, motivation and actual performance, implying inherent righteousness. This use of terms and idioms appropriated from the vocabulary of Zionism creates a Palestinian facsimile which mirrors the Zionist settler pioneer of old, complete with selfless sacrifice (below) and perfect fit between professed and actual action.

The image of the demonic, external adversary who cunningly acquires the most effective strategies of the in-group thus comes full circle. The localized, essentially urban Palestinian-Israeli interface of Natzerat Illit is reunited with the ostensibly omnipresent rift between two mutually exclusive national ideologies whose key encounters are at the battle field and over rural expanses. This enables – if not obliges – Israelis to identify the practice employed by Palestinians as imbedded in an ideology of the collective. It feeds their constant assumptions of an organized, highly motivated and essentially malicious Palestinian effort which they fear could victimize them.

The predicament of the trapped minority and the exigencies of the borderzone exacerbate the tension. The anxieties of Israelis are not diminished by the fact they are dominant in the region. The sensation that the Palestinians – in Galilee as well as in Israel at large – are capable of laying down the bridgehead which might serve an infinitely larger reservoir of their compatriots across the borders, haunts Israelis. The in-but-out status of the Palestinians immediately invokes the notion of permeable and transient boundaries. This ruptures the illusion that the well-defended borders of the state present a firm protective shield against Arab penetration.

Israelis sometimes use the metaphor of illness, including cancer, for the Palestinian citizens of Israel. *Sarṭan begūf hamedina* ('cancer in the body of the state') was an image used frequently in the 1980s as part of Rabbi Meir Kahana's spoken and written propaganda. The idiom featured from time to time amongst the Israeli residents of Natzerat Illit. A young man renowned in Natzerat Illit for his unrelenting opposition to the presence of Palestinians, who had been known for active participation in provocations against would-be Palestinian residents once told me: 'For me they are not a nation. They are a disease'.

The suggestive metaphor is based on the functionalist conception of the state and the nation as a living organ. Its core belief, however, is penetration. Illness, cancer in particular, arrives from nowhere, unannounced, unnoticed. Its presence in the body does not sever its initial affiliation with an aggressive, external, ever-multiplying stock which could spell further catastrophe. The worst imaginable scenario has the body–state being taken over and destroyed by penetrating agents. It immediately implies urgent directives, such as treating all Others – few as they may currently appear to be – as if they represent a menacing, potentially disastrous throng. Coupled with the suggestive idiom of military movement (above), this realm produces a powerful mixed metaphor of military conquest *and* disease.

While national minorities, which I define as *entire* groups living under foreign domination, may be politically problematic, their discrete boundaries are simpler to think of, thus somewhat less perturbing for the dominant majority. Likewise, fourth world groups are well bounded, smaller in scale, and clearly not connected to dangerous large stocks across the borders. Immigrant ethnicity, for its part, is displaced by definition. Out of its element, it lacks the rootedness which gives homeland groups their zest and impetus. The dangerous ambiguity of trapped minorities, on the other hand, might trigger paradoxic reactions of the kind I witnessed in Natzerat Illit..

Exclusivity in settlement

Fears of an imminent Palestinian takeover are not the only issue which makes the Palestinian presence in Natzerat Illit unacceptable for Israeli residents. The Palestinian presence is also at odds with a major tenet of Israelis' self image as a nation, namely exclusivity in settlement.

Gershon Shafir (1989:147–54) argues convincingly that the Zionist notion of pure settlement is linked to the German and Austrian influence on early Zionism (see Singer 1971:151–9). Shafir argues that Otto Warburg, Arthur Rupin, and of course Theodor Herzl, all of whom contributed richly to the practical policies of Zionism in the formative early years of the century, were strongly influenced by Franz Oppenheimer's *siedlungsgenossenschaft* (settlement cooperative) thesis (1913), as well as by the 'internal colonization' policies advocated by the Junkers (see Reichman and Hasson 1984), all of which centred on collective rather than private ownership of land.

Unsuccessful as the programme may have been in Germany and Habsburg Austro-Hungary (Shafir 1989:153), its compatibility with land tenure laws and cultivation restrictions in Ottoman Palestine made it highly suitable for Zionism. Moreover, since the penniless pioneers could not purchase land anyway, centrally financed acquisition of land that would later be made available for settlement was an ideal solution.

The adoption of this policy in 1907 led to the formation of the Jewish National Fund (JNF), whose charter and operative guidelines were designed not only to enable acquisition of land in Palestine on behalf of the Jewish people, but also to frustrate transfer of right in lands to individuals. With time this mechanism grew into a *de facto* guarantee of collective Jewish control of land and, by implication, of Jewish exclusivity in settlement.

As Shafir (*ibid*) demonstrates, the arguments put forward by the protagonists of the pure settlement approach at the time were practical in nature, hardly ideological. With time, however, the means became enshrined as ideology.[7] The concept of collective ownership of land by and for the Jewish people progressed from pragmatic politics into ideology, soon to be canonized as an inherent, primordial component of Zionism and Israeliness.[8]

This is pertinent to the place of ideology in Israel at large and to the problems highlighted by the material from Natzerat Illit in particular. Does ideology act as *avant garde* which sets the course for the mass movement, as mainstream Zionist would have us believe? Or are courses of action selected *ad hoc* in response to external pragmatic considerations and constraints?

The fact that people use ideologies in surreptitious ways does not necessarily reveal how they really view them, or to what extent they actually subscribe to them. Indeed, how would we ever know? My point here is not necessarily conscious, cynical manipulation by Israelis of explicit ideologies. Rather, certain junctures breed convergence between pragmatic moves and ideologized options, thus easily concealing the conjectural nature of 'real' choices people make on theory and practice.

The problem can also be expressed in terms of levels of ideology which interact with levels of practice. A constant game of give and take existed, and still exists, whereby ideas have influence on people who take action and make processes happen. Ideological horizons, which are never purely detached from pragmatic considerations and feasibility judgements, are in turn swayed by new circumstances and so on.

The Zionist movement, at least in Europe and America, thus assumed a two-pronged course: the epistemology of Jewish consciousness (the discovery of being part of a Jewish 'nation'); and the push for a new beginning somewhere. Both, in retrospect, seem closely involved in political practice and pragmatic achievements. Both, however, also take on ideological forms. This duality was in itself an efficacious form of cultural discourse, particularly suited to communicate the message of affiliation and pioneering to European Jews – both intelligentsia and proletariat. And it seems as efficacious in contemporary Israel. Israelis, I argue, do not regard ideology as an unassailable pronouncement, a maxim to be either obeyed or disregarded. Their agency effectively reflects their understanding of it as a context-related construct, to be negotiated and redefined.

This notwithstanding, the Israeli residents of Natzerat Illit take exclusivity in settlement and collective ownership of land most seriously. Their agency and statements display little tendency to construe these tenets as mere pragmatic variables. They clearly ideologize these principles, striving to present them as existential, fateful and composite.

The Palestinian inhabitants of the Nazareth hills defy the stereotypes which mainstream Israeli narratives of history assign to Arabs. They are well educated, proud, well rooted, and show no inclination to back off upon first sight of the self-righteous and powerful Israeli presence. Rather than quietly evacuate the hills and vanish over the border or across the sea, they cling tenaciously to the mountains in and around Nazareth. Worse still, they move to Natzerat Illit with money and skill, invading newly acquired Israeli territory, becoming legitimate settlers in their own right. The impact which the reversal of this linear historical trend has on the Jewish community cannot be overemphasized. It questions the very course of time.

This is profoundly pertinent to the ideologization of local conflict. The representation of the situation in terms of the reversal of historic roles allows Israelis to appropriate key scenarios from their own experience, such as the military idiom (above) and apply them to contemporary Palestinian practices, thus emphasizing the abhorrent nature of the present.

One such key scenario is based on the tropology of Zionist settlement. *Homa Umigdal* – 'wall and tower' – was the name of Zionist settlement operations which took place in the late 1930s, in which prefabricated huts, watchtowers and fences were erected overnight to enclose the residential compound of a new *kibbutz* (see Shohat 1989; Katriel and Shenhar 1990). After the establishment of the state of Israel the scenario was transformed in essence and in appellation. *He'aḥzūyot* (literally 'clingings') were transitional camps, half barracks half *kibbūtz*, established since the 1950s by a special section of the IDF called *Naḥal* (Hebrew acronym for 'Fighting Pioneering Youth') in areas hitherto unsettled by Israelis such as the Arava valley or the Judean hills. Many were later converted to fully fledged *kibbūtzim*. Later still, the concept was adopted by religious Zionism groups, notably *Gūsh Emūnim*, whose early settlements, often established overnight as counter-establishment operations, were labelled *Hitnaḥlūyot* – the biblical term for Joshua's seizure and settlement of the land of Kenaan in the twelfth century BC. Most recently, the Israeli army (IDF) has made symbolic use of a similar image. During the Intifada, the Palestinian uprising in the occupied territories since 1988, Palestinians have occasionally used hill tops overlooking main roads in the West Bank and Gaza to attack vehicles carrying Israeli settlers or security personnel. The IDF often reacted overnight by establishing new military observation stations on the spot. Such posts were labelled *Ma'aḥazim* – literally 'places to hold on to'.

In all four phases the principal image is that of members of a smaller, weaker outgroup settling a previously empty hostile territory, against all odds. The IDF team moving on to a windswept cul in 1991 is a clear attempt to link up with the symbolic load associated with the 1930s Jewish settler, who worked against the British mandate and the rural Palestinian population on whom he forced himself as neighbour.

The attribution to contemporary Palestinians of similar levels of collective determination, organization and almost mystical potency, emphasizes further the reversal of temporal order. The past represents a time whereby brave penetration, dynamic seizure of land and the pioneering fighting spirit was a monopoly of righteous Zionists. The present, disappointingly for Israelis, is a time in which such valour is not reserved to them alone. It can be, and in the case of Natzerat Illit indeed has been, appropriated by the opposition.

To sell or not to sell

The difficulty which Israeli residents of Natzerat Illit experience with the Palestinian presence are thus founded on a non-problematic interpretation of the Zionist project and its ideologized versions of history. And yet, as I have tried to show, this rather foolproof world view fails to determine the course of individual action. 'I shouldn't but maybe I will' is an apt representation of the conduct of Israelis in Natzerat Illit when it comes to selling their individual properties to Palestinians.

Elie Azulay was one of the few estate agents who were active in Natzerat Illit in the late 1980s. I was introduced to him a few months prior to my move to Natzerat Illit, courtesy of an Israeli couple who had used his services a few years earlier, when they had sold their old apartment and moved into a private house in a fashionable new section of Natzerat Illit. When they heard that we were looking to rent a house they immediately suggested we should see Elie. 'He is both honest and efficient' they said, 'always representing the best properties in town.'

Elie had an office in a shopping centre in the southern part of town – a concrete built complex designed around an elongated, rather badly lit passage, tucked on to an office block. There was a small department store, a travel agency, one or two boutiques, a gift-shop, a quick food joint, a sports shop and a stationary booth. Workshops for light industry and little warehouses protruded along a service road at the back. 'You have a home here' Azoulay said warmly at the beginning of our first encounter, pouring coffee in small cups. We chatted. He made genuine inquiries into my forthcoming research, showing more interest in it than most local Israelis I encountered during fieldwork.

Elie was obviously eager to be heard and be involved. His alertness impressed me as one of an exceptionally enterprising person trapped in a community with an economic pace far slower than he wanted. He clearly saw himself as more than an estate agent in a small town with a stifled property market. He promised me he 'had a lot to tell', a prophecy aptly fulfilled in years to come, when he proved easily the single most important and comprehensive source of information I had on Natzerat Illit's real-estate market. He knew more instances of purchases and rents by Palestinians than most people did, and was well versed in the particulars of Israeli compliance with and counter measures to this flux. The commission he was expecting for finding us a rented house was obviously secondary for him. It was the notion that his insights could be of value which drew him.

Elie came to Natzerat Illit with his parents from Morocco in the early 1960s, when he was a toddler. He is married to a native of a Central Asian republic of the former Soviet Union whose family came to the town in the 1970s. The couple have a spacious, carefully decorated house in one of the smarter neighbourhoods of Natzerat Illit. Once, when we sat in their living room, Elie looked at me and said:

What I know about this place and of the people here I know from life. Not from people's mouths, but from looking at them and seeing the little things they do. And you can rest assured: there is nothing like the real-estate market in this town to teach you all you want to know about a person – an Arab, a Jew, whatever.

This intuitive grasp of the essentials of ethnographic methodology notwithstanding, Elie displayed a paradoxic mixture when it came to Palestinians in Natzerat Illit. Deeply and openly distrustful of Palestinians and of Arabs generally, he at the same time showed a great deal of respect for them. He was particularly outspoken about their generosity and proper business etiquette. He would lecture me at length about the dangerous, malicious attempts of Palestinians 'working on instructions from the PLO to take over Natzerat Illit', only to go on moaning on how mean, stingy and pathetically distrusting Israelis are, and what a pleasure it is to deal with Palestinians, 'whose word in business is as good as gold'.

Forever blowing the horn of danger against the Palestinian onslaught on Natzerat Illit and on Israel at large, Eli's critique and genuine apprehension stood in marked contrast to the instrumental part he himself played in their advance. He never tried to hide the fact that much of his professional and financial success during the 1980s – the years he built his practice and got himself established – was based on deals whereby he furnished Palestinian buyers with properties for rent or sale in Natzerat Illit. This notwithstanding, his accounts, which often set-off with mild factual descriptions of anecdotes and cases, almost invariably catapulted themselves to generalizations of 'the problem'. Every Palestinian buyer became a symptom of a larger, darker picture; every Israeli seller grew to be a sign of imminent moral and demographic collapse.

Festinger's work on cognitive dissonance (1957) predicts that actors in situations such as Elie's, where ideology and practice are so markedly at odds, would strive to narrow the gap by either remodelling behavioural patterns (not selling properties to Palestinians) or by modifying cognitive horizons. This argument, so suggestive for social psychological theory since, cannot be substantiated by my experience of Natzerat Illit. Elie is a crystal clear example – though certainly not the only one – of someone whose actions and belief over two decades display no urge to narrow cognitive gaps – a phenomenon which has long become a staple of anthropological observations.

People do, however, employ a variety of other strategies to cope with this mis-match between theory and practice and its attendant tension. First, the belief of many Israeli residents that the Palestinian presence is the town's chief drawback hinges on a systematic misrecognition of the simple fact that demand for real estate by Palestinians in the 1980s was a singularly positive feature in the otherwise ailing local economy. A minimal estimate of the revenue generated in the 1980s by real-estate purchases and rentals on the part of Palestinians and by their payment of local taxes (not including their purchases in local shops and services) is 14 million US dollars.[9] This sum is larger than development funds invested by central government in Natzerat Illit over the corresponding period. Significantly, none of the Israeli residents with whom I raised the issue ever acknowledged this aspect of the Palestinian presence – a point which gains significance below, when Israeli perceptions of the public good are briefly introduced.

Second, Israeli residents develop a vocabulary of justification and rationalization to account for gaps between their practice and cosmology. One argument is based of course on plain material logic. Thus, decisions by individuals to sell to Palestinians for a slightly better price were invariably attributed to the dire financial situation of the seller. Conversely, when referring to the exceptional but well-known case in which a resident, determined not to sell to Palestinians, turned down handsome offers by potential Palestinian buyers and eventually sold to a fellow Israeli for considerably less, commentators tended to qualify their exaltations. Repeatedly portraying him as noble, they nevertheless omitted to present him as a model for all to emulate. In fact all those who spoke to me about his case commented that his willingness to do the ideologically correct thing was inextricably linked to his financial independence.

A third strategy to cope with this basic tension invoked resistance to being dubbed a sucker. Elie, for one, explained his position as follows:

If I don't get involved in those deals, somebody else will. Everybody wants a piece of the action – [Israeli] builders, brokers, advertisers, owners. So why should I be left out? Why should I be the *freier*?

Luis Roniger and Michael Feige (1992) describe *freier* as . . . 'not merely a sucker who loses in market transactions . . . but mainly the one who mistakingly and even grotesquely contributes to collective efforts and the public good'. They depict the emergence of the term in Israel since the 1960s primarily as a critique of the previously dominant concept of the *Halūtz* – a person willing to make endless sacrifices for the public good with no demands for returns. This eclipse from *freier* to *Halūtz* reflects an important trend in Israeli culture in terms of the relationship between the private and the public domains. While their point is relevant enough to Israelis in Natzerat Illit, this eclipse, as I shall argue, cannot by itself account for the mis-match between what people say and what they do.

Fourth, Israeli residents often treat their own case of selling to a Palestinian, (or, for that matter, the case of relatives or friends who did) as the marginal exception which hardly matters. Handling a negative example as the freak exception clearly eases the tension between a person's conviction and his reluctance to live up to its practical demands. It is certainly more convenient than allowing each case to stimulate a searching ideological discussion, and force uneasy choices over matters of sombre national consequence (Barrett 1984:152–3; see Slater 1976:580).

Finally, another look at what I referred to earlier as the split real-estate market. The concept of a split market (see Bonacich 1980) is based on situations (particularly rife in the labour market) whereby one actor sells (his labour) shorter then another. Clearly, the two have conflicting interests.

The situation in the real-estate market in Natzerat Illit is not quite that. Differentiation occurs not due to market consideration (one actor decides to drop or raise prices due to economic calculations), but because some Israelis refrain from selling to Palestinians on ideological grounds. The interests of Israeli sellers are not in conflict: the property of those who would not sell to Palestinians still increases in value, although exchange may be arrested.

On the side of the buyers, where Palestinians are willing to pay more for properties, the conflict between Israelis and Palestinians is much more tangible. Still, in a perfectly split market we should have witnessed Israeli buyers attempting to exclude Palestinian entry, with its inflationary tendencies. This they could have done by organizing in associations or in other market-oriented outfits, or through attempts to persuade potential Palestinian buyers not to pay more. That none of this occurred indicates that the thoretical term 'split market' for the real-estate realm of Natzerat Illit is only partly valid.

Pragmatic idealists

Israeli residents of Natzerat Illit emerge as pragmatic in their pursuit of personal material objectives. At the same time, however, they display a genuine awareness of the 'correct' ideological tenets – those which the state and the Jewish people ostensibly expect them to go by, and which imply selfless resistance to the temptation of selling to a potential Palestinian buyer. These notions reflect the glorious past of a few decades ago, when people supposedly thought, spoke and acted in one miraculously integrated manner, personified in the self-sacrificing *halutz*. The images which emerge from this endorsement of old values thus select for unequivocal allegiance to the collective above all forms of individual gratification; for a strong emphasis on action and actual achievement rather than rhetoric and effigy; for a belief in territorial segregation and in a specific, ethnocentric concept of time and history whereby Israelis incessantly take gains at the expense of Palestinians.[10] Put bluntly, the true Zionist of old was supposedly a perfect social cooperator, a person who acts rather than talks, and an agent who makes the 'right' sort of history by endeavouring to enhance Jewish expansion and territorial segregation.

The Israeli residents of Natzerat Illit thus face two dilemmas. One has to do with strategies of action, and entails a choice between the Zionist directive (not letting Palestinians in) and lucrative practice (selling to the highest bidder); the second has to do with strategies with which to represent reality, and entails the choice between fidelity and faithlessness to old Zionist values. Each of the two dilemmas has one choice which represents integrity (compliance with Zionist vision and fidelity) and one which represents self seeking (lucrative practice and faithlessness to values).

Some Israelis, as I have shown, explain away the problem by simply saying they are not *freiers*. However, the fact that the few who have elected to put collective considerations above individual gains are not depicted as *freiers* is indicative. Having selected sound material practice *and* fidelity to values (selling property to Palestinians *and* holding on to the 'Palestinians out' ideology), Israelis in Natzerat Illit emerge as willing to carry the costs of mis-match between prophecy and practice, but less prepared to bear the brunt of faithlessness to central Zionist values. Resorting to the 'I am not a *freier*' idiom would have effectively annulled the value of selfless sacrifice in the service of the nation. This did not happen.

That totally altruistic or otherwise morally pure behaviour is not necessarily viewed with much favour in all circumstances is a theme familiar from ethnographc inquiries elsewhere. Michael Herzfeld, for example, suggests that Greeks are perfectly willing to be contemptuous of people who allow themselves to be 'had', but much less ready to reject Christian values of kindness and mutual help in any categorical way (1993).

Actors can also choose to view the situation along divergent temporal horizons. Personal considerations such as buying or building a better home (which justifies demanding the highest price for the old one, whoever the buyer) can be portrayed as matters of the short term. Wider considerations such as the demographic balance between Israelis and Palestinians in the town – and, by implication, countrywide – can be portrayed as matters of the longer term.

Alternatively, this dichotomy may be conveniently invoked to ascribe responsibilities. Selling and buying one's home is an act which mainly effects the seller and members of his or her family. In this context they are answerable only to their relatives, particularly their dependents. In fact the better deal a person gets from selling the old apartment, the more responsible he or she is. The demographic balance of the town and the nation, on the other hand, are long-term problems which effect the collective, and can thus be easily construed as the responsibility of government.

Not surprisingly, Israelis in Natzerat Illit often express an expectation that central government would exert influence so as 'to put the (Palestinian) problem right' (*Davar* 1982; see also *Hotam* 1982; Rabinowitz 1990:61). This, in fact, is a perfect avenue to shift responsibility up, as is voting in elections. Casting a ballot paper in favour of a party whose policy accords with your own views on Palestinians can neatly transfer accountability to the party and to its elected officers, thus allowing you, the actor, to follow your own material interest. This, of course, is not unique to Israel. Holding the government responsible for larger problems whereby individual agency ostensibly has little impact is part and parcel of representational politics everywhere.

Social dilemmas

The anthropological and sociological literature offers a variety of concepts and perspectives which could be used to analyze the problem faced by Israelis seeking to sell properties in Natzerat Illit. These include short-

and long-term exchange (Bloch and Parry 1989), social exchange (Ekeh 1974; Befu 1977), altruism (Karilowsky 1982; Oiliavin and Charng 1990), and social dilemma (Dawes 1980). In Dawes's terms, Israelis in Natzerat Illit have consistently opted for a higher pay-off as a reward for their socially defecting action of selling properties to Palestinians (thus allowing them a foothold in the town, against the 'national' interest). All of these perspectives hinge this way or another on the distinction between the private and the public – an issue central to western liberal statism and the philosophy which guides it.

As I have shown in chapter 2, the Israeli residents of Natzerat Illit see Palestinian individuals quite benignly. They often portray Palestinians they are in personal touch with as reasonable neighbours and as legitimate members of what could be identified as the community of daily routine. Palestinians are people with whom a person may chat over a cup of coffee, whom he may greet in the staircase or at the parking lot, or even sell an apartment to. Individual Palestinians in Natzerat Illit, as far as Israelis are concerned, are to most intents and purposes 'People Like Us' (PLU). Palestinians as a collective, on the other hand, are perceived as out to get the Israelis. They are, quite literary, PLO – an entity which, prior to the September 1993 accord between Israel and the Palestinians, was held by the majority of Israelis as the epitome of evil and anti-Israeli malice.[11]

Individual Palestinians are thus contained within the fold of Israeli liberal pluralism. It is the Palestinians as a collective whose marginalization, discrimination and racialization is effectively legitimized in Israel. The Palestinian other thus appears as janus faced: half private, amicable, self-seeking, rational; half public, demonic, maliciously motivated by hatred, dangerously bent on dominating. Just like the Palestinian turned soldier and *ḥalūtz*, this too is a mirror image of the Israeli: part mobilized, intransigent, disciplined according to the needs of the collective; part private, calculating and defecting.

This dichotomy between private and public is no stranger to Jewish and Israeli cosmology or, for that matter, to liberal thought in general. 'Be a Jew at home and a person abroad' was the maxim of liberal pre-Zionist Judaism in Europe, particularly in Germany. It is based on the assumption that people are one thing as individuals and quite another as members of collectives. This ambivalence typifies the liberal wing of Zionism at least since the beginning of the century. It features, on the one hand, a benevolent willingness to tolerate Palestinian individuals and to grant them most rights and privileges, while at the same time displaying a chronic failure to come to terms with the Palestinians as an ethnic, cultural and national collective. This, incidentally, is reminiscent of the way Palestinians of the more intransigent opposition factions within the PLO are willing to include Jews – not Israelis – in a future Middle Eastern settlement: individualized, atomized, depoliticized.

In the early 1980s, when Natzerat Illit first hit the national media as a locus of unrest, liberal Israelis were appalled. Public expressions of disgust and disbelief at the intolerance, racism and hostility exhibited by the Israeli residents of Natzerat Illit abounded (for a representative example see *Yediot Aharonot* 1983). Liberal leftist commentators made conscious – and totally unsuccessful – efforts to underplay these attributes, portraying the Israeli residents of Natzerat Illit as more tolerant, humane, and compromising than the image projected by 'a handful of extremists' (see *Al Hamishmar* 1984, *Hotam* 1984, *Davar* 1982). These beautifying exercises did not stick, and most liberal Israelis still relate to Natzerat Illit as an embarrassment.

Liberalism tells us that people possess equal opportunities, make unhindered choices, enjoy personal freedoms and equal access to resources. My point, grounded in the case of real estate in Natzerat Illit, is that this discourse of civility, based on the rights of individuals, works to personalize and thus decontextualize political conflict, blurring it into a string of unrelated personal cases. Israelis in North Tel-Aviv can afford being appalled by the thought that Israelis in Natzerat Illit are not prepared to have Palestinians living near them. Unlike liberals elsewhere, however, those living in non-hybridizing borderzones cannot suspend inter-group reality as an abstract, hypothetical sphere, or limit it to the realm of values concerning individual rights. In Galilee, the simple fact that one collective marginalizes the other and denies its right to a dignified future can no longer be couched in liberal jargon. Decisions as to whom you admit as a neighbour or whom you sell your flat to may not come daily, but push does tend to get to shove a lot more often, forcing uneasy choices.

The tendency of Israelis elsewhere to portray Natzerat Illit as a pocket of racism is thus problematized. It tends to produce an artificial disassociation between the town and the rest of Israeli society, enabling mainstream Israel to emerge self righteously as ostensibly humane and civilized. This allows Israelis, including liberals, to treat the general predicament of their Palestinian fellow citizens as less grave than it really is, in turn enabling the state to persevere with a selective application of its liberal norms.

4

Differentiated space

The lost neighbourhood

I gradually noticed that virtually all instances cited by Elie Azulay to lend support to his laments over 'the problem' of 'the Arab onslaught' in Natzerat Illit were properties that had been sold or let to Palestinians in the mixed compounds. Al-Kūrūm, the exclusively Palestinian neighbourhood (see chapter 2) remained conspicuously absent from his discourse of 'the problem'.

In practical terms, his silence over al-Kūrūm is understandable. Deals over land and properties in al-Kūrūm were cut exclusively between Palestinians, who seldom use the services of estate agents.[1] The area was thus outside Elie's – or any other estate agent's – domain of activity and information.

Al-Kūrūm and the rest of the north-western corner of Natzerat Illit, with over 250 private homes of Palestinians, still represents approximately one-third of the Palestinian residency in Natzerat Illit. Moreover, since most houses in al-Kūrūm are built on land privately owned by Palestinians, most residents have no intentions whatsoever of moving out – this in marked contrast to Palestinian residents of mixed residential areas 'inside' Natzerat Illit. If anybody needed a clear-cut case of Elie's worst scenario materialized, there was al-Kūrūm: a recent assertion of Palestinian presence within a predominantly Israeli town and a perfect example of Palestinian momentum acquired at the expense of Israeli control.

Elie's tendency to overlook al-Kūrūm was not an exception. The most impassioned of accounts given by other Israeli residents of the existential dangers associated with the Palestinian presence in Natzerat Illit made no reference to the exclusively Palestinian neighbourhood. In fact when asked to trace the town's perimeter, many Israelis omitted al-Kūrūm altogether. When challenged, one man explained that al-Kūrūm was 'not really Natzerat Illit'. Another said it was 'more like a part of Nazareth'. Not surprisingly, acts of Israeli intimidation of Palestinian residents or prospective residents – an occurrence known in virtually all other parts of Natzerat Illit – have never been attempted in al-Kūrūm.

This uncharacteristically relaxed attitude of Israeli residents was mirrored in the policy of the council *vis-à-vis* Palestinian presence and development in al-Kūrūm. In the early 1970s the council of Natzerat Illit collaborated with that of Nazareth (both councils were controlled by Labour at the time), to initiate and construct a housing estate for Palestinian civil servants and Labour Party activists from Nazareth. The result was a compound with forty-eight apartments, built at the top of the slope which later came to be occupied by al-Kūrūm, and known as *Shikūn al-Akhdar*: a mixture of Hebrew and Arabic for 'the green housing estate', after the green plastic shutters fixed in the front which overlooks Nazareth. Little did anyone anticipate then that the estate would form a nucleus of development and construction by Palestinians and for them. Additionally, Natzerat Illit's council has since been generous in granting planning permissions to Palestinians wishing to buy and build on the slope – a policy which proved conducive to further development by Palestinians.

Two decades on, many Israeli residents of Natzerat Illit openly declare their willingness to relinquish al-Kūrūm altogether. During the municipal election campaign of early 1989, when a new local Palestinian list of candidates emerged, Natzerat Illit's Labour branch correctly anticipated a collapse in the traditional support of Labour amongst the Palestinian residents. This realization pushed Labour officers to contemplate gerrymandering, specifically the surrendering of al-Kūrūm to the jurisdiction of neighbouring Raina. Although the notion never surfaced as part of the official campaign, it evidently was and probably still is on the agendas of most Zionist parties in Natzerat Illit (see chapter 9).

A tendency to give up territory hitherto assigned to your control is unusual under the most relaxed of circumstances; it is particularly perplexing in a place like Israel, where land reclaimed from either the Palestinians or the wilderness features strongly in the national pantheon of symbols; it becomes a paradox in Natzerat Illit, where 'Judaizing Galilee' is a central Israeli *raison d'etre*.

Clearly, some Palestinian moves into what Israelis perceive as their territory invoke deep fears in Israelis. Other moves, including ones of larger territorial scale and significance such as al-Kūrūm, fail to attract attention and concern. Observations from elsewhere in Israel suggests that differentiated attitudes to Palestinian presence in various parts is not unique to Natzerat Illit.

Ben-Artzi and Shoshani's account of the recent history of Palestinian presence in Haifa (1986) indicates that prior to 1948 the northern town had some 45,000 Palestinian residents, living mainly in the lower part of the town, nearer the port. During the 1948 hostilities, the majority of Palestinians were forced to leave their homes (see Morris 1987). The 3,000 or so Palestinians who remained, predominantly Christians, were transferred by the Israeli authorities into a well-delineated enclave at Wadi Nisnas in the older inner city. Most properties which had belonged to refugee or displaced Palestinians were taken over by the state and given to new immigrants arriving in Israel in 1949 and the early 1950s.

Between 1949 and 1986 the Palestinian population of Haifa multiplied by a factor of five. This growth is accounted for mainly by Palestinian immigrants from villages in Galilee during the 1970s (Ben-Artzi and Shoshani 1986:34–8). By then, many of the new immigrants who had settled in the old Palestinian properties had already improved their economic situation, and were moving away to newer, more prestigious parts of Haifa. To facilitate the move they sold or let their old residences, often to Palestinians. The 1970s and 1980s thus saw many parts of Haifa which had been predominantly Palestinian prior to 1948 regaining their demographic composition of old, with Palestinians rapidly becoming quantitatively prominent.

A similar process, albeit on a smaller scale, took place in Jaffa, another major Palestinian town decimated in 1948. Jewish immigrants, mainly from the Balkans, were settled in empty Palestinian properties in the early 1950s. Later, when many moved to newer neighbourhoods elsewhere in the Tel-Aviv metropolis, Palestinians resumed renting and buying properties, moving back to live in Jaffa. This process, which continued steadily throughout the 1970s and 1980s, has made a significant mark on Jaffa's public life (see Shokeid 1982:55–60). The phenomenon of trickling but substantial Palestinian return is known also in the old cores of Lod (pre-1948 Palestinian Lidd) and Ramla (previously al-Ramlah), where Palestinian new-comers from a variety of origins, including Negev Bedouins, have been taking up residence in numbers since the 1950s (for a detailed account see Kressel 1976:24–7).

Significantly, these moves, however pregnant with territorial ramifications, hardly became foci of attention – let alone anxiety – for Israelis. Locally as well as nationally they have largely remained as non-events.

The Palestinian tendency to build relatively few residential units per unit area brought about substantial physical expansion of most Palestinian rural communities in Israel, often at the expense of previously agricultural land (see Sofer 1989). The Israeli public is generally aware of this development and is critical of it, but does not display any real signs of apprehension over the matter. Public reaction is generally weak, and seems to revolve around what many Israelis see as blatant disregard on the part of Palestinians towards planning procedures. And while extreme right wing political parties periodically criticize the willingness of the administration to put up with the situation, the territorial ramifications of the process have never stirred a widespread emotional response within the Israeli public.

There are, on the other hand, cases of Palestinian presence in predominantly Israeli areas which do trigger powerful reactions. In October 1989, the (Jewish) New Year edition of Israel's best-selling newspaper *Yediot Aharonot* featured a story (Ringel-Hofman 1989) concerning 160 or so Palestinian families who live in Carmiel – a development town established in 1964 in the heart of a densely populated Palestinian area in central Galilee. The story reflects deep apprehensions on the part of many of Carmiel's 22,000 Israeli residents regarding the Palestinian presence. A right-wing Likud council member summed up prevailing local emotions by saying:

The process began in the early 1980s. First, they [the Palestinians,] find work in the town. Later they open a little business. Then they rent a flat and bring the family to live in town. Eventually they buy the property. Around Carmiel there are some 100,000 Arabs. It is enough that 5 per cent of them decide to immigrate to Carmiel, to make 5,000 – a quarter of the town's population (*ibid*).

Such remarks are occasionally echoed in other peripheral new towns across the country. Examples include Tsefat (Safad) and Hazor in Upper Galilee, two development towns where a number of Palestinian families have recently bought properties; Acre, where Palestinians move away from the old city into blocks of flats in the new suburbs; and the southern towns of Beer-Sheva and Arad, where a number of local Bedouin families as well as Palestinians from the north of Israel have taken up residence in recent years. Similarly, new Israeli suburbs built around Jerusalem in the 1970s on previously Jordanian rural land – Neve Ya'acov and Hagiv'a Hatsorfatit are two examples – have been the scene of Israeli apprehensions *vis-à-vis* Palestinians buying and renting. On several occasions in the 1980s this led to attacks on apartments occupied by Palestinians and fire bombs against Palestinian residents' motorcars.

Finally, negative Israeli reactions to the notion of the Palestinian presence are an unmistakeable feature of *kibbutzim* and *Moshavim*.[2] In both settlement forms, the general assembly of each settlement has final say on membership admittance. So far, virtually all attempts by Palestinians to become members have been denied. This veto, often explicitly based on the applicant's affiliation, stands in blatant contradiction to the socialist and universalist ideology to which the *kibbutzim* and (to a lesser extent) the *Moshavim* movements ostensibly subscribe. This double standard is a source of tension and embarrassment within individual settlements as well as in the movements generally. This notwithstanding, exceptions or a change of policy are yet to come.

Some Palestinian citizens of Israel – Bedouins, Druze, Christians, and more recently a handful of non-Bedouin Muslims – serve in Israel's defence forces. The fact that Palestinian candidates for membership in *kibbutzim* and *Moshavim* have included ex-servicemen has had no bearing on decisions by general assemblies regarding candidates. The barrier against Palestinian participation in *kibbutzim* and *Moshavim* is even more rigid than the notion of Israeli exclusivity in the sacred realm of national defence.

Territorial control in Zionism

Barukh Kimmerling's analyses of the place of territory in Zionism and in the Palestinian-Israeli conflict (1977, 1983) specifies presence, ownership and sovereignty as the three components of territorial control. The three components form the basis for his conceptualization of the conflict: an ongoing struggle in which both sides attempt to gain as much control over as much territory as possible.

This framework goes some way to account for the variations in Israeli reactions to the Palestinian presence. Al-Kūrūm, it could be argued, differs from other parts of Natzerat Illit in the extent and nature of Israeli control. All parts of Natzerat Illit are part of the sovereign state of Israel, and fall within the municipal jurisdiction of a town perceived by everyone as Israeli. Sovereignty over the territory is thus indisputably Israeli. As for ownership and presence, al-Kūrūm stands out from all other parts of Natzerat Illit. Land and property in it is privately owned by Palestinians (i.e. full Palestinian ownership). Palestinians also make up the entire residency (i.e. overwhelming Palestinian presence).

Al-Kūrūm displays a pattern of control whereby Israeli sovereignty is not accompanied by ownership and presence – a situation characterized by Kimmerling as pattern E (1983:22). Elsewhere in Natzerat Illit, where

Israeli sovereignty is matched with Israeli collective ownership of land and individual ownership of property, as well as by a decisive majority of Israeli residents, Israeli control is total. The combination of sovereignty, ownership and presence, creates, in Kimmerling's terminology, a pattern of complete control (pattern H, *ibid*).

This variance in control over territory, the argument would go, can account for the variance of Israeli reactions to the Palestinian presence. In the predominantly Israeli parts of town, where Israeli control is virtually complete, the Palestinian advent is viewed with fear and apprehension. In al-Kūrūm, where Israeli control is only nominal anyway, the Palestinian presence meets milder Israeli sentiments.

Kimmerling alludes to the morbid Israeli fear of the reversibility of territorial processes. In his study of the public debate in Israel in the 1970s and 1980s regarding the potential return of evacuated Palestinian villagers to their homes and land in the villages of Ikrit and Bir'im near the Lebanese border, he cites the arguments put forward by politicians representing mainstream Zionism against such a return. A leading member of the Labour party is quoted as telling the press that 'The problem does not only relate to the Galilee or the Negev, but to other places as well: Tel-Aviv too' (*ibid* 1977:165).

The quote, by no means a freak utterance, reflects a tendency within mainstream Zionism to evaluate its own territorial advent as tentative and fragile. Decades after the establishment of the state of Israel and the systematic seizure of most Palestinian land within its boundaries, Zionism continues to hold itself susceptible to counter-measures by the weakened Palestinians. This point is crucial for a fuller understanding of the Israeli attitude to land and, by implication, to territorial compromise. In this respect, once again, the peculiarities of a trapped minority, particularly the ambiguous status of borders and boundaries between it and its father ethnos, play a significant part.

Kimmerling asserts that such expressions on the part of Israelis are anchored in a broader ideological context. Israeli spokesmen, he argues, tend to link each local territorial dispute – the one over the two remote and tiny villages of Ikrit and Bir'im in the north is but one lucid example – to the entire history and suffering of the Israeli people, including the trauma of the Holocaust.

This trend is evident to date. For example, right-wing Israeli ideologists consistently portrayed the *Intifada* (the Palestinian uprising in the occupied territories since 1987) as an all-out war for the whole of the country, not just the territories – explicitly using the term *milḥama* for it. This approach reflects a genuine belief in the intent and capability of Palestinians to export the uprising across the 1967 borders into Israel proper. The implication is that giving way to Palestinians in one part necessarily invites total collapse all over.

During the Gulf War in early 1991 prominent Israeli public figures appealed to the citizens of Tel-Aviv to stay put during the height of Iraqi missile attacks. One of the many statements made by Shlomo Lahat, Mayor of Tel-Aviv, reads as follows:

We must stay put. If our contribution to the state is to get hit by Scuds, then that is what we must do... People must not act just to save their own individual skins. Today people leave Tel-Aviv, tomorrow they will leave Jerusalem. Next they would leave Israel all together. This is what Sadam wants (*Haaretz* 17.2.1991:a4).

Such 'domino effect' visions, and their reification in public debates during the Gulf War, reflect a deep anxiety that every individual incident involving Israeli presence in a given territorial segment carries enormous historical and ideological consequences regardless of context and conjuncture. Shlomo Lahat, formerly a general of the Israeli army, goes down this line of argument as far as losing touch with the distinction between military effectiveness (with which staying put in Tel-Aviv under threat of scuds had nothing to do), and the resilience which saved the day for the Israeli collective in previous wars, particularly in 1948, when presence really mattered for gaining control over disputed territory and holding on to it.

In 1994 and 1995, the campaign staged by the Israeli right against the return of the Golan heights to Syria was once more phrased in existential terms, predicting the imminent annihilation of Israel without the Golan. This discourse is careful to suspend projected features of future warfare, conveniently overlooking the reduced salience of territorial bases.

The case of Ikrit and Bir'im presents a mirror image to that of Natzerat Illit. In both cases newly acquired Israeli sovereignty stands against what Israelis perceive as a Palestinian onslaught. The move of Nazarene urbanites to Natzerat Illit becomes equivalent to the attempts of villagers from Ikrit and Bir'im to return to their demolished villages. In both cases Zionism, ever conscious of the wider ramifications of letting the Palestinians in (or back), closes ranks to keep the Palestinians out. In the case of Ikrit and Bir'im the state machinery prevails: all evacuees and their descendants have so far been barred from reinstatement. In Natzerat Illit, where Israeli individuals yield to market forces and are tempted to sell to Palestinians for a handsome price, Zionist ideology caves in. The argument linking each individual case to the grand vision of precarious history – a claim which carried so much weight in the debate regarding Ikrit and Bir'im – is found in Natzerat Illit only in the proselytizing laments of the aftermath.

To sum up this line of inquiry, Zionism emerges as inherently insecure regarding the durability of its territorial achievements. Israelis are particularly apprehensive regarding Palestinian advances in territories where state control has been safely established through sovereignty, ownership and presence. Palestinian expansion in places such as al-Kūrūm, where Israeli control is tenuous anyway, seem to attract far less Israeli attention.

And yet, plausible as this argument may be, its explanation of the situation in Natzerat Illit is incomplete. In the 1950s and 1960s, Israeli ownership and presence in the old parts of Haifa, Jaffa, Lod and Ramla signified what Kimmerling typifies as full Israeli control. This notwithstanding, the substantial return of Palestinians, so clearly present in the cases of Haifa and Ramla, turned the situation on its head. If, as the argument would imply, the key to Israeli reactions is the threat of reversed control through depletion of Israeli ownership and presence, then how can we account for the dispassionate Israeli response to the costs in terms of Israeli hegemony in those other urban examples?

Kimmerling's model must be augmented if these peculiarities are to be accommodated. The symbolic role of *hityashvut* is suggested as the missing link.

Settlement, environmental transformation and appropriation

Williams and Smith interpret nation building as a symbol-laden sphere of human action:

without which the nationalist dream must remain a mere blueprint, but whose acquisition allows the nationalist to translate his utopia into practical realities. The 'land' allows him to realize his goals of sovereignty, fraternity, identity and regeneration – in practical works of construction. It is, after all, 'the land' that can be renewed, regenerated, rebuilt; and through that act of rebuilding, people can be changed, their outlook revolutionized, their capacities enlarged. *(1983:510)*

Elsewhere Smith points out that work on the land, which creates the infrastructure of the nation, helps form an homogenous group out of an unrelated conglomerate of individuals (1981). E. Weber notes that nation building helps state structures and agencies substitute intermediate and regional institutions (1976).

These writers, while not problematizing the necessarily inventive nature of nationalism, nevertheless point to a salient aspect of it. Acquisition of land, identification, mobilization and 'homogenization' of the people, and transformation of the natural environment into a political territory through physical construction are elements which for the actors single out legitimate participation in the nation-building effort. In the case of Zionism these three elements are perfectly enshrined in the concept of *hityashvūt*. Technically speaking, the term denotes 'settling'. In the Zionist vocabulary it became a generic noun for the entire sphere of settlement. This includes the federations of settlements (also referred to as 'movements' or 'streams' of settlement) – such as the four historic federations of *kibbūtzim* and one of *moshavim*; the institutions and bureaucracies affiliated with these federations; all physical entities on the ground, and the settlers themselves.[3]

My argument rests on the contention that *hityashvūt*, more than any other sphere of life in Israel, is and has always been exclusively Israeli. Land acquisition, the mobilization and recruitment of people through immigration (''*aliya*'), and the transformation of the environment through construction and development, form the *raison d'etre* – as well as the basic structure – of the World Zionist Bureaucracy, and have dictated the Zionist agenda for almost a century. Zionism implies, by definition, that ownership of land, '*aliya* and *hityashvut* must remain exclusively Israeli, or lose their very meaning.

This is where al-Kūrūm differs from the rest of Natzerat Illit. Municipal affiliation does not define national territory. It is *hityashvut* – settlement in its specific Zionist connotation – which engenders the final Judaization of terrestrial space. Al-Kūrūm, like Palestinian villages and towns elsewhere in Israel, is a territory which has not been subject to environmental transformation by the Zionist apparatus. The terrain may have been somewhat improved, but has never been reconstructed by any agency of Zionism. Likewise, locations in the old quarters of Haifa, Jaffa, Lod or other towns which became mixed may have been settled by Israelis at some stage. But temporary Israeli ownership, presence, and even sovereignty are not enough to qualify these sites as genuine components of national redemption. Israeli presence and ownership in downtown Haifa and Jaffa could thus be reversed without stimulating an emotional response on the part of Israelis. The cultural meaning and powerful symbolism of *hityashvut* simply does not apply there.

Visible environmental transformation, while obvious to Palestinians too, carries a powerful symbolic load for Israelis. Beyond providing housing, loci of industry and services, commerce and recreation, new development is expected to erase old landscape chapters and their attendant cultural content. The environmental transformation associated with

Zionist settlement thus marks the sanctification of land as national social space, initiating it into the realm of Israeli nation building.

The terrestrial space of 'the Israeli state' is thus less uniform than hitherto assumed. While the legal sovereignty of the state could be perceived – by Israelis, at least – to denote uniform Israeli dominance, the diverse patterns of control over territory, supplemented by the superimposition of *hityashvut*, creates a complex jigsaw. Only those parts which have or are being transformed through *hityashvut* are affectively (and hence effectively) perceived as 'Israeli' territory. Once qualified, such places become core sites of the new mythology, usurping specific figurative loads. As perceived incarnations of progress and redemption, they carry the imperative to be protected at all costs from intrusion by non-members. Mixed settlement on such sites becomes abominable for Israelis as it signifies the ultimate evil they dread so deeply: the deterioration of collective achievements through rapid dissolution of control over the territory.

These sentiments are supplemented by an inherently orientalist outlook, so prevalent in Israel, which portrays the outpost, in fact the entire Zionist project including *hityashvūt,* as a singularly positive, if not redemptive element in an otherwise wild and primitive Middle East. This becomes doubly powerful in the borderzone, where ostensibly evil attempts to erode Israeli exclusionism, identity and eventually presence seem all the more apparent and mundane. The borderzone comes through as a site of particular tension between liberalism and exclusionism, acted out through the idiom of *hityashvūt.*

5

The limits of liberal education

Educational segregation

During a conversation about the schooling of Palestinian youngsters in Natzerat Illit, a veteran Israeli resident, formerly a member of the municipal council, once said to me:

If only they wanted, they could easily send the whole educational system of this town spiralling into havoc. All they need to do is stage a wave of applications to our schools, wait for the first denial of admission, and apply to the supreme court. Their risk of losing such an appeal is minimal.

The speaker's nightmare has not materialized, nor is it likely to. The Palestinian residents of Natzerat Illit, including those who have been living there long and plan to stay indefinitely, display no desire for their children to attend primary, secondary or high schools in the town. They are indifferent to the political implications of turning all-Israeli schools into mixed institutions. Sending their children to schools in Nazareth seems to them a matter of course – a state of affairs which Israelis in Natzerat Illit view with evident relief. One official in the education department put it to me in clear and simple terms: 'Why should they attend our schools here? They have their own schools in Nazareth, where they belong. They go there, we are here, and everyone is happy.'

The universal lack of interest in mixed education on the part of Palestinians in Natzerat Illit is linked to the obvious advantages of the schooling system of Nazareth. Schools in the Palestinian town, especially those run by church institutions, have outstanding academic reputations. The atmosphere tends to be competitive and achievement oriented. Discipline is strict. Although the main medium of instruction is Arabic, strong emphasis is placed on either English or French as a second language. Many graduates proceed to Israeli universities, particularly Haifa and Jerusalem. Some obtain higher education in Europe and North

America. Not surprisingly, schools in Nazareth have been attracting Palestinian pupils from rural communities all over the country for decades.

Apart from the academic consideration, there is the familiarity factor. Most adult Palestinians currently residing in Natzerat Illit are natives of Nazareth. Graduates of the local educational system, they are acquainted with individual institutions as well as with the municipal bureaucracy. Their capacity to handle their children's affairs with the same confidence and ease in the exclusively Israeli, Hebrew-speaking corridors of peda- gogic power in Natzerat Illit is much more limited.

Geographical distance to schools in Nazareth is not a major considera- tion. Most Palestinian households in Natzerat Illit have at least one member whose workplace is in Nazareth, and own at least one motorcar. One Palestinian parent put the conveyance issue into perspective by saying that:

This journey of 3 kilometres, which takes no more than half an hour, even in the morning rush hour, is not a factor in our decision to have the kids at school in Nazareth. Compared with the time when I was at school it is a joke. Only thirty years ago, kids from villages used to walk to school an hour and a half every morning. Some came on donkeys.[1] Anyway, Nazareth is our home town. It's only natural for our children to study there.

School children who have specialized educational requirements and are compelled to seek them away from their own settlement are entitled by Israeli law to have their travel expenses reimbursed by their own local council – an obligation the council of Natzerat Illit promptly fulfils in the case of Palestinian youngsters who live in the town and who go to school in Nazareth. A form of busing is thus created, the sole purpose of which is to segregate – exactly the reverse of what was intended in mandatory school busing in the US.[2]

Above all, however, is the issue of Palestinian sense of identity and belonging. Significantly, Palestinian parents who had attended Israeli schools as youngsters seem to be most lucidly aware of the disadvantages associated with sending their children to Israeli schools. One parent once asked rhetorically:

Why should my child be treated as a stranger, and be alienated from the rest? I want her to be treated like everyone else, not be singled out as a member of a minority group which the majority still see as hostile and dangerous.

Another parent said that,

Identity and language are as important as future achievements at university.[3] And anyway, kids do well in universities in Israel without having had to leave their own society and culture for their secondary studies. The price is too high. The dividend no longer seems proportionate.

Attempts at mixed education

The rule of educational segregation between Palestinians and Israelis in Natzerat Illit, while in line with the situation countrywide (see Mar'i 1978, 1985 and Sarsur 1988), has a number of exceptions.

First, the few children born to mixed couples of Israeli women and Palestinian men tend to attend Israeli schools.[4] Born to Jewish mothers, and thus recognized by the Jewish code and by the bureaucracy as Jewish, children of such couples are welcome in Israeli schools, and are often encouraged to enrol. Second, a small number of all-Palestinian families send their children to Israeli schools. In 1989 one fourteen-year-old Palestinian boy attended the local secondary school, while a handful of younger children (including, in one case, three siblings) attended primary schools. Israelis commenting on these cases seem to believe this used to happen more often in the past. It would appear however that there were never more than three or four Palestinian children in any school at any particular time.

A Palestinian who chose to have his child attend the Israeli primary school in 1988 explained his choice by saying it was:

primarily for the sake of the child. So she can know Hebrew well. After all, we are bound to live in this country, where Hebrew will always be the most important language. I want the child to speak it well, like everybody else. This way she can move up in the world, study and become an engineer, a lawyer, something good like that, and be respected.

Israelis in Natzerat Illit are vaguely aware of the occasional Palestinian child attending the local schools, but are not particularly worried. One Israeli woman, a teacher, once told me that:

As long as it is a few, it really does not matter. If they start arriving in numbers and take over the school, that is a different matter. But a boy here, a girl there, this makes no difference. And anyway, their lives are made such a misery by the rest of the (Israeli) kids, that most of them make sure they stay a good distance away.

Attendance of Palestinian children in all-Israeli nursery schools in Natzerat Illit is sporadic too, not least since the isolated cases are manipulated by the education department so as never to exceed one or two for each age-group. Palestinian parents whose children are admitted tend to be submissive, often projecting an air of gratitude to the authorities for allowing their children the right to be there in the first place.

The more significant – and institutional – exception to the rule of separated education systems is nursery schools run by the municipality of Natzerat Illit for Palestinian toddlers.

In 1978, the department of education designated a nursery school in the northern section of town to admit Palestinian children. Five toddlers whose families resided in the neighbourhood were enrolled that year, joining the existing cohort of twenty-five Israeli toddlers. The staff, which previously included a head teacher and an assistant, both of them Israeli women, was joined by a new recruit, a Palestinian woman whose job description was *ozeret safa* – Hebrew for language assistant. Her task, as she put it to me a decade later, was 'to help out the Arab children, none of whom could speak any Hebrew when they first came to the nursery'.

Nicole, a professional employed by a welfare agency in Nazareth and mother of one of the Palestinian toddlers admitted in that first cohort, told me in 1989 that the nursery had been:

. . . perfect. Warm, cosy, clean, and virtually on our doorstep. The staff was good, and I could happily go to work every morning, knowing my daughter was well cared for. My next-door neighbour Rutti, an Israeli, had her daughter there too, so the little ones were inseparable: mornings at nursery, afternoons at either home. We were all quite content.

Not for long though. In early 1979 a number of the Israeli parents approached the council's education officers, demanding the removal of the Palestinian children from the nursery. Rutti, it soon became apparent, was a leading figure in this initiative. In 1989, embarrassed, she conveyed her version of the episode:

I really do not know what came over me, going to the council and placing that unjustified demand. I guess it was still the aftermath of leaving the Kibbutz. You see, it is not that our standard of living in Natzerat Illit was any lower than in the Kibbutz – in fact our housing conditions improved remarkably once we moved. It was the general tatty appearance of things, and the feeling that the wholesomeness of being Israeli, of belonging to a place I loved – something I took for granted in the Kibbutz – was irreparably missing. This place, full of new immigrants with whom, apart from good will and idealism, I had so little in common . . . it was difficult. And then, on top of all this to have my daughter educated with Arabs . . . I guess for me it spelt another step away from the Israel I knew and loved, and the culture I was educated to believe in.

Nicole, not surprisingly, took her next-door neighbour's move as a personal betrayal. She initiated a confrontation, which she later reconstructed in the following words:

Next day I saw her and said: 'hey, Rutti, come here' (demonstrates an authoritative 'come here' motion, her palm turned up, her index finger repeatedly arching).

'What is this I hear about you, demanding that Arab kids will be ousted from the nursery?' To which she said: 'it is not against you. You are not.' 'What do you mean I am not?' I insisted. 'You'd better get used to the idea that if you are against Arabs then you are against me as well. I am Arab.' And so it went on, she insisting that I am 'not', and me emphatically stressing: 'I am Arab.'

Next, Nicole demanded a meeting of the parents:

They all came and I said: 'now what have you got against Arabs?' I wanted to see whether this was against a particular child, or just sheer racism – people rejecting kids just because they were Arabs. Because of course, had there been an offensive child, dirty, or with lice or what have you, I would have been bothered just like them, and would have supported a move to expel him.

I insisted on getting a reply, until one mother finally said: 'a boy urinated on my daughter'. I laughed. This is a minor thing that sometimes happens amongst children. For this to have all Arab kids expelled? It was obviously a racist thing, and I said it. And to their credit, I must admit they took the point. Eventually Rutti was the one who called the council and said: 'That's it. I retract. Drop the issue.' And that was the end of it, for then.

Na'ila, the Palestinian assistant whose own son was one of those admitted, was impressed with Nicole's public performance. In 1989 she recollected:

When that Rutti woman said she didn't want her child to play with Arab children Nicole stood up and gave her hell. 'If you won't have your child play with Arab children, how come she and my daughter play together every afternoon at home?' she said. 'And if this is the way you see it, then I am no longer having either your daughter or you coming into my house.' She spoke well, did Nicole that day. You see personally, because I was employed there, I could not really make any comment. But as a mother I very much resented what Rutti did.

At that stage Nicole's husband, a well-known professional in his own right, stepped in and discontinued the child's attendance at the nursery. The newly elected Communist-led municipality of Nazareth had just established the first ever day-care centre in the town, and he had no difficulty securing a place for his daughter, who went on to attend primary and secondary schools in Nazareth. Her brother, four years younger then her, attended a *Na'amat* (trade union women's section) day-care centre in Natzerat Illit between the age of two and three, then proceeded to primary and secondary schools in Nazareth. The couple's youngest daughter began attending a day-care centre in Nazareth in 1987, when she turned two. All three children incidentally had Israeli child-minders when they were under two – typically women of North-African origin living nearby.

Decisions taken by Nicole and her husband suggest that like most Palestinians in Natzerat Illit, they draw a clear line between school education (including nursery schools), for which they turned to Nazareth, and child-minding and day-care centres, for which they chose Natzerat Illit. Nursery schools, with their more intensive pedagogic intervention and tighter administrative control, clearly represent the arbitrary and exclusive nature of the education system in a manner which day-care centres do not. At this junction, affiliation with the municipality of Nazareth – not only Arabic-speaking and Palestinian but also dominated by the communist party, so clearly disassociated from the state – became the natural choice.

Rutti, a liberal-minded person who had spent endless hours at Nicole's apartment, found herself in a tight corner once the toddlers were enroled at nursery school together. The nursery school was a part of the official education system, and so the situation was injected with new meanings. Matters now went beyond questions such as who plays with whom, where or when. Rutti clearly found the public aspects of having her child educated with Palestinian toddlers taxing. Her own apologetic retrospective account invokes her need to being 'wholesome Israeli' – an experience which could not be embodied in a code of practice that would remain compatible with liberalism.

Invisible school

The education department of Natzerat Illit took no further action regarding the mixed nursery school in 1979 or 1980, when the number of Palestinian children went up to thirteen – almost half the total intake of thirty (Natzerat Illit 1980). However the following academic year, beginning in September 1980, saw change: the mixed nursery ceased to admit Palestinian toddlers.[5] Instead, that year the municipality set up two new nursery schools for Palestinian toddlers in the north-western corner of Natzerat Illit, an area covering al-Kūrūm. One school catered for three- and four-year-olds, the other, occupying an adjacent building, was designed for four- and five-year-olds. Both started out with Israeli head-teachers and Palestinian assistants. One of the assistants was Naʿila, the language assistant at the old mixed nursery school.

Naʿila did well there, and her relationship with the education department went from strength to strength. In 1984 she was promoted further, becoming head-teacher of a new nursery school established in a residential street in the newer and more popular southern part of town, designed to cater exclusively for Palestinian toddlers. There she serves to date, aided by an Israeli assistant.[6]

Israelis in Natzerat Illit invest considerable effort in playing down the Palestinian presence in the town, often attempting to conceal it altogether.

The nursery schools for Palestinian toddlers are thus anomalous. They are, in fact, the only formal institutions specifically catering for the Palestinian community.

The two schools situated in the all-Palestinian north-western section of Natzerat Illit are physically invisible for most Israelis, who simply never go there. Na'ila's school, however, is located in the southern part of town, on a residential street inhabited predominantly by Israelis. But is it less invisible?

The nursery building is situated on an elevated terrace. Entering it from the street involves opening a little gate, climbing a flight of steps and walking around the side. The yard facing the street is narrow and untended, so all outdoor activities happen on the far side, virtually unseen from the street. Significantly, the only institution provided by the local council for the Palestinian community remains invisible to Israeli eyes.

It is in that 'dark' side of the nursery that toddlers, who attend Monday to Friday from 08:00 to 13:00, spend most of their time on dry days. A large tree supplies shade for a sand-pit, swings and several wooden climbing frames. Na'ila and her assistant monitor activities seated in wooden chairs under the tree, where they also entertain friends, relatives, officials and anthropologists.

The invisibility of the nursery has a bureaucratic aspect too. The academic year beginning in September 1987 saw 1,746 children under five attending thirty-nine nursery schools in Natzerat Illit (Natzerat Illit 1989). The official list indicates that the thirty-six schools which cater for Israeli children were named after Hebrew names of native flowers (nine schools); fruit species (four schools); trees and bushes (twenty schools); and geographical regions of the country (three schools). The three nursery schools catering for Palestinian toddlers are essentially nameless, simply called after the neighbourhood or street in which they stand. The impression one gets by merely looking at the list is of a system forced to incorporate an ambiguity, an entity it systematically refuses to recognize and internalize.

The building itself is divided into two separate units. The nursery occupies the large room to the east, while the symmetric large room to the west is used from 12:30 onwards as *a moadonit* (female form of 'club', used only in this context) – a day-care centre for primary school children who need professional adult supervision after school hours. The nursery and the *moadonit* have separate toilet and wash facilities, but share the kitchen in the middle section of the building and some storage space in the basement. The *Moadonit* and its inmates are stigmatized as irregular and problematic, so the association between it and the nursery creates a twice-marginalized environment.

Na'ila was in her forties during my fieldwork in the late 1980s. Having been involved with nursery education for Palestinian children in Natzerat Illit for at least a decade by then, she had a close working relationship with the council. In particular she cherished the ties which she and her husband maintained with the deputy mayor of Natzerat Illit between the 1970s and his death in 1993. The deputy, a veteran Labour Party man, commanded an efficient network of contacts with Palestinian families and individuals. Regarded by his Israeli colleagues as chief emissary on behalf of the council and the party amongst the Palestinians, he is fondly spoken of by local Palestinians to date. His Palestinian contacts, a good example of which were Na'ila's family, were typically people coopted into the votes-for-favours system of patronage which formed the chief basis of Palestinian participation in local level politics until 1989 (see chapter 9). Na'ila, a native of a village in Galilee whose own father died when she was an infant, often referred to the elderly deputy mayor as 'my father'.

Na'ila was highly regarded by the officials of the council. One of them described her as 'a self-made woman' who, 'having begun as an assistant with no formal knowledge or experience', slowly 'worked her way up to become head teacher, educating herself in the process'. Another official once confessed that 'many (Israeli) people who know her wish there were many more Arabs as faithful (*ne'emanim*) as she is'. 'Faithful' in this context implies primarily identification with the state, coupled with personal loyalty to Israelis in the person's immediate work environment – the epitome of what Smooha, after popular usage in Israel, has labelled 'A good Arab' (1992).

Officers in the education department were particularly impressed with the discipline and order Na'ila administers at her nursery school, so fundamentally at variance with the atmosphere in Israeli nursery schools. One official once attested how impressed he was with:

. . . the way these children are well behaved, respectful. They are so obedient, and quick to respond to her demands and directives. Compare it to the chaotic goings-on in any of the Jewish nurseries, with shouts and rowdiness and clamour, and you see it really is to her credit. Though of course, it is also a cultural thing. The Arabs are not like us. They have respect for authority, and age. Their children see adults as the ultimate authority.

This is an instance of a way of looking which 'orientalizes' while superficially appearing to compliment. Being disciplined befits a group which in other contexts is charged with fatalism and chaotic despotism. Such an appraisal thus becomes a vicarious instrument (as well as an expression) of control by the dominant group.[7]

Na'ila's nursery school is indeed a restrained environment. Children wishing to address either Na'ila or her assistant, use *mū'alamti* (my teacher), rather than the teacher's first name. Space is meticulously controlled: when all play outside, children wishing to enter the building to use the toilet have to present themselves to the teacher, explain their reason to go in, and only do so once permission has been granted. When I once exclaimed how well-mannered and well-ordered the children were, Na'ila beamed. In line with the essentialist view expressed by the official quoted above she said that:

This is how it is amongst us Arabs. The young obey the old. They are disciplined. My son, at eighteen, still has to ask my permission if he wants to go out. And when I say he must be back at this time or the other, or do something, he knows: that's it.

Palestinian parents, it appears, are as appreciative of Na'ila as Israeli officials are. Their attitude to her and other staff is clearly deferential. One celebration I attended ended with a few of the families staying in the main playroom long after the event was over, clearly enjoying a chat with Na'ila, offering to help and tidy up. Likewise, Na'ila has never had any difficulty recruiting parents to the parents' committee, whose main task is to raise and manage small sums of money for supplementary equipment and activities.[8] A leading member of the parents' committee summed up the attitude of parents towards Na'ila by saying:

This business of the committee, managing the funds for the nursery, is really only a formality. To tell you the truth, we do not really get involved with the nitty-gritty. We trust Na'ila completely with it. We know that every penny she asks from parents is for a good cause which she could not fund otherwise. And we know she uses the money in good faith. She is good with the children, and good for the nursery. We are here to help as much as we can, not to supervise her. We have every confidence in her and in her professionalism.

Na'ila's assistant Rosa is an Israeli of North-African origin. More or less Na'ila's age, her official title, *ozeret safa*, (language assistant) is identical to that which Na'ila held when she became involved with nursery education a decade earlier. Significantly, however, its meaning in the present context has been reversed. In the old mixed nursery, under an Israeli head teacher, *ozeret safa* was a title given to a Palestinian assistant whose task was helping Palestinian children who spoke no Hebrew. Rosa's task in Na'ila's nursery, where the medium of instruction is the children's native Arabic, is different. She is there to teach the Palestinian children Hebrew.

'Whenever I can, I switch to Hebrew with them', she once told me, as though disclosing a clever ploy on her part. 'It is, after all, part of my job here – to make sure they learn some Hebrew.' The pride she took in the pedagogic responsibility invested in her was evident.

While Naʻila's role in the predominantly Israeli nursery school a decade earlier had been to help the Palestinian children get around, Rosa's role in the predominantly Palestinian nursery was to push forward the frontier of the dominant culture. Being a native Arabic speaker herself (albeit in a North-African dialect), Rosa finds it easier and more efficacious to perform in Arabic, switching to Hebrew mainly for teaching Hebrew songs (below), or to impress a visitor. This, however, does not change the way she and her Israeli superiors portray her role in nursery – always *ozeret safa* – 'language assistant', not merely 'assistant'. Her role as representative of the hegemonic order mitigates the danger that she should be perceived as an ordinary assistant to Naʻila, thus easing her structural disadvantage as an Israeli subordinated to a Palestinian.

Rosa evidently cherishes this role. It is, after all, a task she rightly perceives as delegated to her from yonder. Enshrined in an official title, it establishes her as a frontier sentry on behalf of Jewish Israel, facing potentially dissenting and subversive Palestinians, however young. She is part of a system which nostalgically perceives transfusion to Palestinians of 'genuine identification with Israel' as an important and unproblematic aspect of the Zionist project.

By attending schools administered by Natzerat Illit's municipality, Palestinian teachers, parents and guardians acknowledge and reify the power structure underwriting the system's pedagogic authority. Language is a central issue here. Practical competence in language, Bourdieu suggests, is an essential component of power:

Language is not only an instrument of communication or even of knowledge, but also an instrument of power. One seeks not only to be understood but also to be believed, obeyed, respected, distinguished. Whence the complete definition of competence as *right to speak*, that is, the right to the legitimate language, the authorized language, the language of authority. Competence implies the power to impose reception.   *(1977:64, quoted in Thompson 1984:46–7).*

Hebrew is the dominant medium in the system. Rosa's agency and presence – one Israeli in an all-Palestinian environment – is a constant reminder that Israeli power permeates the pedagogic environment and dominates it.

Contents and curriculum: the toddlers' agenda

The absence of a systematic curricular agenda tends to obscure nursery schools' pedagogic mission and ideological thrusts. Clues must thus be sought in texts and practices accompanying junctions such as religious, national and personal celebrations – a project undertaken in Weil's (1986) account of birthday celebrations in Israeli nursery schools, and by Handelman and Shamgar-Handelman (1990) in their account of kindergarten holiday ceremonies.

Israeli holidays are celebrated either in the classroom or in public events in the community. In both cases, agendas are ultimately supervised by local council officers. Teachers and principals are issued with recommendations for procedures in classroom affairs. Grander celebrations are often organized and conducted by school principles or by other officials on behalf of the municipal council.

Natzerat Illit's education department, like those of other Israeli new towns, has always emphasized community events on public holidays. The calendar of centrally organized ceremonies includes strictly national events, Jewish feasts, and occasions which embody both. The way Palestinian toddlers are incorporated into these public events presents a fascinating case of exclusion through contrived inclusion.

First, Israel's Remembrance Day *(Yom Hazikaron)*, which comes one day before Independence Day *(Yom Ha'atsmaut)* – the two tend to occur in May.[9] Independence Day is a national holiday when all schools are shut, so Remembrance Day, occuring one day earlier, remains the obvious opportunity for staging formal school and town events. These events tend to highlight the solemnity associated with the memory of war heroes and the exaltation of the pinnacle of Jewish nationalism – the declaration of Israel's independence on 15 May 1948.

The venue for this and other holiday ceremonies in Natzerat Illit is the municipal football stadium, where school children arrive *en masse* in buses hired by the local authority. School goers of all ages thus make the bulk of the attending audience in what often becomes the major formal event of the day.[10] Local politicians and religious figures attend and speak. Teachers and pupils read poems, make music and sing. Reels of flowers are placed, fire torches lit, flags are lowered to half mast.

The entire cohort of local school goers is expected to attend the ceremonies; the Palestinian toddlers are no exception. Like other nursery teachers Na'ila and her Palestinian colleagues are issued with detailed operational guidelines and timetables, transportation schedules to and from the football ground, rules of conduct and other pieces of information required for a smooth event. Like Israeli toddlers, the Palestinians and their teachers dutifully arrive on site waving little flags of Israel, mumbling the songs laboriously taught by Rosa, presenting nicely packaged boxes of collectively purchased sweets to IDF representatives – a custom known as *shay laḥhayal* (Hebrew for 'gift for the soldier').

The nationalistic overtones of Israel's Remembrance and Independence Days are obvious. More than any other event this dual celebration embodies the exclusionary nature of Israeliness. It is the time when perceived common descent, citizenship and sentimental belonging are most vividly interlinked to blood: Jewish blood generally; the blood of fallen Israeli soldiers in particular.[11] It is, essentially, an event whereby non-Jews, albeit citizens of Israel, are categorically excluded. The very definition of the state, enacted in the ritual, hinges on the 1948 victory over the Palestinians and their allies in the Arab states.

One official happily remarked that 'the *shay laḥayal* gifts which the Arab nurseries bring on Independence Day are always the nicest, the biggest and the most beautifully wrapped'. This observation came back to me a few weeks later when I visited Naʿila at the nursery. It was early afternoon, and parents were collecting their children.

Naʿila and Rosa were busy tidying up toys and furniture around the playroom when an Israeli head-teacher of an adjacent nursery school walked in. There followed a genuinely amicable exchange of jokes and greetings – Naʿila and the visitor have been colleagues for over a decade. Then the visitor revealed the reason for her call. She has just realized she is completely out of small flags of Israel, which she needs for decorating the nursery for an approaching end-of-year celebration. Could Naʿila help her out?

Naʿila, as pleased to do a favour as she was flattered by the nature of this particular request, produced a bunch of blue and white flags from a drawer. The visitor was grateful, but clearly not completely satisfied. She needed more. Naʿila moved fast and businesslike, disappearing downstairs to the school's store room and soon returning with a mail-bag full of clothes and oddments. She opened it in front of her colleague, producing a large, tidily wrapped bundle of little triangular flags of Israel, all sewn together on a long cord, ready to be hoisted. Smiling proudly at her own efficiency and tidiness, Naʿila handed the bundle to her colleague. The visitor was grateful and relieved. 'I knew that I could count on you', she said to beaming Naʿila.

The determination on the part of Israeli officials to drag the Palestinian toddlers through the elaborate motions of Remembrance Day, complete with its linguistic idiom and imagery which they can hardly comprehend, is intriguing. It is imbedded, paradoxically, in the liberal tenets of the municipal bureaucracy. Palestinian toddlers are constituents of a system whose directives ostensibly apply to every individual regardless of religious, ethnic or national affiliation. It is only when directives are translated into motions on the ground, when rows of children begin entering the stadium mumbling songs they cannot hope to fathom, that their exclusion becomes so apparent. When the flags are hoisted and the speeches sound, the Palestinian kids become mute witnesses to a foreign ceremony which signals their very marginality. The liberal officials who generously invite them in the first place are those who take a leading role in the construction of the stonewall which grows between them and the rest. Nominal inclusion notwithstanding, the hosts become indifferent to the difference of the guests, to use Herzfeld's (1993) suggestive term. The cruel overtones of exclusion grow tangible and inescapable.

A second example is *Shavū'ot*. In its contemporary Israeli guise, *Shavū'ot* is a holiday premised on a medley of Jewish religious symbols and the Zionist idea of a return to the rural fatherland. Paramount amongst these icons is the notion of the seven plant species (*shiv'at haminim*) with which, according to the pentecost, the land of Israel has been endowed. Once assembled on the football pitch, the thirty-nine nursery schools are divided into seven prearranged groups, each forming a circle on the pitch to represent one of the seven species. Like their Israeli peers, Palestinian toddlers too bring their collective 'harvest basket' to the ceremony every June.

The performance is narrated in a language the generative base of which is not only profoundly Jewish, but also clearly nationalistic. It takes the form of a dialogue: a teacher relays questions from the stage, the children respond in unison from the floor. The first few questions, including 'what festival are we celebrating today?' and 'how many species, children, has our land been endowed with?' establish the essential features of the situation, settling two key issues which hence will go unquestioned: whose land this is, and whose festival is being celebrated. This sets the stage for the predictable procession which follows, whereby members of each of the seven groups awaits their turn to hurry to the stage and to present their 'harvest' of fruit – or graphic representations thereof. Each presentation is accompanied by an appropriate Hebrew song, describing the merits and uniqueness of the species.

Local council officials seemed proud of the incorporation of Palestinian toddlers into the ceremony. On one occasion, a senior council official proudly produced a bunch of colour photographs taken at the previous year's *Shavū'ot* event, pointed at a circle of four-year-olds seated on the grass and said:

Look at those Arab children and their teacher here. You couldn't really tell the difference between them and the rest, could you? Ever so well behaved, obedient, clean and calm.

The official was genuinely proud to recollect and demonstrate success in what appears to be the worthy project of having all children of whatever creed and colour join the action. The highly exclusionary aspect of the affair was simply not registered. It was neither problematized on the day nor pondered on the occasion of its photographic reconstruction a few months later.

Like all other toddlers in Natzerat Illit, the Palestinians partake in the mass tree-planting event on *Tu-bishvat* in January. *Tu-bishvat* has a rather obscure mention in the *Mishna* as 'new year for the trees'. In modern Israel, however, it has become a nation-building celebration, complete with mass tree-planting as token participation in the Zionist transformation of the land. Its narrative focuses on the national duty and privilege to 'redeem' the land (*geulat haa'retz*). Trees are not planted merely for timber, shade, or as a means to combat soil erosion. Rather, planting creates new social space. The motto is represented in a famous nursery rhime:

Dūnam po vedūnam sham,
adama nikhbeshet,
kakh nigʻal admat haʾam...

(an acre here, an acre there,
land is being conquered,
thus we redeem the nation's soil...)

Wet and muddy weather on the January day in 1989 notwithstanding, the Palestinian nursery children, accompanied by staff, diligently attended, dutifully planted.

During the morning ceremony each nursery school was assigned a ninth-grade schoolboy or girl to help the teacher and the toddlers negotiate the muddy climb which separated the road where the buses alighted from the planting area. The Israeli youngster who joined the Palestinian children, fourteen-years-old Gadi, was no stranger. Living near the nursery school, Gadi had been a more or less regular volunteer in aid of the nursery for the previous two years. He often came to the nursery after returning from school in the afternoon, to help the teachers carry things to the store-room, tidy up, do minor repairs. The children all knew him by face and name, and were evidently delighted to see his familiar face amongst the crowds on *Tu-bishvat*. Talking to me of the event, teachers and council officials went out of their way to emphasize the joyful reunion between Gadi and the toddlers. This encounter – probably the only positive interaction between the otherwise bewildered toddlers and any of the Israelis present – was clearly the single gratifying aspect of the day for them.

Jewish and national Israeli holidays do not feature significantly in the classroom of the Palestinian nurseries. Rosa may teach a Hebrew song or two, primarily so that the children can reproduce them on public events, but not much more. For them attendance at the public ceremonies remain isolated, at best insignificant events.

The majority of children in the three nursery schools for Palestinians in Natzerat Illit are Christian.[12] So are all five Palestinian women teachers and assistants. When it comes to Christian holidays, the teachers are encouraged by the education department to model celebrations on patterns known in church-run nursery schools in Nazareth. Thus, unlike schools for Israeli children which operate six days a week and close on Saturdays, the nurseries for Palestinian toddlers in Natzerat Illit are closed both Saturdays and Sundays. Friday, the Muslim holiday, is a normal school day.

The special holidays are naturally Easter and Christmas, both celebrated in the nursery complete with nativity play, a Christmas tree, presents, Papa Nawal (Santa Claus), Easter eggs, and the appropriate array of carols and hymns sung in Arabic. Both occasions involve an early evening ceremony attended by the parents, for which the children and the staff prepare laboriously. Senior council officials are often present at the Christmas ceremony, with Na'ila's patron, when he was still alive, often attending as the guest of honour. The teachers present officials with Christmas presents. If an official fails to attend, the presents are promptly delivered to his or her home or office. At least one official displays these presents in her office, referring to them as tokens of the 'good relations with the Arab nurseries' and 'their smooth incorporation into the educational system of the town'.

Symbolic violence, manipulative clients

Bourdieu and Passeron's discussion of symbolic violence (1977) underscores the reproductive nature of education systems. The main social task of education, they argue, is to ensure the reproduction of dispositions and, eventually, of *habiti* most favourable for 'society' or, to be precise, for the hegemonic groups therein. Symbolic violence is the means: a tool of the trade aimed at 'the imposition of a cultural arbitrary by an arbitrary power' (*ibid*:5).

This immediately problematizes the notion of pedagogic authority. Bourdieu and Passeron go on to argue that this authority hinges on forces which have nothing to do with knowledge, but are directly linked to power structures placed outside the pedagogic context (*ibid*:6). The dominant pedagogic authority will always cater for the interests of the hegemonic groups, not only through its capacity to determine what is imposed but also through control of the boundaries of the population on whom this content is imposed (*ibid*:7).

When Israel put together an education system for its Palestinian citizens in the 1950s, the vision was quite simple: to inspire confidence amongst the Palestinians in the state of Israel, if possible in Zionism. This created a rather predatory approach to curricula and to staff appointments – two areas writers have alluded to in some detail (see Mar'i 1985; Benziman and Mansour: 1992 chapter 8). And while the situation is more relaxed today than it had been before, the Israeli system nevertheless remains involved with Palestinian education in search of a political objective.

The system still carries signs of the attempt to create the elusive 'good Arab', an entity which official Israel fondly believes to have existed in the past and, more significantly, to be resurrectable. Some ministry of education officials probably still believe that a genuinely 'faithful' Arab breed – docile, non-political, grateful for the gift of modernization endowed on him by Zionism and the state – can be sustained and nourished for the good and glory of the state and for the benefit of the Palestinians themselves.

But Israeli educational bureaucracy is by no means monolithic. Its evolvement into a less predatory and far more liberal system has produced considerable variations in the extent to which Israeli officials are motivated and in fact prepared to get involved in control at grass-root levels. The point, however, is that by now this is no longer necessary. The system has produced such a large and powerful cohort of coopted Palestinian supervisors and teachers that personal intervention on the part of Israeli bureaucrats is virtually superfluous. Self censorship is quite enough to keep the system going.

The Israeli officials in charge of the educational bureaucracy in Natzerat Illit are in an awkward situation. Lacking any training, experience or willingness to cope with such situations, they find themselves managing a considerable cohort of Palestinian toddlers. The classic problem of bureaucratic power which grapples with keeping people out is stood on its head in Natzerat Illit, where officials are forced to cater for those forced in by the system but who are, for the officials, essentially aliens.

There was only one direction the Israeli bureaucracy could turn to for guidance on how to treat this section of its own constituency: the essentially liberal ethos of individuality. The Palestinian toddlers were to be treated just like anybody else: same place as other nursery schools on the football pitch on Remembrance Day; an equal place along the rows of planters on *Tu-Bishvat*; an equivalent role at the presentation of the harvest on *Shavū'ot* and so on.

What the system could not find the strength to do, given the peculiar context of Palestinians' presence in Natzerat Illit, is to treat the toddlers as a collective with separate and legitimate perspectives and an alternative narrative incongruent with that of Israelis and their system. The insistence on equality based on individualism eventually produced the grotesque marginalization of unsuspecting four- and five-year-olds, attending ceremonies which are as irrelevant to their culture as they are exclusionary to them as persons.

Bourdieu and Passeron's (1977) assertion that hegemonic groups are able to delimit *who* studies (i.e. impose degrees of exclusivity) and determine *what* is studied (i.e. control curricula), is supplemented by the argument that they can also exercise control over the *mode* of imposition (i.e rules of conduct within the pedagogic realm). This approach is echoed in Illich (1970) and Kapferer (1981), who emphasize the 'political' functions of schools – the implicit features of the system which prompt students to accept the dominant school culture, thus tacitly supporting it. Gehrke (1979) likewise elucidates the notion of 'hidden curriculum' the primary goal of which is socializing students into the dominant order, as does McLaren's analysis of the ritual structure of school conformity (1986:81–139).

Israeli bureaucrats in Natzerat Illit try to control who is educated where. They try to ensure that the quota of Palestinian toddlers admitted into predominantly Israeli schools and nursery schools remains below a certain threshold. They were behind the creation, near-dismantling and final dissolution of the mixed nursery in 1978–80. In 1980 and 1984 they moved to establish separate nursery schools for Palestinian children.

Palestinian parents, staff and other representatives were virtually excluded from consultation and decision making along the process. Not surprisingly, the interests, tendencies and idiosyncrasies of Israelis were paramount – a point most lucidly illustrated in Rutti's testimony of the reasons behind her 1978/9 move to re-segregate the nursery school attended by her daughter. For her, as for other Israelis, educational exclusivity was evidently a precondition for a true sense of being Israeli. This was profoundly threatened by the notion of mixed education. Her complaint was an efficacious reminder to the council to regain control over the crucial matters of boundaries around the system they were running.

Israelis consistently make key decisions on *what* is taught to Palestinian children in Natzerat Illit. The annual events imposed on the children, in which they play the part of silent, thankful visitors, carry a clear message of power, one which persists even on Christian holidays celebrated in the relative intimacy of the classroom. The attendance on such occasions of Natzerat Illit's exclusively Israeli political leadership is ostensibly to honour the distinguished guests, but at the same time creates the perfect opportunity for them to act as supervisors and inspectors. It is on such occasions that the nursery school displays its ultimate adherence to the directives imposed by the system: non-Palestinian, non-Arab identity. *Papa Nawal* (Father Christmas) is the faint, benign Palestinian equivalent of the strong nationalistic symbols so emphatically present on public celebrations of Jewish and Israeli holidays.

Head teachers naturally have total powers to create, interpret and implement the rules of daily life at nursery – rules committed to the reproduction of hierarchical order based on power vested in age and in administrative authority. This hierarchy, so fiercely guarded in the Palestinian nursery, is a significant departure from the boisterous, often wild atmosphere which typifies Israeli nurseries. Israeli officials, however, make no effort to encourage Palestinian teachers to adopt standards of discipline more prevalent in the Israeli system. Officials are evidently proud of the rigid discipline and order which characterize the nursery schools which cater for the Palestinians. Their approval of the pedagogic framework which stabilizes traditional age and status structures, thus ensuring full supervised control, is significant. It obviously overrides any ambition on their part to reform these standards and make them more compatible with laxer norms which guide most other sections of the system.

Finally, another look at power relations, their concealment, and the role of educational systems in buttressing and legitimizing them. Neo-Marxist perspectives such as the ones quoted above hold concealment of power relations as imperative for the upholding of pedagogic authority. Bourdieu and Passeron (1977:39) in fact describe pedagogy as a snowballing, self-perpetuating system which breeds misrecognition of its own arbitrariness.

The problem which immediately presents itself in the case of the Palestinian citizens of Israel is simple: do individuals really misrecognize the 'true nature' of the system? Do Palestinian citizens of Israeli or, for that matter, members of any minority group in a similar predicament, really fail to read domination in every aspect of the structure which determines their precious intellectual, scientific and vocational progress?

I argue they do not. Palestinians recognize the power structure which underscores the education system in Natzerat Illit infinitely more clearly than do the liberal officials who run it. While Israeli officials are often fooled by their own creation, the Palestinians, who on one level are clearly the marginalized victims of the system, emerge also as its cool and calculated users. The bureaucracy offers them free education for toddlers, which enhances the ability of women to become employed and earn. Moreover, the educational milieu in question is relatively safe: a Palestinian teacher, Arabic as medium of instruction, the privilege of having their children as members of the in-group rather than as marginalized constituents in a predominantly Israeli peer group.

Yes, there is a price to pay: the teacher is stigmatized as deeply co-opted, participation on Israeli national holidays can be degrading and confusing, attendance of officials on Christian holidays is irksome. But then, these elements can be and are routinely rationalized. Why not learn of other people's festivals when you are four or five? What is so fundamentally wrong in hosting dignitaries on holidays? Most significant, however, is that the whole thing is temporary. The consistent choice on the part of Palestinian parents to later send their children to primary schools in Nazareth indicates that a problematic system which may be tolerable at nursery level is clearly a non-starter later.

The refusal of Palestinian parents to remain the starry-eyed and faithful clients of the system and their level-headed usage of it, problematizes Bourdieu's prediction that pedagogic authority must disintegrate with the unveiling of the arbitrary power which upholds it. The notion of Palestinian residents as sophisticated users of the system, not only its helpless victims, is a theme which will come up again in chapter 9, where I discuss the place of Palestinians in municipal politics in Natzerat Illit.

6

Reflexivity and liberalism

Surprise recruitment

In January 1989, as I was entering my second year of fieldwork in Natzerat Illit, the Palestinian residents were putting together their first ever bid for political representation in the municipal council. Determined to get a Palestinian elected to the municipal council, they formed an independent list of local candidates – an undertaking I discuss in some detail in chapter 9. All activists were united behind the need to attain 'Jewish-Arab coopera-tion' – a code for inclusion of Jewish Israelis in the official list of candidates.[1]

A month-long chase after potential Israeli partners followed, in which the Palestinian activists held several meetings with representatives of left-of-centre Zionist parties, but all to no avail. The disappointing outcome was conveyed by the leader of the list in an election rally in January 1989. He gave an account of each of the frustrating encounters, gradually intro-ducing his all-Palestinian audience to the new situation: cooperation with Israeli partners was not about to happen.

Then, out of the blue, one of his deputies turned to me with a direct and public proposition. 'Well', he said, 'what about you? You are officially a resident of the town, hence eligible for office, are you not? Why don't you stand with us?'

Seen in retrospect, the attempt to recruit me is perhaps understandable given the circumstances. I was, after all, the only Israeli interested in their project. I had attended meetings and rallies, laboriously and visibly taking notes. I regularly spent time with the activists, asking questions, expressing sympathetic views. And yet, the public suggestion that I should join their ranks took me by complete surprise. Here I was, four months before the termination of my fieldwork, being offered an unexpected opportunity to enter local politics. The offer had a local significance of which, I suspect, those offering were scantily aware. My situation in Natzerat Illit was tenuous. Like all anthropologists I still perceived myself as marginal. Most of my Israeli acquaintances knew by then that my presence was short term. Some of them must have been aware of my misgivings about their community and its exclusionary attitudes towards the Palestinians. This notwithstanding, acceptance of the proposition on my part could have been an unprecedented departure. Joining the Independent Palestinian List would mean appearing in the local Israeli community as someone who endorsed the other side of a struggle generally perceived as winner takes all – a zero sum game in which an actor can only be on one side.

The moment became definitive. Anthropologists have been forced to choose for or against further immersion in field situations before. This time, however, the choice was not simply another inward step towards exotic native culture, of the kind anthropologists sometime weigh against conventions of their own culture and ethics. What was at stake here was denunciation of what my Israeli host community stood for and, even more significantly, of aspects of my own personhood I was not quite ready to forgo yet. It was a tempting invitation to cross the lines and go politically native. I knew I was not ready to accept it.[2]

The circumstances and my embattled, deeply embarrassed state of mind were hardly conducive to a full public exposition of my reasons to decline. In fact some of my observations here are crystallizing only as I reconstruct the event to write it up almost four years on. As it happened I stood up slowly and attempted, completely unrehearsed, to explain where I stood in relation to an elusive line which remains one of the mysteries of anthropology. I said something about my position as a researcher, and how difficult it would be if I became officially involved in a campaign which was to form a major part of my study. Although I took their offer as a compliment, I said, unfortunately I had to decline.

Some of those attending may have anticipated my reaction, others not. The matter was not raised again, not even in private, by anyone to date. I, however, remained with an uneasiness which, while suspended since, has never disappeared completely: the awkward aftertaste of letting down good people who put their trust in me. That moment catapulted me right into the heart of the paradoxes of Israeli–Palestinian relations, as well as into an unexpected facet of the oxymoronic dilemma of participant observation.

Memories from the grotto
In the 1960s, a young woman came to live in our house. She was the new *Ozeret* – Hebrew for (female) help – hired to clean, wash, iron and do

other household chores. Youngest of four siblings and aged only five, I was just old enough to note a difference between her and the women who had worked for us before. The other women had full names such as Ḥanna Sabaḥ and Naomi Jereshi. The new young woman, who called herself Shoshana, had no surname – or none we were aware of. Significantly, when in the summer of 1993 I asked my mother and older siblings about Shoshana, I soon discovered that none of them could recollect ever knowing her surname, let alone what it was. But then, that could be expected: the women preceding her had all been Israeli *Mizrahiyot* – Jewish women whose families had come to Israel from Arab countries. They may have been racialized and marginalized, but were fundamentally perceived as part of 'us'. Shoshana, on the other hand, was Palestinian: hence ambiguous, unsettling, enigmatic. That we did not know her properly was inevitably linked to the fact we hardly recognized her people.

Even her first name was not quite hers. Shoshana, we knew, was a crude transliteration into Hebrew of her original name, Rosette. A Christian native of a village in Lower Galilee, her Hebrew name must have been assumed as a self-imposed distancing from her Palestinian self in an attempt to find a job – and hold on to it – with Israelis in a fashionable part of Haifa.

Like her predecessors, Shoshana – I cannot think of her with any other name, and anyway, I need it here as a reminder – had room and board with us. Like them, she too lived in a space known as 'The Cave'. Situated at the very centre of the house, The Cave was not quite a room. Roughly 3 metres long and one and a half wide, it had been designed as a passage between the western, more public section of the apartment, where visitors would enter through a little ante-room into a set of three large guest salons, and the eastern wing which had the bedrooms. But we never used The Cave as a passage. Its western end was blocked by a permanently locked door with thick translucent but distorting glass frames. The eastern end remained wide open to the corridor connecting the living area with the bedrooms. It had no door, no partition. Some members of my family remember a curtain, others are not quite sure.

The space inside The Cave was offered partial defence by the door which separated the main corridor and the dining room. Once ajar – which it was and still is, most of the time – it partially covered The Cave's opening. Being somewhat narrower than the opening, however, it failed to block it properly. Locking The Cave for privacy and safety was thus out of the question. In fact anyone walking along the corridor could have a comprehensive view of the only bit of space defined as Shoshana's own: the large bed; the open cupboard with her few belongings; the yellow bulb hanging from the ceiling on a single thread.

I now think of Shoshana as a Palestinian equivalent of Elsie, whose gloomy image in the 1923 poem by William Carlos Williams, says James Clifford, displaces a literary tradition which treated servants and domestic workers as 'domesticated outsiders of the bourgeois imagination' (1988:4 fn. 1). She was not shy, but her broken Hebrew often silenced her. I cannot remember a word she ever said in the presence of more than one or two of us, none she ever uttered in the presence of my father or my older brother. She smiled a lot and was as pleasant and submissive as the job required.

Bright and curious, Shoshana had stacks of newspapers and journals she kept in the cupboard near her bed, to browse through whenever she had free time. The literature must have been left by the *Ozeret* who occupied The Cave before her. Most of it would have been completely out of reach for women in her native village: foreign women's fashion magazines, Israeli weeklies such as *La'isha* ('*For the Woman*') which specializes in family matters, romance, and features articles on people not important enough to make the major papers. There were even issues of '*Olam Hakolno'a* ('*Cinema World*').

One afternoon Shoshana and I, the teenager and the five-year-old, sat on her bed, leafing through a magazine. We turned a page, and there they were: African women, photographed bare-breasted. We giggled, embarrassed. The taxing moment, not unusual between adults and children, brought on board some fundamental issues. Sexuality was one of them, but even more demanding was the need to clarify the cultural similarities and differences between us, the onlookers. Shoshana was first to regain composure. She pointed at the picture and said with clemency: 'They are not like us, you see. They simply do not understand.'

Her recreation of the tree of knowledge episode was like a magic spell. The clear mark she delineated separating 'us' – fortunate enough 'to understand' – and others – ignorant and thus forgivable Africans – bailed us out of our embarrassment. With time her distinction became our working code. 'I saw a picture of some more who do not understand', I would indicate to her. Soon we were in her dim dwelling once again, exploring the varieties of consciousness in darkest Africa.

But here, with hindsight, is an alternative perspective of Shoshana's life amongst us. A Palestinian woman, sixteen years of age, alone in an alien city, away from home and family, at the mercy of her employers *cum* hosts *cum* jailers. Her nights are spent in a dusky alcove, where members of the household cannot help but look. Her need and right for privacy and dignity forgotten. Her intimacy robbed.

My family was and still is perfectly liberal. Evil thoughts and low-brow generalizations about The Arabs hardly surfaced – I guess my father's genuine subscription to non-ascriptive individualism rubbed off on us quite naturally. But this precisely is the snag: the need for privacy and intimacy has little to do with stated ethics. It has a lot to do with power, which in our house, like everywhere else, was never symmetric. If seeing is power, then a glance from the well-lit fairway of the corridor into the darkened dead-end alley of The Cave has piercing potency. When the person lying there in silence is a young woman whose sense of self-respect, decency and worth is culturally enmeshed in modesty, seclusion and chastity, the imbalance becomes acute.

My parents' intentions *vis-à-vis* Shoshana were probably as benevolent as my intentions towards the Palestinian residents of Natzerat Illit during the 1989 election rally, and equally anchored in universal liberal ethos. But intentions did not carry the day in either case. Other factors interfered, stopping us from matching heart-felt conviction with actual practice. Whatever our ideas, the Palestinian actors ended up marginalized.

The moment of Shoshana in The Cave belongs here as a painful early memory of failed liberalism – a theme which forms the theoretical backbone of this book so far. My family in the 1960s and myself in 1989 are not freak phenomena. The great majority of middle-class Israelis, Natzerat Illit no exception, share the basic tenets of a non-ascriptive, benevolent and liberal attitude to Palestinians, to Arabs and to others generally. What the experience of Natzerat Illit conveys, I think, is that such values, intrinsically agreeable as they may be, are not enough.

On reflexivity in anthropology

Reflexivity in anthropology has style and form, as well as a coherent epistemological development. Ricoeur's (1969) *Le Conflit des Interpretations* was introduced into anthropology a few years later by Geertz (1973), producing a licence to interpret which would later become theoretically and ethically overburdened. This tension, combined with the impact of Said's *Orientalism* (1978), brought a generation of anthropologists – including some of Geertz's disciples – to question the validity of ethnographic representation as previously practised, creating what has been dubbed the crisis of representation in anthropology. A body of work emerged whose outlook – whether on a particular ethnographic project or on anthropology as a whole – stressed, among other issues, reflexivity.[3]

This turn in anthropology redefined old demarcation lines. The notions of the 'discrete' field and the impartial anthropologist as 'data collector', of ethnography as 'data processing' and the final presentation to the reader of 'ethnographic findings' were fruitfully questioned and re-negotiated. New light was shed on anthropologists' authority and on authorship, as well as on questions of the politics of domination and control. In due course the trend was introduced to ethnographic monographs and essays on Middle-Eastern groups.[4]

Some critics see this attempt at ethnographic writing as narcissistic and ego-centred, founded in writers' immature reluctance to face the inevitable consequences of authorship and editorial control. It has been labelled vain, indulgent navel-gazing.[5] I myself have sometimes found sections within this discourse somewhat trying, more to do with the writer's person than with the realities of those whose story is purported to be told. I am still undecided whether key-words such as dialogical, experimental, reflexive, post-modern and post-structural are indeed the idioms of a brave new chapter in anthropology, or just components of a fashionable important footnote.

But rather than nominate my overall winners in this debate over theory and ethics, I prefer to think of the efficacy of reflexivity in terms of the ethnographic context in which it is deployed. Some ethnographic situations gain little theoretical or analytic depth from exposé's of anthropological trials and tribulations. Others become more vivid and more valid once the reader has the opportunity to place the narrator in his or her particular field situation and personal context.

Occasionally, however, there are ethnographic projects of a third variety – those which are incomplete, inaccurate, even dishonest unless the reader is allowed some insight into relations between the anthropologist and those for whom the field is home. While a comprehensive characterization of such projects is beyond my scope here, one obvious criterion comes to mind. The more formal and one-sided the power relations between the anthropologist's metropolis and the group he studies and eventually represents, the more essential reflexivity becomes. My situation in Natzerat Illit is clearly of this third variety.

Research projects of Palestinians written so far by Israeli academics – most of them men, incidentally, and many of them orientalists – tend to gloss the writer's subjectivities and sensitivities *vis-à-vis* the situation he describes.[6] This scholarly tradition is well established in Israel, and its validity has gone unquestioned far too long. For me, a similar attempt to convey 'observations' from Natzerat Illit or anywhere like it as nothing but 'objective data' is untenable. As far as studies conducted by Israelis of Palestinians and of other Arabs are concerned, a diversion from the axiomatic authority which earlier generations of researchers took for granted is not only timely, but long overdue.

I would like to think that the reflexivity which I endorse here is of the *collective* kind. In this I mean an approach which has one reading less about the anthropologist's spiritual (mis)adventures and more about past and present social, political and cultural constellations and their impact on ethnographic conduct and its outcomes.

I am an Ashkenazi Jewish male, born and raised in Israel into a reality in which my kind were and are still dominant, and in which others, particularly Palestinians, were and are still essentially powerless. My insights of the field were shaped by my biography, but also by the ways my informants saw me. The bureaucracy regarded me as a potential settler; Israelis identified me as a comrade on the demographic frontier; Palestinians considered me a trusted, well-placed ally. To think all this had no effect on where I looked, what I saw, what I allowed to register and how I tended to interpret would be naïve. To think I know precisely how this process happened would be pretentious.

My diverse personae in the field were often incompatible. Judaizing Galilee has always been anathema to Palestinians, my own acquaintances no exception. Most Israeli residents of Natzerat Illit, on the other hand, while generally happy with personal contact with individual Palestinians, would have regarded my solidarity with the local Palestinian collective as tantamount to treason. The question of loyalty thus crept into my vision of myself and my research. What does my Israeli neighbour really mean the morning following a dinner party we had for Palestinian friends when she utters across the lawn with a jocund smile, 'so you had visitors last night, now didn't you?'. How would my Palestinian informants react if I told them what some of my Israeli acquaintances – including ones I am quite fond of – think of 'the Arab problem'? Mercifully, none of my stints on active military service in the IDF since the 1970s have been in the occupied territories. But had I been called up for service in the West Bank or in Gaza during the Intifada, could I find anyone in this town with whom to share my choice between obeying orders and carrying out policies which I regard as unacceptable and being jailed for refusing to take part?

In the turbulent and highly charged atmosphere of the Middle East today these questions go beyond the realm of theory or intellectual debate. They form a concrete part of life. Whether we are Palestinians, Israelis, social scientists or social 'actors', we all deal first and foremost with aspects which could determine our future here and that of our descendants. I know these questions remain largely unanswered. I hope the willingness to raise some of them is some contribution.

PART 2

RESISTANCE?

7

Hospitality and the engendering of space

Hospitable voyagers*

30 January 1989. Having spent the morning interviewing in the southern part of town, I head towards the stop near Dado shopping centre, to await the bus home. Rajeba is at the stop, beaming as she sees me approaching. In her mid-forties, she is probably only a dozen years older than me. Yet when I see her I feel as if she is of another, older generation. It is a sense I often have regarding Palestinian women: regardless of biological age or appearance, they seem older and more senior. As women and as Palestinians, they are marginalized twice over. The difficulties and humiliations packed into a day in their lives, I sometimes think, must be equivalent to strife others experience in weeks or months. They see a great deal and age rapidly.

Rajeba's children, some of whom I met, are in their early twenties. She asks about my one-year-old. I tell her she is fine. It crosses my mind that our lives, including the luxury of not becoming parents until our thirties, are a sheltered, spoilt affair.

Rajeba inquires which bus I am awaiting, and where I hope to go. 'Oh yes, the number 5', she says knowingly. 'I am waiting for it too. It should be here any moment now. Ten minutes after the hour. You'll be home in no time.'

I detect a tendency on Rajeba's part to assume responsibility for my journey. My suspicions strengthen as we mount the bus. First I notice how she actively protects me from the others in the queue, gently elbowing my way in front of her. She then climbs quickly at my heels, greeting the driver in Arabic from the step behind me. He smiles and waves me in without attempting to collect my fare, then turns to Rajeba. They carry on a bit. The seasoned engine roars. Their voices are kept low, their exchange rapid. Abbreviated

---

* This section of the book features entries from my field diary. These appear here in italics, each beginning with a date line.

signs are snapped in brisk, staccato diction. I cannot hear them, let alone decipher the dialogue. Then, before I know it, it is over. Rajeba has paid my fares and now nudges me along into the half-empty bus. I acquiesce, feeling distinctly like a piece of merchandise changing hands.

The journey is short, giving us but a brief opportunity for small talk: something about the nursery school for Palestinian toddlers in Natzerat Illit, where a mutual friend of ours works. She has heard I sometimes go there to sit with the children, chat with the teachers under the shade of the old carob tree in the back yard. I notice how alert she is, as if on duty, responsible, protective of passengers on board. Or is it only me she looks after?

The bus climbs up the ridge nearer my house. Rajeba makes sure I know where we are and how to get home. Has she forgotten what I know she knows – that I have lived here over a year now? Why has she taken this unrelenting command of my journey? What compels her to make a final audible reminder to the driver, making sure he is about to halt at my stop even once the stop signal had sounded? I alight with a mixture of bewilderment and relief.

The incident gained import not long after, when two more Palestinian acquaintances behaved in a similar fashion on two different occasions when we bumped into each other aboard the local bus. Both were men, considerably younger than myself, who had been briefly introduced to me before. As with Rajeba, there was nothing in our respective relationships which could imply an obligation on their parts towards me. This notwithstanding, as soon as I was on the bus they sprang to my assistance, insisting on paying my fare, clinching a deal with the driver without consulting me, then handling me as if I was a child.

Disenfranchised franchise holders
In the 1920s, the British administration granted the 'Afifi family from the village of Saffurya [1] a franchise for public transport in northern Palestine. The franchise included destinations such as Haifa, Damascus and Jenin, as well as Nazareth and its rural hinterland. One peripheral service the 'Afifis operated connected Nazareth with 'Ain Mahil, a village 8 kilometres east of the town, now bordering Natzerat Illit to the east. As it happens, the old road from Nazareth to 'Ain Mahil runs along the ridge where the first residential areas of Natzerat Illit were built in the late 1950s. The new town thus found itself within an area included in a public transport franchise owned by Palestinians.

Pre-state Zionism, with its preoccupation with movement of people over land, placed great emphasis on public transport. Threats to buses, taxies and lorries were invariably interpreted by the Jewish settlers as anti-Zionist brigandry fuelled by indiscriminate hatred of Jews and backed by Palestinian and pan-Arab nationalism.[2]

Later, with the advent of Zionist settlement, the capability of providing transport to and from outlying posts became three-pronged: a logistic necessity, a means to assert territorial presence and an issue involving national pride. After the establishment of Israel in 1948, bus companies in various parts of the country were expected to dissolve and surrender their franchises to Egged, the nationwide bus cooperative. Egged, which enjoys a virtual monopoly in subsidized public transport to date, gradually became identified with Israeli hegemony over space in all parts of the country, and grew into a recognized and popular part of Israeli national sentiment. Egged's mission, after all, involved the periphery, hardship and adventure, a pioneering spirit, an ongoing contact with the Palestinian frontier. While some Palestinian citizens of Israel have been admitted as members, Egged is owned by an overwhelmingly Israeli membership. It has a *tiyūlim* department for educational exploration tours into hidden sites and landscapes of the newly discovered homeland, and takes great pride in having extended logistic assistance to all of Israel's armed conflicts.

Pre-1948 regional franchise operations owned by Jewish individuals or institutions tended to view the merge with Egged as their duty to the nation. The 'Afifis, like other Palestinians in their situation, failed to share this sentiment. The new monopoly notwithstanding, they simply went on serving the rural hinterland of Galilee. Most of their lines connected villages with Haifa and with Nazareth. With few Israeli settlements around, Egged was first unperturbed by the competition. Only later, with the establishment of Natzerat Illit, did the issue of the franchise over urban public transportation within Natzerat Illit present itself.

A legal battle ensued involving the 'Afifi family, Egged, the municipality of Natzerat Illit and the Ministry of Transport. The matter was finally resolved in court, which upheld 'Afifi's rights as granted by the old franchise, complete with the licence to operate local bus routes throughout Nazareth and its environs.

As a result, the Nazareth Bus Company (herewith NBC), of which the 'Afifi family is chief owner, now operates Natzerat Illit's local services as an integral part of its Nazareth-based metropolitan network. One of its local lines, which traverses the northern section of Natzerat Illit, terminates in the village of 'Ain Mahil, thus in fact making use of the old franchise connecting the village to Nazareth. As for intercity lines, while most bus connections between Natzerat Illit and the rest of Israel are operated by Egged, the profitable line to Haifa, which had been part of the 'Afifi's franchise prior to 1948, is an exception. The court forced Egged to share it with GB Tours – a sister company to NBC, partly owned by the 'Afifis. Egged and GB Tours thus supply alternating buses on the line, which runs from Natzerat Illit through Nazareth to Haifa.[3]

Locally, however, NBC buses remained the only means of public transportation – within Natzerat Illit as well as between the town and Nazareth.[4] In fact all local routes which serve Natzerat Illit either begin or end their journey in downtown Nazareth. Each journey crosses over from Nazareth to Natzerat Illit at least once.[5]

While passengers include Palestinians as well as Israelis, the social space inside the buses is clearly Palestinian. Israeli residents refer to the vehicles, as well as to the service generally, as 'the Arab bus' (*ha'otobūs ha'aravi*). There are visual differences: while Egged buses are red, new, and by the late 1980s, mostly air-conditioned, NBC buses were green, considerably older, and technologically inferior. Many of them in fact are old Egged stock purchased by NBC. All NBC drivers are Palestinians.

Like elsewhere in Israel, one of the duties of the driver is to collect fares and dispense tickets. NBC drivers thus have to chose between Arabic and Hebrew every time a passenger steps aboard. They know many of the Palestinian passengers personally, but even Palestinians they do not recognize are greeted amicably, befitting age and gender. This is not the case with Israeli passengers, with whom drivers tend to be more curt. Fairly fluent in Hebrew, they nevertheless tend to be reserved, bestowing Israelis with minimal attention. They seldom err in their identification of a new passenger as either Palestinian or Israeli.

The radio on the bus is normally tuned to a station broadcasting in Arabic, usually the Israeli Broadcasting Authority's (IBA) programme in Arabic. Most Israelis are unaware of the differences between IBA's Arabic programme – often described by Palestinian citizens of Israel as a clumsy tool of state propaganda – and pro-Palestinian stations broadcasting in Arabic from Syria, Lebanon, Cyprus or France. For Israelis, the language seems to be the crucial point: '*radio be'aravit*' (radio in Arabic) is the generic, derogatory expression.

Palestinian children, generally restrained in the presence of adults, tend to be uncharacteristically boisterous while on board NBC buses. This is conspicuous in early afternoon, when many of them make the return journey from school in Nazareth. They radiate a sense of security, most

probably grounded in the presumption that the likelihood of public repri-
mand by Palestinian adults in the presence of Israeli passengers is low.
Israeli children travelling on NBC buses, on the other hand, tend to be less
clamorous than their usual manner.

Role inversion and resistance

My Palestinian acquaintances' conduct aboard the Palestinian looking,
Palestinian owned and Palestinian driven NBC buses had them acting as
my hosts. Having assumed and established this role, they tended to reduce
the drivers to minor members of the household, collaborating with the
chief performer, running errands to ensure the ritual goes smoothly. This
ritual of hospitality, I argue, which used space aboard the bus as pre-estab-
lished Palestinian turf, was at the same time aimed at reasserting it as such.

Hospitality is a pillar of Arab culture, Palestinians no exception. It is a
duty so closely associated with pride and honour that the right to perform
it has turned to a prerogative. Lavie (1990:289) alludes to the ambiguities
of Mzeina Bedouin life under the Israeli occupation of the Sinai, whereby
values of honour, often derived from being Bedouin hosts, were mitigated
by the precarious existence they had as powerless subjects of their uninvited guests.

The paradoxes facing the Palestinian citizens of Israel in their relationship with Israel and Israelis are similar. Respective roles of honourable,
dispossessed native host (the Palestinian) and uninvited guest, intruder,
colonizing ruler (the Israeli) remain unresolved and fraught with tension.

This becomes particularly complicated in the border situation of
Natzerat Illit, where Palestinians grapple with the baffling and frustrating
situation of being unwanted guests on their ancestral land. Forced to
display gratefulness for the little they can get access to, their acquiesence
suggests a mental capitulation, with limited ability to stand up to the dominant Israelis.

Extending hospitality to Israelis thus emerges as a unique chance for
Palestinians to resist, an opportunity to reinstate the underlying natural
order by which the native acts as host to the new-comer. Hospitality has
hosts setting up agendas and guests adhering. Once the parts are given and
tacitly accepted, even temporarily, the guest is trapped: dependent, helpless, his very presence reaffirms the host's positioning and privilege. It is
the Palestinian at home who can, for once, determine the locus, the procedure, and the duration of the interaction with his Israeli guest. One routine
example is the emphatic and effective protestation *bakir*! (hey, early yet)
produced by Palestinian hosts when guests attempt to break away. When

guests are Israeli, this pattern temporarily suspends routines of Israeli dominance, using code and etiquette to temporarily transfer control to Palestinians.

In a political context such as Natzerat Illit, whereby spacial dominance has been turned on its head since 1957, the Palestinian rites of hospitality assume new meaning. Rather than a performance dictated by mere 'custom', hospitality is asserted, becoming a means by which to tackle the paradox of being displaced in your own homeland.

The conduct of Palestinian 'hosts' on board NBC buses was analogous to that of Palestinian friends I sometimes bumped into in downtown Nazareth. There too, the rituals of hospitality were invoked, complete with concern for my safety, efficient orientation and other aspects of well-being on the main street. Naturally, this warm attention on the part of Palestinians was never replicated in chance meetings which took place in public spaces in adjacent Natzerat Illit.

Perhaps it is allegorical to the Palestinian predicament in Israel that the only public space where Palestinians in Natzerat Illit feel free to assert their uninhibited presence through hospitality – the space within buses – is transitory. Local buses are not only in constant movement, but also form a space where contact is essentially short term. My Palestinian friends could push their hospitality partly because the short duration of the encounter did not allow the parties to fully confront the meanings of Palestinian strength in a public space shared by Israelis. Their resistance to Israeli dominance was tentative, temporary, tenuous.

Preoccupation with resistance on the part of anthropologists studying colonial and post-colonial contexts goes hand in hand with the current interest in representation, historiography and the power relations which foreground them. Abu-Lughod (1989) cites French feminist theory and studies of specific subordinate groups such as working-class youth in England, plantation workers in the Caribbean, peasants in South East Asia, subaltern groups in India and in South Africa as well as women in the USA, as fields in which key terms such as resistance, voices, subversion, dissidence, and counter-hegemony guide theoretical discourse since the late 1970s and throughout the 1980s.[6]

The theoretical terrain in which these studies are located was sketched initially by Gramsci in his Prison Notebooks (1971). Later, his line of thought has been extended and expanded by Foucault in *The History of Sexuality* (1978) and *Power/Knowledge* (1980), by Bourdieu in *Outline of a Theory of Practice* (1977a) and by Edward Said in *Orientalism (1978)*. I shall return to these, and in particular to Gramsci, in due course.

Julie Peteet's work (1994) on the place of beatings and bodily damage inflicted by Israeli soldiers on Palestinian men during the Intifada, highlights how Palestinians transform a situation ostensibly humiliating and degrading into a locus of male honour. She argues that the role of bodily harm in turning children into boys and then into responsible adults ready for leadership – a kind of rites of passage into manhood – turns the initial contact with the occupation army upside down. Rather then successful agents of repression attaining acquiescence, the Israeli soldiers are depicted by the Palestinian actors as acting in spite of themselves in the interest of the Palestinian cause. This they do, she argues, by galvanizing the resilience and efficacy of young males who confront them and suffer from their hands, which in turn enhances the youngsters' status.

Peteet's point of departure is Schiefellin's argument (1985) that the efficacy of ritual lies 'less in the text and its cultural categories', more in the relations between performers and other participants (Peteet 1994:32). Peteet then goes on to suggest, after Kerzer (1988), that:

... if ritual performances take place in a highly charged atmosphere of domination and crisis and are then cast as relations of power, they may inform a political agency designed to overthrow the domination of one set of performers (*ibid*).

The point of this argument is that certain rituals can outgrow the old mould which has them merely reaffirming and protecting the *status quo*, to actually accomplish things.

Hospitality, even if performed on board a bus or in a street corner, is a highly ritualized human activity. The situation between Israelis and Palestinians in Israel reflects a lopsided relation of power, albeit far less prone to crisis than the reality of the Intifada. It is Peteet's heavy reliance on theories of ritual performance and, in particular, her uncritical view of the suggested linkage between ritual and change which I disagree with.

Abu-Lughod (1989) provides a lucid warning against the tendency of humanist anthropology to idealize resistance. Anthropologists, including her own earlier writings, she confesses, tend 'to romanticize resistance, to read all forms of resistance as signs of the ineffectiveness of systems of power and of the resilience and creativity of the human spirit in its refusal to be dominated' (1989:41–2). This critique must surely be extended all the way back to Gramsci, who fondly – and humanistically, no doubt – believed resistance to be a salient precursor of the revolutionary overthrow of the hegemony.[7] This point later enables Abu-Lughod to argue that the analytical and theoretical value of resistance is not so much in its capacity to indicate a future revolutionary change towards a better world. Rather, it is the capability to analyze power and domination as encountered in the field which is enhanced.

Kaplan and Kelly (1994) caution against interpretations of Gramsci's work which rely too heavily on Raymond Williams's work, and which focus primarily on consciousness. Gramsci, they argue, saw resistance as a largely unconscious activity, with revolution being only possible through active agency – the sort instigated by 'organic intellectuals' who are 'so conscious that they understand the current hegemonic order . . . and their new, higher, emergent civilizations' (Kaplan and Kelly 1994:126). The embarrassment of latter day writers to deal with Gramsci's suggestion of vanguard revolution as the intellectual's calling, say Kaplan and Kelly, blurs the edges around resistance, pushing the term to include too many types of activities. The chief distinction thus shifts to that between 'conscious' and 'unconscious' resistance, thus taking away much of the potential theoretical efficacy of the term (*ibid*:126–7). As a result, rather than expanding the idiom of resistance, Kaplan and Kelly try to move away from 'myths of a conscious elite and superconscious revolutionary vanguard' (1994:127). 'The extreme alternative to the merely resisting, hegemonized, and fragmented subaltern', they suggest, 'is not the organic intellectual but the alienated one, self-aware and critical to the point of incapacity' (*ibid*).

Let me suspend the argument regarding resistance for a while, and move on to introduce three more Palestinian men whose conduct in Natzerat Illit might have been counted within the hazy Gramscian category 'resistors' so readily adopted by some contemporary anthropologists. The ethnographic account of their agency will set the stage for a more conclusive theoretical remark about resistance later.

8

Risk, rationality and trust

Illiberal squad

Natzerat Illit has one competitive basketball team, *Hapoel Natzerat Illit* (henceforth HNI). Formed in the 1970s, when it joined the bottom (fifth) division of Israel's National League, the team took a few years to be promoted to the fourth division (*liga Bet*), where it competed from 1984 to 1990.[1] Affiliated with the nationwide network *Hapoel*, the sports arm of the *Histadrut* trade union federation, HNI was and still is operated and financed by the local workers' council (*Moetzet Hapo'alim*), the standard name for local branches of the *Histadrut*.[2]

The 1988–1989 squad offered a fairly representative cross section of the Israeli population of the town. The eldest player was a twenty-eight year-old driving instructor. The youngest were three seventeen-year-old school-boys. There were two conscripts, a policeman, a shop-keeper, a technician and a bank clerk. Five players were of North African origin, seven were East European – three of them natives of the Soviet Union who arrived in Natzerat Illit as toddlers in the early 1970s. There were no Palestinian players on the team.

Having played for clubs in higher divisions of Israel's national league, I joined HNI soon after moving to the town. At thirty-four, I was past the zenith of whatever basketball career I may have had, and was looking mainly for exercise to stay in shape. Being more or less on a par with the team in terms of ability, my position as an active player on the squad was self-explanatory. Players as well as management were vaguely aware that I was engaged in a social study of the town as part of some university degree. Like myself, however, they saw no link initially between my presence on the team and my investigative persona. None, in fact, seemed particularly preoccupied with the details of my research. This was unlike my experience in other arenas in Natzerat Illit, where my identity as an investigator was always paramount. More on this shortly.

Much of the material presented in this work so far attempts to depart from the stereotypical view of Natzerat Illit as an island of bigotry and racism. My argument has been that Israelis in Natzerat Illit are, on the whole, as liberally minded as their compatriots elsewhere. Rather, it is their unique circumstances which expose the failure of liberal ideology to prescribe behaviour to match ideals and principles it ostensibly stands for.

The case of HNI players, most of whom displayed stark illiberal worldviews, presents a further twist. Whereas many Israelis in Natzerat Illit are critical and apprehensive about the specific case of Palestinian presence in their town, most HNI players were also loud and clear regarding 'Arabs' generally. One of the conscripts, a military policeman, was stationed as a warden at a nearby military prison, guarding Palestinian prisoners apprehended during riots in the *Intifada*. On one occasion, when the team was at a restaurant for lunch, he gave the rest of us a chilling and totally unreflexive account of a riot which had taken place in the prison a few days earlier and of the measures taken to suppress it. His gleeful, gruesomely detailed anecdote had clubs and hosepipes, black eyes and blue faces, streaks of blood, broken toes, twisted fingers and heavily breathing Palestinian prisoners. The undivided attention he was getting at the table may have pushed him to overplay the brutality of the affair. But even allowing for some exaggeration, his account was truly sickening.

Most of his audience was as sympathetic as he was proud. When one of the younger players queried whether 'you guys ever show mercy', the answer was a recitation in unison by two or three of the older players to the effect that 'these sons of bitches, who throw stones at our soldiers and hurl abuse at the state and the army – they deserve no mercy'. Towards the end of his account two players inquired eagerly whether they could possibly visit the prison with him. They said they wanted 'to take part in the action, you know. Have some fun, club some Arabs, do our bit.' Astonished, I heard the interlocutor promise to check the possibility with his CO.

Another player, a police sergeant, was occasionally summoned with his unit for tours of duty in Jerusalem, to police the Friday prayers at the *al-Aqsa* mosque on Temple Mount (*Ḥaram al-Sharif*). On one occasion he announced that he was going to miss an approaching training session. 'We are going to Jerusalem', he explained, 'to beat and blow those Arabs to bits. Show them the cost of messing with the police'.

One player complained on several occasions that his family's transport business was systematically ruined by unfair competition from local Palestinians. On one occasion he told me of his plan to move to adjacent Migdal Haemek[3] since, as he put it:

Natzerat Illit is gradually becoming an Arab town. They are allowed to come in here, rent, buy, take us over. In Migdal Haemek everybody knows: no one moves into the town without approval of the mayor. And he has said on various occasions that he is not allowing a single one of them to move in.

In December 1988 a Pan American airliner was blown up above west Scotland killing hundreds – an event known as the Lockerbie disaster. The event coincided with an initiative on the part of the United States for *rapprochment* with the PLO. A player on HNI, an avowed supporter of Meir Kahana's ultra-right *Kach* movement, had this to tell me about the affair shortly after it happened:

That's good. It will teach the Americans who Yassir Arafat really is, and that they should not deal with him. That is what the Arabs want to do to everyone. This is how they are, and this is why I don't want them here or anywhere else.[4]

These statements were admittedly made in public, in the context of a relatively young, all-male, exclusively Israeli sports team, where discursive survival hinged on lucidity. Debates, many of which took place in a minibus on the way to or from away games, tended to consist of short, bold statements, often breeding verbal extremism. In private conversations some players came across somewhat more restrained. The overall picture, however, was clear enough. HNI players, more than many others in Natzerat Illit, had definite ideas regarding Palestinians who, as far as they were concerned, were as dangerous to the state as they were detrimental to the town. At the end of the day they are out to get all Jews and Israelis, who must in turn get tough.

The Palestinian coach

As the 1988/9 season approached,[5] HNI management began looking for a new coach who would harness the talent and ambition they believed was present in the squad and help promote the team to the third division. Financial limitations and a shortage of qualified candidates in the region narrowed the choice considerably, until the team administrator, a devoted volunteer on behalf of the local workers' council, came up with a surprising choice. In August 1988, following extended negotiations, he hired Ra'id Riziq, a thirty year-old Palestinian from a veteran Christian family in Nazareth, as team coach. Riziq, who teaches physical education in a government school in Nazareth and who had been coaching basketball for nine years, came with an impressive record. Six previous seasons saw him coach three clubs, all of which were promoted under him by at least one division. One of the three, the YMCA club of Nazareth, was promoted from fifth to fourth to third division in two straight seasons, missing further promotion the following season by a whisker. This was corrected in 1987–1988, Riziq's fourth year as coach, when history was made: the club was promoted again, becoming the first ever Palestinian club to make Israel's National Basketball League Division Two – a fully professional, big league.

Typical of many peripheral clubs in Israel, once promoted to the senior division, the club chose to drop their local coach and hire a better known one – in this case a veteran Israeli coach from Haifa, experienced in the major leagues. Raʿid Riziq was thus fired after his most successful season. Frustrating as this may have been for him, it enabled him to respond positively to HNI's offer and to become the first Palestinian ever to coach an all-Israeli team in Israeli team sports.[6]

10 August 1988. 19:55, at the gym. HNI players are casually warming up for the first official practice of the new season.Club officials watch them intently from the sideline. Standing next to them in a fashionable track-suit is a well-built young man, with a whistle on a cord around his neck. The new coach, Raʿid Riziq, has come for his first practice session.

20:00: Riziq stands up and nods to the team manager, who calls the players to the bench. Basketballs stop bouncing instantly, their thuds replaced with squeaks of rubber soles on the wooden floor. Then an attentive silence settles in as the players seat themselves on the low bench along the wall.

The new coach walks slowly to face the row of players. Muscular, tall, his posture is impressive as he waits there motionless, hands behind his back. He glances at his watch, obviously ready to begin. The team administrator appeals for a few more moments while he goes out to look for one other official. The coach nods his consent. The administrator goes out shortly, then returns alone. Riziq does not wait for an introduction and begins:

First of all, if any of you consider being late even by one second for a practice, or for any drill I set, he'd better not come at all. Likewise, if anybody has a pain in his hand, in his leg, in his stomach or whatever, he'd better stay away. I don't like these stories. This must be understood now. My Hebrew is good enough. You will understand whatever I have to say.

You probably know me, or have heard of me. So far, every team I coached was promoted. And I intend to go on that way. You will all have to work hard. I may not be *here next year, but you will. You remain here. This is your team. I shall insist that you give everything (to the team), which you will.*

I did not come here to make new friends. I do not want you to be my friends, I don't need it. My wife back home, she loves me, and that is enough for me. We are here to work, and work hard. I shall not let you off or exempt you from anything. What I want is to practise as much as possible. We have a month and five days until the first match. I would like us to practise five or six times a week, including a concentrated day of training on Saturdays, from morning to evening, or at least from morning to noon. If anyone has a problem with this, let him speak out now.

The players are silent, somewhat overwhelmed. The tone and content of the speech already represents a quantum leap for this essentially amateur club. A brief but inconclusive discussion of dates and times for approaching sessions ensues, and the practice gets under way.

The team walks on court. The coach explains the first drill. It is a standard one: players running to the basket in file. A team-mate, waiting stationary at the corner, passes the ball to each running player, who takes it to the basket. A simple move, but Riziq introduces a snag. He insists that each running man should call out for the ball. This act, so natural in real game situations, looks contrived during a practice, when all moves are prescribed, repetitive.

Two minutes into the drill Riziq whistles and the action stops. He assembles the players in the circle at the centre of the court. 'I do not hear you calling', he says. 'All together now, call out. I want to hear you calling together as if you are asking for the ball.' His demand – half-way between an educational exercise for a particularly slow group and a punishment for unruly youngsters – verges on authoritarianism. After all, the players are adults. Incredibly, we all respond, shouting in somewhat embarrassed unison: **'op. op. op'**. The coach is still not satisfied, and wants it louder. The cries go stronger: **'op. op. op'**.

Practice commences again. Riziq proves concise and eloquent, meticulous in his demands and very tough. Players are penalized with extra runs for imperfect execution of exercises, including failure to complete drills within time budgets allocated. The practice is not only relentless, but also exceptionally long. The coach does not smile, makes no jokes, and reprimands players who attempt to exchange hushed words with one another. Two short intervals for drinking water is all we get in the way of repose. The intervals are timed – three minutes each. Players are not allowed to sit on the floor during these intervals or, for that matter at any other point.

22:00: Two strenuous hours after he began the session, Riziq finally blows the whistle to signify that it is over. He utters a rapid 'good night' and is out of the gym. Exhausted players, distorted with pain and effort, collapse on the *floor. One of them exclaims: 'This is not a training session. It is the Intifada.' Another adds that 'this guy has had specific orders from the PLO: he is here to kill us'. Nobody laughs, and there are no more remarks. People pensively collect their gear and leave.*

Riziq's opening speech, outlining a contract with the players which would determine the atmosphere for the weeks and months to come, shattered a number of implicit assumptions which Natzerat Illit Israelis, like Israelis generally, have regarding interpersonal relations with Palestinians. The very role of a Palestinian publicly addressing Israelis in public broke the mould of Palestinians as obedient, silent listeners. The speech, moreover, had a dominant, confident, often threatening Palestinian resolutely issuing commands to Israelis. This he did in immaculate, authoritative and confident Hebrew, including the prediction (or was it an order?) 'you will understand everything I have to say'.

The coach's disposition, more like an army officer talking to subordinates than like a Palestinian addressing Israelis,[7] portrayed Riziq as an ambitious, successful professional, by no means an underdog. His hidden message was that in the present company it is Israelis, not Palestinians, who are prone to under-achievement ('I may not be here next year. You stay here'). It had a proud Palestinian rejecting the potential closeness of his Israeli counterparts ('I do not need you as my friends'). The introduction of an invisible but loving woman, unattainable for Israelis by virtue of being both Palestinian and married ('my wife back home loves me. That is quite enough for me') further accentuated his autonomy.

I had known about Riziq before. Some Palestinian friends in Nazareth, aware of my interest in basketball and in the recently promoted all-Palestinian YMCA club, had told me of the club, its players and the unusually talented and tough coach. I even wrote a newspaper feature article about the club's promotion in mid-1988, although I did not speak to Riziq whilst preparing it.

When later that summer I heard that Riziq, a Palestinian, was about to become coach of the all-Israeli team I had just joined, I realized that this sporting aspect of my routine was about to take a surprising turn. The practice session and the speech preceding it convinced me that I faced a unique conjuncture, an opportunity which anthropologists seldom manage to create, but are sometimes fortunate enough to stumble on.

My original intentions notwithstanding, HNI gradually became a central arena for me as an ethnographer. I was immediately forced to make a number of decisions regarding my relationship with team-mates, the visibility of my investigative persona, and how to manage and present my own positionality. As often happens during ethnographic fieldwork, the need to differentiate between myself as anthropologist and me as person took me by surprise. Rightly or wrongly, I judged the situation in which I found myself in HNI – a legitimate participant and only marginally an observer – as beneficial.

Not wishing to compromise this unexpected vantage point, I decided to carry on just as I had done before the team became so promising a scene for my research: refrain from positive acts of inquiry and limit myself to silent observation. I hardly posed questions to those around me, and when I did it was in passing, mostly leading to one-off exchanges rather than fully developed discussions. I never had a notebook, writing utensil or a recorder with me in practices, matches or team meetings, and certainly did not conduct anything remotely like an interview with any of my team-mates. The only exception here was Riziq, with whom I became friendly in 1989, after the end of his period as HNI coach. I visited his home on many occasions, had him and his wife visit our home, and held prolonged discussions with him about basketball, his time as HNI coach, politics. I let him read a draft of a journal article (Rabinowitz 1992c) based on his story, where he appears under the disguised name Shafik Daher, before I had it published. In April 1995 I read him the final draft of this chapter, receiving his consent to use his real name.

Most of the material I present on HNI here, however, pertains to the time before Riziq and myself grew closer. While my special relationship with him may well have coloured my emphasis and interpretation, the ethnographic detail I present here is based exclusively on observations written at nights, immediately as I returned from practices, matches and meetings. Fortunately, the gym was only minutes away by car from home.

Boundary concealment: who are 'we' anyway?
Riziq's capacity to depart from stereotypical modes of behaviour which Israelis expect to find amongst Palestinians was demonstrated on various occasions. He was, for example, astutely inquisitive and matter of fact when conscripts and army reservists had their military service clashing with practices and matches.

22 August 1988. Following a practice session, a player approaches Riziq with a problem: he had been called up for a stint on active military duty

*which was planned to last fourteen days, beginning the following Sunday.
The stint coincides with the build-up for the season – the player is about to
miss a number of practices and pre-season matches. The following dialogue
ensues:*

Riziq: *Any chance of you getting a sick-note[8] and giving this call-up a miss? I once
knew a player who used to do this regularly and quite effectively.*
      Player: *Well, technically it is possible. But I would really feel uneasy about it. The
unit I am with is very easy-going, and people are really considerate. If you have a real
problem, others will help you out, including the CO and officers. There is trust. So if I
do this, not show up at all, I will really be letting them down.*
      Riziq *(nodding in understanding): I see. What about matches, though. Could you
have an evening or two off for matches?*
      Player: *Yes. That will definitely be all right.*

Riziq was quite prepared to draw his own discourse and metaphors
from the domains of military valour. *Esprit de corps*, fighting spirit in
battle, mutual dependence under fire and control of territory popped up
more than once.

*26 August 1988. Approaching the end of a practice session. Riziq requests
a particularly demanding drill. He is adamant on perfect performance, and
counts aloud the final seconds from twenty downwards. The players are
pushed to the limit, and as his count goes under ten, two or three cheat by
relaxing and letting the clock run out. One gives up altogether and stops
running five seconds before time. Riziq assembles everyone at the corner of
the gym, and turns to him:*

Riziq: *You stopped five seconds from time. Why?*
      (Tense silence).
      Riziq: *Don't you know it is the final seconds which are the most important in bas-
ketball? Why did you give up? Would you stop running in the last and crucial moment
in a battle too? Would you leave your mates without cover in war and just stop
running? Do you know how many bullets you will get? (points at his own belly repeatedly, as if being hit successively by bullets).*

This discourse deviates sharply from the image Israelis have of
Palestinians as people who shy away from anything remotely linked to military affairs. The place of values such as military valour, camaraderie and
soldier-like responsibility to the definitions of Israeliness in general and of
Israeli manhood in particular has been alluded to by several writers.[9]

Israelis find great difficulty in extending these values and applying them to non-Israelis, least of all to Palestinians – citizens of Israel no exception. Riziq's resilience and choice of metaphors thus effectively appropriated these values from their normal Israeli exclusivity.

Riziq often used the terms 'us' and 'our mentality' for the team, thus temporarily obliterating the all pervasive abyss between Palestinians and Israelis – two groups normally assumed to be as different as they are distinct. For example:

26 August 1988. At the end of practice, a birthday party. One of the players, twenty-six today, rushes to the changing room, returning shortly with a plastic bag. Out come a rich birthday cake, complete with cream and icing, disposable cups, bottles of soft drinks. Using a chair as a makeshift surface to work on, he hurriedly cuts the cake, pours the fizzy drinks, then dishes them out to the players, seated on a bench along the wall. He remains standing near his chair.

Riziq is on his feet as well, but slightly to the side. Someone makes an improvised speech. There is laughter. Then Riziq asks: 'What about songs? Don't you people sing on birthdays?' His suggestion and question are met with silence. First, birthday sing-along is somewhat out of place in the context of an Israeli men's basketball team. Secondly, his use of 'you people' is ambiguous. Does he mean 'you Israelis'? 'People in this town'? 'This particular basketball club'?

Someone cracks an unrelated joke. Grateful, we all return to nibble at the bits of cakes we hold in paper napkins.

Throughout his period as HNI coach Riziq strictly avoided direct reference to his national identity. He took great care, for example, not to use Arabic words in his speech.

28 August 1988. A practice session in the gym. Riziq explains a new drill, clear and concise as ever. On route, however, a mishap: he bridges two sentences with the Arabic word yaa'ni. *The term, whose meaning in this context is 'in other words' – makes perfect sense to the players:* yaa'ni *is one of an assortment of Arabic words fully incorporated into spoken Hebrew. This notwithstanding, Riziq is acutely embarrassed. He fumbles, as though he had just committed a terrible* faux pas, *then stops dead, shaking his head disapprovingly. Finally he takes a deep breath and starts the sentence all over again, replacing the unfortunate word with its proper Hebrew equivalent.*

14 August 1988. At the end of a practice session. Riziq announces that he and the team administrator are planning to attend a tournament elsewhere in Galilee, involving top professional clubs from Tel-Aviv. They think it would be nice if as many of us players came along. 'The tournament will take place in Ṣamaḥ', Riziq tells us, then quickly realizes this appellation is inappropriate. Ṣamaḥ is the Arabic name of an old Palestinian village which once stood at the southern tip of the Sea of Galilee (Kineret in Hebrew, Baḥrat Ṭabariya in Arabic), and was destroyed in 1948. The site, which Israelis have since named Tsemaḥ, now has local government buildings and other facilities, including a large conference and sports centre, the venue of the approaching tournament. Having realized he just used the Palestinian name of the place, Riziq quickly regains control and corrects himself: 'no, that is Arabic. I mean...Tsemaḥ'.

The few acknowledgements of his identity as Palestinian which Riziq did allow were of a folkloristic nature.

19 August 1988. At the end of a practice session, near the gym's door. Riziq turns to some of the players and says:

Amongst us (the Hebrew word he used was etslenu) there is a saying that if you eat Zaa'tar you become leaner, have much energy and speed and, most important of all, your head is 'opened', you think more clearly. So before you come to the next session make sure you have some.

Zaa'tar, the Arabic word for thyme, is also the name of a popular spice, made in many rural Palestinian households by grinding thyme with other herbs. In recent years, however, it has become immensely popular amongst Israelis, who can buy it in most supermarkets, ready-made and packaged. And while the name *Zaa'tar* has been incorporated into Hebrew with no alteration, every Israeli knows its Arabic origin. Its use by Riziq, including the sharing of popular Palestinian belief about its potency, all prefixed by '*etslenu*' was a clear and conscious reference to Riziq's own identity and culture.

14 August 1988. At the end of a practice session in the gym. The team attempts to fix an extra practice session for the following week. Players' schedules and priorities are not easy to coordinate, but Sunday emerges as a practicable time. It is almost agreed, when Riziq, who is normally the one pushing for extra practices and training sessions, in spite of his rather lax players, is forced to decline. He tells the team that:

This time it is I who cannot make it. My cousin got married this week, and having spent all evenings this week in practices,[10] I have not yet been able to visit and greet him. Sunday unfortunately remains my only available evening.

Riziq's explanation meets instant sympathy and understanding. The practice is rescheduled.

While extended formal wedding celebrations are known in some communities of Mizrahim in Israel, its practice amongst Palestinians is almost taken for granted by Israelis. Riziq's reference to a family wedding, or for that matter to the beliefs regarding the use of *Zaa'tar*, thus had clear signification of his cultural and national identity. These references, however, were essentially 'soft'. They coloured his Palestinism in folkloristic, depoliticized shades, while at the same time breaking the silence which shrouded his otherness. This enabled a relaxed treatment of a loaded issue. The alternative – an unbroken, ambiguous silence regarding his identity – might have been construed by players as more menacing.

Later I discovered that Riziq's political inclinations reflect the consensus amongst young Palestinians in Nazareth *vis-à-vis* the state, namely accepting it as a necessary evil. It is a stance which many Israelis in Natzerat Illit regard as tantamount to treason. A choice on his part to delve into issues of identity and politics would have strained his relationship with players and management to the limit.

Authority questioned

The weeks just prior to the formal season and immediately after its commencement exposed a growing rift between Riziq and his players. The players, most of whom had never played professionally, found it exceedingly difficult to adjust their demanding basketball schedule to their professional, familial and social commitments. The main problem was attendance at practices and matches. Many sessions took place with less than ten men – the all-important quorum needed for exercising game plans. Ra'id Riziq grew bitter and frustrated with these lapses in attitude and commitment, and made no secret of his misgivings.

19 September 1988. The team is about to leave Natzerat Illit on its way to a friendly match in adjacent Migdal Haemek. Some have already gone in one minibus. I find myself with Riziq on the pavement outside the gym, awaiting the other hired vehicle. Riziq laments the slack discipline of players as well as of the management. He is clearly preoccupied with the issues of order and authority. The conversation turns to earlier experiences in his career as coach, and he offers his interpretation of the events which led to his departure from Nazareth YMCA the previous year, following the most successful season he and the club have ever had:

I was becoming weaker, less authoritative, yielding. You have to understand, the way I was in YMCA throughout my time with them was not at all the way you see me here. There I had always been hard on the players and on the management. I was genuinely tough. I had my ideas and I pushed them and never gave way[11]. Then, last season, I softened. I started giving way. I was letting people off the hook, was not single-minded enough. This was the beginning of the end. One thing then led to another, and at the end of the season, with all this historic success, I was out.

Unfortunately, now as I am coaching here, I have had this mentality rubbed off on me still further. One guy is late. Another has a pain in his hand. A third, something is wrong with his sister, a fourth has troubles with his grandmother. And I... go along with these things. I tell you, I am becoming soft, like you Jews. It is really bad.

The first matches in September brought less than satisfactory results. Defeat in the first two matches made the season look unpromising. The players' attendance did not improve, and an early crisis was clearly in the making. We also learnt that Riziq had not been getting as much support as he expected from management, particularly from his official employers at the local workers' council. Most of them, I later discovered, had been uneasy all along about hiring a Palestinian as coach.

In mid-October, an emergency meeting was convened by one of the veteran players and the team manager. Attendance was for once complete: all players, the coach, the team manager. During the meeting another fact emerged: Riziq, who began coaching more than two months earlier, in August, was still awaiting his first salary. The meeting ended with pledges on the part of the players to attend all practices, coupled with promises by management to recruit more players to the squad and to facilitate the smooth running of the team for the rest of the season.

Earlier conversations between players reflected their preoccupation with Riziq's motivation to coach a fourth division club so soon after promoting his former club to the second. The new situation deepened people's bewilderment: why was he willing to go on for so long without pay? One day, when the team was in the minibus returning from an away game (Riziq was travelling in his private car), a highly regarded veteran player volunteered an explanation: Riziq, he said, elected to coach HNI simply to demonstrate that he can manage an all-Israeli team. 'He needs to prove it' said the player, 'it is the key to his future career as coach.' This interpretation, which was evidently plausible to most players, was adopted as the standard solution to the riddle, to be repeated by various other players on subsequent occasions.

In the aftermath of the mid-October meeting, however, Ra'id Riziq was convinced that the promises were futile, and that neither wages nor new blood were forthcoming. He decided to suspend himself for two weeks. His idea, he later told me, was to see if management was going to make drastic changes, and thus to decide whether there was any point in carrying on with HNI.

This move had considerable repercussions – though hardly in the direction Riziq anticipated. The team administrator, who had recruited him in the first place, and who remained the mediator between him and the local workers' council, immediately resigned. Three volunteers from outside the inner ring of Labour activists quickly stepped into the void, becoming the new management committee.[12]

The new committee embarked upon an energetic and successful fundraising effort. Unrestricted by any moral obligations to the self-suspended Riziq, they appointed a new provisional coach – a player whose long experience with HNI, considerable natural leadership and immediate availability made him the obvious choice. The new player-coach ended up coaching the team for the rest of the season, doing reasonably well.

By the time the team seemed to be functioning smoothly under the new management and coach in early November, the local workers' council had lost even the limited interest they may have had in Riziq as an employee before, effectively disowning him. His claims to be paid for the time he had worked were not met, the council claiming he had left the team unilaterally, thus breaching contract. His court claim against his ex-employers dragged on until late 1992, at which point he was granted compensation in court.

The players too were quick to lose sight of their former coach. Riziq's considerable professional impact on the team was soon eroded by the ideas and emphases of his successor. His name was hardly mentioned any more.

3 December 1988. During practice at the gym. The (new) coach explains a drill. One of the players finds it similar to a drill he already knows. He turns to his mate and says:

This is like the drill we used to have with...this guy...He used to do this with us, remember? What was his name?...the Arab.

Doctors and patients

Like most new towns in Israel, Natzerat Illit suffers from a chronic short-age of physicians. None of the doctors serving the community are long-term residents of the town. Many, particularly specialists, live elsewhere, attending local clinics once or twice a week. There is no hospital in Natzerat Illit. *Kupat Holim Klalit* (KHK) – Israel's largest health insur-ance scheme, run by the *Histadrut* trade union federation – operates two medium-sized clinics, but requires patients to travel to Afula or even Haifa for most non-routine checks and treatments. *Macabbi*, the second largest health insurance scheme, has one clinic in Natzerat Illit.

Neighbouring Nazareth, on the other hand, has a thriving medical com-munity. It has three hospitals (all run by Christian organizations), and a large number of resident specialists, all Palestinians who are either hospi-tal staff themselves or have ready access to hospital facilities. A decade-old crisis in public health in Israel, which has left KHK impoverished, dis-courages specialists in Nazareth from making themselves available to patients exclusively through KHK. One result is that private health care thrives, with most physicians operating private clinics.

Dr Nawaf Sa'adawi, a resident of Nazareth, is a paediatrician. Originally from a village in western Galilee, he is one of a handful of Palestinian citizens of Israel who graduated from the prestigious medical school at the Hebrew University in the 1960s. After his graduation he worked for KHK for a while, then moved to Nazareth, set up his own clinic and quickly gained a reputation which spread to neighbouring Natzerat Illit. Veteran Israeli residents often described Sa'adawi as 'the doctor who raised our children'. Upon arrival at Natzerat Illit to begin fieldwork, my spouse and I inquired about medical care for our baby daughter. An Israeli resident, herself a mother of four, said with deliberate exaggeration: 'there is only one paediatrician around here. His name is Doctor Sa'adawi.'

A keen, experienced diagnostician, Sa'adawi commanded an up-to-date knowledge of therapeutic methods and a close acquaintance with special-ists. Operating mainly from his private clinic in Nazareth, he was also available three afternoons a week in a Natzerat Illit clinic run by one of the large health insurance schemes.

It took a while to discover that many of the Israeli patients who testified to Sa'adawi's excellence came across on other occasions as strongly anti-Palestinian. One example is Brakha Benisho, an Israeli resident of Moroccan origin. Aged twenty-five at the time of fieldwork, she had just given birth to her second child. Returning from the maternity ward of the regional medical centre in Afula, she said of her experience:

It was OK generally. But the Arab women really brought me down. They really are like cattle, giving birth year in year out, no fail. They are so primitive – you should have heard them scream in the labour room. It made me so angry. And they take so much space. Imagine – Arab women all over the place, with millions of noisy relatives around them, all chattering in Arabic. It is disgraceful, the way the hospital authorities put them with us Jewish women. The least they could do, if they insist on helping the damned Arabs multiply, is put them separately.

On another occasion Brakha complained about KHK, of which she is a member. She talked of queues, of rude service, of incompetent doctors. Finally she related the following incident:

My older daughter was once ill with a rare infection which no one in KHK tracked down. It went on and on. The child was suffering. We had no sleep for weeks. Eventually it was too much to endure, and I went to Sa'adawi. Imagine – going to his clinic in the *shūk* [Hebrew for market] in downtown Nazareth. All those Arabs, and the dirt. So foul. But then, Sa'adawi, I swear, had one quick look at the poor child, and knew exactly what was wrong. He told me, then and there: it was an infection. A rare one. He wrote the prescription. I got the medicine. The child was well within a day. Not that it did not cost. It did, and how: those Arabs know too well how to take money. Especially from us.[13]

Dina Hirsh, an Israeli resident of European origin, aged twenty-seven at the time of fieldwork, was a mother of a one-year-old then. She was once present when a neighbour, who had recently given birth in the medical centre in Afula, told of a Palestinian woman who had given birth to a still-born baby. 'She was so stupid and primitive, that Arab woman', the raconteur said, 'that she completely lost control, and the baby ended up suffocating.' Dina's reaction was instant and spontaneous: 'Oh good. One less Arab.'

This notwithstanding, Sa'adawi was Dina's ultimate authority on child-care – from nutrition through hygiene to treatment of real and imagined illnesses. There were times when she attended his clinic three or four times a week. She refused to consult any other doctor, insisting that the efficacy of his treatment was unsurpassed.

Brakha Benisho and Dina Hirsh obviously hold extreme views regarding Palestinians and their relations with Israel and Israelis. For Benisho, everything about her experience with Sa'adawi which is objectively 'Arab' (the location of the clinic in Nazareth, the *sūk*, the people on the way) is negative and threatening. Conversely, all aspects of the experience which are objectively negative (the cost, the distance, the dirt in the *sūk* at the end of a business day) she subjectively links to 'Arabness'.

Hirsh, on the other hand, resolves the problem of Sa'adawi's identity by other means. Being a member of the health insurance scheme with which he is affiliated, she is not normally forced to attend his private clinic, and is thus spared the 'Nazareth experience' which Brakha Benisho so resented. In the context of the Natzerat Illit clinic where he sees Dina Hirsh and her infant, Sa'adawi's national identity is virtually forgotten. His (real) family name is not stereotypically Palestinian. His forename, a more typical name with obvious Muslim connotations, is omitted from spoken and written communication. His immaculate Hebrew, often sprinkled with English and Latin, radiates authority.

Brakha Benisho's single episode with Sa'adawi, while obviously trying, had one aspect which stood out for her in glorious isolation. She attributes her daughter's recovery to a magic moment in which health was restored through a succession of almost simultaneous acts: Sa'adawi observed, identified, pronounced a diagnosis and cured by prescription. That was the instance in which, for her, Sa'adawi ceased being an 'Arab'.

In the case of Dina Hirsh, who sees Sa'adawi much more frequently, the moment is extended to a routine, and is buttressed by her insistence that this particular doctor's efficacy is unrivalled. As far as she is concerned, it is a professional, trustworthy doctor who looks after her son, not an 'Arab'.

Trusting the untrustworthy

Dina Hirsh, Brakha Benisho and the basketball players of HNI, while subscribing to crude essentialist generalizations regarding 'Arabs', are nevertheless willing, in certain circumstances, to trust and even subordinate themselves to Palestinian individuals.

In *The Rebirth of Anthropological Theory* Stanley Barrett defines the notion of 'contradictions in personal attributes' (1984:150–8). People's stereotypes and preconceptions of personal attributes, he argues, tend to be arranged 'in binary opposition' which 'push toward polar extremes' (1984:157). Thus the 'dumb blonde' syndrome reflects an ostensible contradiction between being intelligent and being beautiful; Falstaff and Cassius reinforce the stereotypical opposition in Shakespeare's mind between being fat and being gloomy, and so on.

Barrett concentrates on the classic contradiction represented by the black professional in North America. White people, he asserts, have certain assumptions about blacks who are:

supposed to be poor; they are slaves, or field hands, or migrant labourers, or factory workers. When one comes across a black physician, which of his (or her) statuses dominates, race or profession? *(1984:157–8)*

The problem had been addressed by sociologists decades earlier. Hughes (1945:355) observed that non-white, female, non-Protestant physicians of 'lower social stock' are accepted by white Americans only in the most acute emergencies or as exotic healers for the desperate. This assertion, while probably more true of the United States in the 1940s than of the reality in certain states today,[14] is nevertheless relevant for this discussion. More recent research indicates that the chief negative characteristics which white Americans tend to attribute to blacks are lack of ambition, lack of competence and intelligence, underachievement, laziness and inconsistency (see for examples E.G. Cohen 1982, 1984). Schuman (1982:346–9) asserts that the psychogenetic beliefs regarding the sources of black underachievement held by American whites in the early twentieth century have been replaced in the second part of the century by a kind of environmental determinism. The key characteristics, however, seem to remain at the level of blacks' performance (see also Campbell and Schuman 1968).

When white Americans face black professionals their difficulty is in reconciling professional performance with the stereotype of blacks as poor achievers – an incoherence revolving around blacks' *capabilities* or, more precisely, the assumed absence thereof. The case of Israelis in Natzerat Illit is different. Exposed to a relatively affluent, urbane and educated Palestinian community, they have long internalized the notion that Palestinians sometimes have impressive careers. The contradiction in personal attributes triggered by a Palestinian professional or a Palestinian in a position of authority is thus considerably weaker.

The negative views of Palestinians held by Israelis have been monitored periodically by means of attitude and stereotype surveys.[15] One striking feature of most survey results is that the qualities which Israelis attribute to Palestinians, including citizens of Israel, are primarily related to intent. When asked to comment on 'the Arabs', Israelis tend to focus on ascribed intentions and conspiratorial designs. Peres, who asserts that 'Attitudes of Jews towards Arabs are obviously dominated by the struggle against the Arab world' (1971:1029), indicates that 76 per cent of Israelis of European origin and 83 per cent of those of oriental extraction believe that 'every Arab hates all Jews' (*ibid*). Peres and Levy (1969) likewise suggest that Israelis view Arabs as potentially violent.

In her much-quoted survey of 1980, Mina Zemach asked Israeli respondents to specify the first five words which spring to mind upon hearing the term 'Israeli Arab' or upon thinking of it. The words respondents came up with were arranged in fourteen sub-groups. The sub-group which had the highest frequency (35.2 per cent of the expressions used) was characterized by Zemach as 'reflecting (the attribution to Arabs of) negative emotions – hatred, fear, suspicion' (1980:82). An additional 13 per cent of labels cited were associated with the Israeli–Arab conflict ('PLO', 'terror', 'murder', 'hatred of Jews', 'the enemy') or with the Holocaust ('concentration camps', 'antisemitism', 'Germany'). This yields a total of 48.2 per cent first reactions directly linked to ill intentions which Palestinian citizens of Israel ostensibly have towards Israelis. Only 16.5 per cent of the expressions cited referred to perceived inherent qualities of Palestinians such as 'dirty', 'lazy', 'family oriented', 'savage', 'diligent', 'ignorant', 'poor', 'miserable'.

Trope indicates that Israelis' stereotypes of Arabs primarily reflect perceptions of Arabs' intentions (Trope 1989:135).[16] In his treatise on Israeli ethnocentricism, Sami Smooha attributes the way Israelis feel regarding Palestinians to the persistence of the Israeli–Arab conflict and to the dissent of Palestinians within Israel (1988, 1989a:150). The stereotypes of Palestinians which Israelis hold may thus be characterized as self-referential, indicating primarily what Israelis think Palestinians want to do to them. It could be further argued that such stereotypes entail the attribution of irrationality, with Palestinians essentially seen as hot-blooded murderers primarily motivated by hatred. Revengeful rather than self-seeking, they are perceived as potentially given to uncontrollable malice, often at the expense of careful choices and designs which could have better served their own best interests.

The notion that any Palestinian can turn his skin at any time, deny his own interests and allow his dark, demonic alternate self to possess him and his actions features regularly in the discourse of right-wing politicians in Israel. Often reflected in printed headlines describing Palestinians' assaults against Israelis,[17] it is present in a more sophisticated guise also in the less-likely quarters of Israeli liberalism. Amos Oz's description of the demonic Palestinian twins in *My Michael* (Oz 1984) is one example. Adir Cohen's study of the image of the Arab in Israeli literature (1987) cites an array of similar depictions.

The problem facing Natzerat Illit Israelis once confronted by a Palestinian citizen in a position of authority is not his faculty. In their view being Palestinian does not exclude excellence *a priori*. Their difficulty is in reconciling being Palestinian with the benevolent *intentions* required for responsible authority and proper professional performance. The issue of trust, not that of aptitude, is at the core here.

Professional trust

Trust has a special place in the relationship between professionals and clients. Willensky's discussion of the service ideal and of the place of trust therein argues that professionals as well as clients must believe that the client's interests are paramount – a belief which cements the client's trust in the professional. This trust in turn secures free flow of information without which the professional is unable to perform (1964).

Goode has argued that wider society grants guilds professional autonomy only when it is deemed essential for adequate performance of the service. In exchange the profession undertakes to exercise effective internal control over practitioners' ethics and performance. The more the clients are exposed to potential damage, the more important it becomes to exercise the checks and penalties that would protect them (1969:292–3). Goode goes on to identify the 'person professions' – those which deal with the individual's body, personality or reputation – as ones in which the public is particularly aware of the professional's capacity to harm the client, intentionally or otherwise. The public is aware, however, that person professionals such as physicians, psychiatrists or divorce attorneys are particularly restricted by codes of conduct, ethics and ideology (*ibid*). Paradoxically, it is in the person professions that clients often feel they are best protected from the potentially hazardous side-effects of being handled by professionals.[18]

Brakha Benisho and Dina Hirsh could thus be seen as taking a double risk with Doctor Sa'adawi. One is the conventional risk that the physician might harm their children or families by misuse of the powerful tools of his trade – his expertise, his prescriptive authority, and intimate details about the family which he may have become aware of. The other is the specific danger that being Palestinian he would attempt to cause indiscriminate damage to his Israeli patients. It is, after all, the same sort of damage which, according to their world view, every Palestinian always hopes to cause to every Israeli, and which they themselves sometimes openly wish for Palestinians, including children.

One conclusion then is that where personal wellbeing is at stake, distrust of Palestinians' intentions is subordinated to the basic faith in the professional integrity of physicians, whatever their national affiliation. Also, in the well-ordered context of their encounter with Sa'adawi, Brakha

Benisho and Dina Hirsh were clearly confident of their ability to distinguish good faith from malice – a certainty which underscores their willingness to trust the Palestinian doctor.

Coaching basketball, at least in Israel, does not constitute a profession in the normal sociological sense. For one thing, neither coaches nor clubs explicitly subscribe to the service ideal. The interaction between coach and players is better described as one where interests are fused – not as one in which the interests of players (or the club) override those of the coach.

Ra'id Riziq poses less of a potential threat to his players and to management than a physician would to patients. This is not to say, however, that danger is completely out. What if the coach discriminates against a particular player because of the player's political leanings? What if he is out to harm the club representing the Israeli town which so obtrusively asserts itself in the coach's Palestinian heartland? What if the coach sees his unusual position, in charge of young Israeli males, as an opportunity for sweet revenge for the humiliation and suffering inflicted by the Israelis on his people for decades? What if he does, after all, get his orders from the PLO, as the remark at the end of the first session jokingly suggested?

As it happened, HNI players ended up displaying a remarkable ability to disregard their attitudes *vis-à-vis* Palestinians and Arabs generally, to trust Riziq and to accept his authority. This is but one of many cases in which Israelis invest trust in Palestinians in a variety of non-professional contexts including commerce, industry and government (see Smooha 1992; Horowitz and Lissak 1990:78–9). This clearly calls for an alternative explanation that would apply beyond the specific realm of professional interaction.

Exorcising the fear of irrational malice

Trust features in sociological literature in two major perspectives (Zucker 1986). One, the origins of which are traced back to Parsons, 'asserts that trust resides in actors', and assumes that participants to an exchange will put self-interest aside in favour of 'other orientation' or 'collectivity-orientation' (*ibid*:57; after Parsons 1939, 1969). The other, which Zucker traces back to Garfinkel, 'rests on some degree of collective orientation at the beginning of interaction, but self-interest is often expected and legitimate at subsequent stages of the exchange' (Zucker 1986:57).

Most discourses of trust in sociology[19] highlight the function of trust as 'a deep assumption underwriting social order' (Lewis and Weigart 1985b:455). Likewise, studies of trust as a social reality (Lewis and

Wiegart 1985a), of trust as a commodity (Shapiro 1987) and of the concerted efforts aimed at creating trust (Zucker 1986; Roniger 1990) depict trust as a 'climate' regulated by society and for it. My perspective here departs from these attempts: it looks at trust primarily in interpersonal relations. More specifically it focuses on the relationship between danger, rationality, risk-taking and trust.

Trust occupies what Spencer-Brown (1971) calls the unmarked space between the familiar and the unfamiliar. Luhmann (1979, 1988) sees this space as the transition zone between cosmology, where the world is assigned with distinct, fixed dangers, and technology – where the sensation of precariousness gives way to a new belief in technical solutions. It is in this essentially modernist middle ground that we meet the rational construction of risk and trust – a complimentary opposition which has become a feature of virtually every venture and decision in modern life. Trust, where it exists, is a tentative bridge, consciously – and culturally – constructed between the impossible and the feasible. This approach informs, to an extent, Hart's depiction of the Frafras of Acra (1988), Gambetta's analysis of the nineteenth-century Mafioso in Southern Italy (1988) and Lorenz's treatment in the same volume of the relationships between industrialists and sub-contractors in France (1988).

For many Israelis, I likewise argue, trusting Palestinians hinges on departure from a state of primordial fears of Palestinians' bad intentions, to a realm in which Palestinians are seen as having rational interests like everybody else. Given the extent to which the orientalist perspective has penetrated Israeli life and consciousness, complete with emphasis on the ostensible irrationality of Arabs (above), this task is by no means trivial.

Raʿid Riziq displayed a persona with which HNI players were quite familiar – that of the determined and successful competitor. This sporting image was buttressed by his consistent avoidance of aspects of his personhood not directly linked to being an ambitious coach. He repudiated personal encounters to the extent of remaining unaware of his players' surnames, or, for that matter, of their ignorance regarding his.[20] A resident of al-Kūrūm since the early 1980s, he was oblivious to the fact that most players erroneously believed him to be a resident of Nazareth. Likewise, he carefully circumvented uncontrolled references to his national affiliation, making sure this emotive issue cropped up only in innocuously folkloristic and depoliticized contexts, wilfully reducing the range of attributes in terms of which the players could relate to him. This restriction was so effective that it arrested most players' personal loyalty towards him – a fact which became painfully evident in October 1988, when the coach found himself isolated from club management and felt compelled to quit.

In 1995, as I read this analysis to Riziq, he had this to say:

> I think you have a point here. In fact this is something which has perplexed me for a while now, as it came up in almost every place I coached. Take the YMCA for example. The squad of 1987–1988 had historic success under me, when we repeatedly broke all previous records of promotion and got as far up as Division Two. When we were finally promoted to Division Two, there was that terrible row with management and I was forced to leave. I sat at home and waited for the players to make a move on my behalf, to raise their voice, but nothing happened.
>
> Or take Shaf-'amr. When I took the team, we started the season with nine wins in a row, and looked pretty good for promotion. But my salary was not paid, and I quit. I thought the players might make a stand, say they do not want another coach, whatever. Nothing. Another coach was hired to replace me, the streak of victories was broken and they failed promotion.
>
> So obviously there is a valid point here, and it probably has to do with my way of dealing with my players, the discipline, the distance which I keep. But let me tell you this: I love the way I work, I think it is professional, and I have total faith in it. I will continue like this, although it is clear to me that there is and will always be a price to pay.

HNI players' preoccupation with the coach's intentions, followed by their conclusion that he saw his stint with HNI as an important stepping-stone, were in line with their interpretation that he was first and foremost after personal success. This discovery exempted them from the endemic search for cryptic explanations for his choice to work with Israelis. Their distrust of Palestinians' intentions, while not eradicated altogether, was easily suspended.

Both Riziq and Sa'adawi were identified by their Israeli counterparts as highly rational and calculating. This represented a significant departure from the stereotype of irrational malice so often attributed to Palestinians. The ambitious coach is interpreted as being there because he seeks a brilliant career. The doctor wants to remain a doctor, and – at least as far as Brakha Benisho is concerned – is out to get the client's money. Likewise, Palestinian keepers of shops in Nazareth, which Israelis regularly patronize, Nazareth garage owners and Palestinian parties to joint-ventures with Israelis have a long-term interest in cooperation which Israelis quickly discern and readily endorse. This gives the Palestinians a solid cover of predictability and hence trustworthiness. The omnipresent Israeli anxiety of Palestinian irrational malice is offered a sensible, context-related exit.

Self interest in the adversarial context

This discussion raises the problem of rational self interest and its place in the adversarial context. As indicated, once Israelis interpret Palestinians as acting out of rational self-interest, the old 'all Arabs hate us all and are out to get us' approach is eclipsed by the essentially pragmatic position that 'Arabs, like all other people, are out first and foremost to help themselves'. This in turn allows Israelis to develop *ad hoc* trust, or minimal trust – at least within specific limits such as commerce, industry or the person professions. Analytical attention thus shifts from the relatively well-documented rationality of actors who *invest* trust, to the less obvious notion of the rationality which actors *attribute* to others as a prerequisite to trusting them.

The fact that Israelis sometimes perceive an actor as rational and cooperative in spite of being Palestinian has a further implication. A Palestinian perceived by Israelis as someone who has somehow overcome his irrational destructive drives and is now willing to cooperate with Israelis so as to serve his own interests is inevitably accredited with a high degree of rationality and calculation. This in turn enables Israelis to invest more trust in him than they would have done in a potential Israeli partner, whose motives for cooperation might always be unclear. If rationality and predictability are indeed so highly valued in business and professional encounters, there follows the paradoxical, counter-intuitive notion that interpersonal trust can in fact be sometimes founded in the adversarial context.

An interesting problem is the extent to which actors tend to generalize from specific interactions involving *ad hoc* trust to wider and more clearly politicized arenas – in this case from the positive experience with a doctor or a coach to Israeli–Palestinian relations generally. My observations from Natzerat Illit indicate no such transference. Neither HNI players nor Sa'adawi's patients allowed their extended encounters with the two impressive men to modify their attitudes regarding Palestinians or Arabs generally. This seems consistent with my impressions of economic cooperation. Israeli partners, customers, employers and employees tend to associate their Palestinian counterparts primarily with the perfectly legitimate *homo economicus*. The initial tendency to see all Palestinians as irrational bloodthirsty creatures may be mitigated by the discovery of familiar calculations. But however effective within specific, recognized contexts, these realizations do not appear to spill over to other spheres.

Israeli attitudes towards the involvement of Palestinians in Natzerat

Illit's real-estate market provide another vivid illustration. Negotiating real-estate deals with prospective Palestinian buyers, many Israelis become aware of the sensible self-seeking aspect of individual Palestinians and their conduct. As mediation unfolds Israeli sellers often learn about specific circumstances and considerations surrounding Palestinians' wish to move to Natzerat Illit. Most negotiations proceed and are concluded in good faith, with both sides treating circumstances and self interest as not only legitimate, but self explanatory and hence acceptable.

Things are not as placid however when Israeli residents, including ones who have successfully completed sales to Palestinians, think of real estate in terms of the more general panorama of 'Palestinians moving into Natzerat Illit'. The same Palestinian who was depicted earlier as party to a rational and mutually rewarding deal, is now construed as part of a sinister and threatening Palestinian conspiracy to take over the town, outnumber its Israeli residents and dominate them (see chapter 3).

The lack of transference demonstrated here suggests that positive interaction between individuals, even where it happens over extended periods and with numerous participants, is not a guarantee for heightened belief in equal co-existence between groups. Only a conviction that the other side *as a collective* guides itself rationally, predictably and in accordance with mutually acceptable rules of play, can facilitate a sweeping shift of attitude. This, I argue, is what happened in the summer and autumn of 1993, when Yasser Arafat's personal predicament, the institutional and economic crisis of the PLO and the political decisions taken by the Palestinian leadership convinced most Israelis that the Palestinians were driven by rational calculations which pushed them towards an accord with Israel. The rationality now attributed to the Palestinians created a swing in the views of many Israelis regarding negotiation with the PLO and the eventual relinquishing of territories occupied in 1967 – two issues which had been taboo in mainstream Israel for decades.

The tension between treatment of individuals and a generalized attitude towards an outgroup is not unique to Israeli–Palestinian relations. A Christian Palestinian with whom I shared some of the notions presented here, had this to say about his strained relationship with Muslim Palestinians and Islam:

Although I lived most of my life with Muslims here in Nazareth, I still find myself referring to them as something different and inferior. I sometimes think of them as *Znūj* (Black Africans) or *Hnūd* (Indians). With time we Christians were educated to believe that we are one step above them. Perhaps by seeing them like this we try to put ourselves in the position of the Jewish guy who looks at us from above.

When I meet a Muslim professor, will he change my view of Muslims? I think not. Meeting someone who is extremely educated will not change my attitude to Muslims as a whole.

And, I know I do not have any faith in their intentions. Perhaps it all goes back to childhood memories. When I was little, we had a Muslim family as neighbours. And when my mother would throw away the washing water through the window, the Muslim woman living underneath would shout: 'first we'll finish off the Jews, then it will be you lot'. This is one reason why although I want a Palestinian state, I am not at all sure I could ever live in it.

Do Palestinian citizens of Israel attribute rationality to their Israeli partners? Arguably they do. True, the relentless preoccupation of Israelis with the formidable problems associated with infrastructure and economic development, housing, agriculture, industry and more has all too often been directly at the expense of Palestinians. It involved seizure and expropriation of Palestinian land and is continuing to fuel discrimination in budget allocation, inequality of opportunities for Palestinian individuals, limited access to resources and more. No one is more aware of the ubiquity and gravity of these inequalities than the Palestinian citizens of Israel themselves. And yet, I argue, most Palestinians in Israel do not attribute to Israelis an irrational obsession to cause them harm at all costs. This is reflected, amongst other things, in the pattern of mobilization adopted by the Palestinians within Israel. As chapter 9 suggests, the level and intensity of involvement on the part of Palestinians in parliamentary and local-level politics as a medium for public action implies a certain faith in a negotiated improvement. This sentiment could hardly be sustained if Palestinians assigned Israelis with irrational malice against all Palestinians always.

A major distinction thus emerges between the Palestinian citizens of Israel and Palestinians and Arabs elsewhere – including those in the territories occupied by Israel in 1967. The overriding interpretation of Israel in the Arab world remains an essentialist, and self-referential one, portraying Israel as an evil entity, irrationally and inexplicably obsessed with dominating Arabs and harming them. The rhetoric of war and politics across the Arab world is rife with references to Israel as driven by satanic forces rather than by reasonable pursuits of realistic goals and interests. Not so amongst most Palestinian citizens of Israel.

Finally, HNI players by no means represent your average liberal-minded

Israeli. And yet, their bigoted, unshakeable dispositions *vis-à-vis* the Palestinians did not stop them from displaying a remarkable level of trust of, cooperation with and even subordination to Ra'id Riziq. Significantly, this took place with no signs whatsoever of what one might be tempted to call consciousness raising. The assumption, grounded in the liberal emphasis on enlightenment, roughly that progress comes with movement from theory to knowledge to ideology to norms to attitude and finally to action, emerges as highly problematic. Likewise the continuum, implicitly assumed in liberal thought, from racist to indifferent to liberal to trusting and cooperating, is constructively ruptured. Paradoxically, not only does this rupture fail to arrest desired progress towards cooperation, in certain contexts it could even enhance it.

Epilogue

April 1995, in Ra'id Riziq's living room. Having just completed reading the final version of this chapter to Ra'id – my free translation of the English text into Hebrew mixed with Arabic – I sit and wait for his response. He is pensive, intent, as if weighing his options. Finally he turns to me and says:

You know, I coached a Jewish squad again not long ago. The youth team of Kibbutz Gevat. It went quite well. We finished second in their division, and they wanted me to continue. I was considering their offer, and suddenly understood this weak point I have. When I work with Arabs, I am as strong as god, and I succeed. I put everybody, even rebels, back in line. No one gets smart with me, not even management.

When I work with Israelis, I go back to that wretched point where it is not only they who look down at me, but I as well. This sort of attitude enters into me as well. Perhaps it is because you see for yourself and you realize that everything on the Jewish side is better. The roads, education, culture, the way people are treated, life in general. The Jewish child gets more social security, better conditions, better support.

I know that I can be as good as any of them, but I also see that they have better lives. Like when I was at the physical education academy at the time. I knew how well I competed with all my Jewish class mates – in physics, chemistry, gymnastics, basketball, volleyball, swimming, English. There were so many fields in which I knew I was better. And yet I felt inferior. And they all made sure I felt that. Not my mates. The system. It works that way.

No matter how much you develop and progress, you still know that you have the lower hand. I feel I am near, but then a silly thing like the way a stupid secretary treats you puts you back in that inferior place.

This is the feeling that takes over when you come to coach a Jewish squad. It is even there when you coach an Arab side with a Jewish star: not only a Jewish guy, but also the star of the club. So you think to yourself: I'll be soft on this guy, considerate, democratic, gain his trust and eventually get confirmation that I am all right. This is the way I felt with many Jewish guys I coached. And I know it is all wrong. It is only *recently, with a Jewish guy I had in the last club I coached, that I started to feel that I have the hang of it. Actually I am waiting now for the next Jewish guy whom I will coach. I tell you, he is not going to have an easy time. I have had enough. And I also think I am more ready than ever to coach a Jewish team again. I just heard from* Hapoel Natzerat Illit *again. They say they want to talk to me about next season.*

9

In search of genuine representation: the independent list

Wrong host, uninvited guest

In October 1988, at the height of the general election campaign for the Knesset, the leaders of Natzerat Illit Labour branch were landed with an awkward mission. Yitzhak Navon, a veteran Labour politician who had served as Israel's fifth president, a fluent speaker in Arabic, was coming for a day trip to the Nazareth area to campaign on behalf of the party. Palestinian Labour activists in Nazareth were putting together a schedule for his visit, including meetings with outstanding Palestinians and a public rally. The Labour branch of Natzerat Illit was to organize a separate programme for Navon in the Israeli town. The Labour party has always enjoyed impressive electoral returns amongst Israeli as well as Palestinian voters in Natzerat Illit, and the local organizers were determined to stage at least one event in which the ex-president would address Palestinians in Natzerat Illit, in which he would use Arabic as his medium.

The obvious choice was to set up a *ḥūg bayit*. Literally meaning 'home circle', *ḥūg bayit* is an election rally organized by a party in a private home, in which national figures rally in front of a hand-picked audience. The relatively small congregation and the homely atmosphere often breed an intimacy which people can hardly hope for on other, more formal public occasions. Principal decisions as to which towns or regions have enough potential voters to justify the effort associated with setting up a *ḥūg bayit* are normally taken at the respective party headquarters in Tel-Aviv.

For local party organizers a *ḥūg bayit* is a two-way showcase. First, it is their opportunity to display prestigious figures to the local public, thus reaffirming their own connections and familiarity with higher office. Second, it is a chance to impress the visiting dignitary with the kind of hospitality, affluence, and loyalty which they as local activists can master.

Having determined to have Navon speak to Palestinians in Natzerat Illit, the local Labour leaders now had to find a venue. It had to be a sumptuous home, large enough to entertain an audience a few score strong with dignity and comfort. Naturally it had to belong to a Palestinian who would be willing to publicly associate himself with the Labour party.

This combination proved difficult to find. A year into the *Intifada*, with Labour's Yitzhak Rabin – then minister of defence in Yitzhak Shamir's government – busy crushing the uprising in the territories, popular support for Labour amongst the Palestinian citizens of Israel was at its lowest ever. It soon became obvious that the handful of Palestinian residents of Natzerat Illit who were known publicly to be supporters of the Labour party and the numerous Palestinians who owned large private homes in the town did not coincide. Since a less than adequate venue could turn prestige into humiliation, the approaching event was a double-edged sword.

Three weeks before the scheduled day, Natzerat Illit's deputy mayor stepped in, taking upon himself to sort out a venue. His first move was to delegate the task to a Palestinian family with whom he had a long-standing relationship, and whom I knew and saw occasionally. His repeated visits and telephone calls brought home the urgency of the situation, indicating that having exhausted his own contacts amongst Palestinian Labour supporters, he was now looking for potential candidates further afield. His client family was expected to help out, which it did. The event was finally staged at the house of a wealthy Palestinian industrialist.

A Palestinian friend, not a Labour sympathizer himself, told me amusedly of the final choice of venue. 'They had Navon come to Rafiq's home', he laughed. 'Everybody in Galilee knows that Rafiq is not only a rich man, but also one of the most active supporters of the communist party.'

The irony is clear. Forty years after the establishment of Israel, a former president of the state and a leading member of the powerful Labour party surreptitiously invites himself as guest of honour to the house of one Rafiq, a pillar of the local communist establishment – a movement mainstream Israel still sees as an abhorrent sign of treason and conspiracy. The little episode offers another angle on hospitality or, more precisely, on awkward uninvited guests who end up paying tribute to the wrong person. It is about sincerity and falsehood, patronage and dependence, presentation of self and honour. It also reflects the troubled role of Palestinians in party politics in Israel.

My analytic focus in this chapter is two-pronged. First, the problematic nature of the claims of Israel – and liberal democracies in general – that the one person one vote maxim offers minorities an equal opportunity in politics. Second, another look at resistance.

Political doing and political being

The ideal democratic system has voters who identify with the system, its norms and institutions, electing representatives. These, in turn, are expected to enhance the electorate's interests and represent their values and identity. The Palestinian citizens of Israel, however, do not operate in an ideal democracy. Their sense of alienation from the state, which sees itself as 'Jewish', makes their political participation complex and trouble-some. Many Palestinians are ambivalent about their very choice to vote, and equivocal even towards those individuals they end up voting for. They are acutely aware of the paradox in which they operate, namely that their involvement in Israeli public life and party politics lends *de facto* legitimacy to a political entity whose very essence obliterates their chance of national assertiveness, and whose persistence marginalizes and racializes them.

One aspect of the paradox particularly relevant here is that throughout the twentieth century those political strategies which helped Palestinians gain better access to state-allocated resources were the most damaging to their perceptions of collective pride and identity. Thus the *mūkhtars* (village elders), coopted and appointed by the Ottoman and British rulers,[1] and later by the state of Israel,[2] were often able to secure minimal levels of state resources for those loyal to them. They are, however, strongly associated in the minds of Palestinians with the untoward patronage by foreigners. Their role is colloquially referred to through the derogatory idiom *bi'a*. Literally meaning 'sale', the term denotes the dishonourable exchange of loyalty and autonomy for dubious favours from unauthentic, morally inferior rulers.

Edward Said (1978) has demonstrated how some analyses of Middle Eastern societies and history unfavourably accentuate the primitive, despotic, nepotistic and unsophisticated nature of the Arabs – a trend not unknown from the literature on the Palestinian citizens of Israel. The orientalist approach attempts to analyze the role of the *mūkhtars* and their relationship with government in terms of 'Arab culture' and 'traditionalism'. Such politically motivated attributions of 'cultural traits' and, even more crudely, of 'mentality', become forceful instruments in the imperial struggle for domination. This attitude, complete with its ostensibly rational grounding, has been taken over by the self-appointed and self-conscious 'European', 'liberal', 'modernizing' discourse so readily adopted by the majority in Israel, to serve as backbone for an emerging eurocentric Israeli identity. It is this view which tends to attribute the performance of Palestinians in modernizing Israeli politics – including their yielding to the *mūkhtar* system in the past – to their 'culture' and 'mentality'.

There is very little about the phenomenon which can be plausibly attributed to 'culture'. If anything, it is the vicissitudes of the political subjugation of the Palestinians which bred this type of dependence. To gain tangible personal and communal achievements, Palestinian citizens of Israel have so far had to resort to clienthood with Israeli political figures and institutions. They have had, as it were, 'to sell'.

The main political alternative to 'selling' in Israeli party politics has been the communist party – its latest parliamentary guise being the Democratic Front for Peace and Equality (DFP, colloquially known as *al-Jabha* – the front). The DFP's attraction for the Palestinian citizens of Israel was and still is its offer of an honourable option: electing non-coopted, anti-establishment Palestinian representatives to parliamentary and municipal posts (See Beinin 1990; Rekhes 1986). This trend has been emulated since the 1970s by other political parties that base themselves on Palestinian votes, including the Progressive List for Peace (PLP, known as *al-Tūqadamiya*) and the Democratic Arab Party (DAP – *al-Ḥizb al-Dimūkrati al-ʾAraby,* led by ʾAbd al-Wahab Darawsha).

The electoral success of these three parties in parliamentary elections in the 1980s and the early 1990s was not mitigated by the fact that none of them effected meaningful long-term improvements in the circumstances and life chances of their constituencies. Palestinian voters in Israel obviously regard the mere presence in parliament of authentic, independent representatives as importantly as they do tangible achievements such as better distribution of resources and access to influence.

Barred from power-sharing by every Zionist party, independent Palestinian members of Knesset consciously limit themselves to declarative statements and assertions. Their electorate too expects them to simply stand up to the Knesset and 'say the truth to Israelis', as one Palestinian once put it to me.

A distinction I shall use here is that between political participation aimed at achieving tangible political goods (e.g. resources, jobs, preferential treatment by the bureaucracy etc.) – a practice which I label political 'doing'; and political involvement aimed primarily to represent – make present – one's voters in the corridors of power, a practice which I term political 'being'. The Palestinian citizens of Israel, I argue, clearly go for 'being', at least throughout the 1970s and 1980s.[3] If nothing else, this dichotomy should productively eclipse the outdated differentiation in the writing of some researchers between 'moderate' Palestinians (those coopted by the Zionist parties, e.g. mukhtars) and 'extremists' (those who refuse to play the game and assert an independent view, i.e DFP and PLP). Representative examples of this perspective are Landau (1969) and Rekhes (1976 and 1979).[4] It also avoids the traditional distinction so well known in the social sciences between 'symbolic' and 'instrumental' behaviour.[5]

While not a solution to the deeper paradox of Palestinian participation in Israeli party politics, political 'being' creates a parallel and slightly more acceptable path for such involvement. This is one reading of Smooha's thesis regarding the politicization of the Palestinian citizens of Israel (1989b), a thesis which has substantial support from other studies. This politicization, refined here to political 'being', while committed to a more vociferous presence, has limited scope for redressing the inherent imbalance of political power in the land.

The place of Palestinians in local level politics in Natzerat Illit: a short history

The 1970s and early 1980s saw limited involvement on the part of Palestinian residents of Natzerat Illit in local party politics. The most significant attempt to harness their support came from the local branch of the Labour party, which has controlled the municipal council ever since the town was established. As in other Palestinian communities in Israel, the party's vote-recruiting strategy hinged on local brokers. Able to promise improvements in environmental care and better municipal services to the Palestinians concentrated in the north west of the town (particularly al-Kūrūm) in return for votes, Labour managed to secure the Palestinian vote throughout the 1970s and well into the 1980s. This exchange was durable not least since the Palestinian community in al-Kūrūm consistently got less than its fair share of municipal resources. This ensured that the residents had a continuous stake in keeping good relations with Labour and the municipal council (Rabinowitz 1990, 1992a). Brokerage and mediation on behalf of Labour was undertaken primarily by two Palestinian men residing in the north-western section of the town, whose pattern of operation resembles the cooptation through patronage of Palestinians into Israeli politics at large. Both brokers were associated with Israeli patrons, notably the deputy mayor. The dyadic relationships he cultivated with them were characterized by durability, an in-built imbalance of power, limited choice on both sides regarding their respective roles and a continuous exchange of discernable 'goods' – indeed most of the features characteristic of patronage in other contexts.[6]

The 1980s saw a gradual and steady increase in the significance of the Palestinian electorate in Natzerat Illit – a trend which coincided with the narrowing of Labour's electoral lead over right-wing Likud in the town (see table 10). While the two trends were hardly related, the electoral success and political survival of Natzerat Illit's Labour candidates – all of them Israeli – grew increasingly dependent on the support of Palestinians.

Polling in Israel is based on residence. Individuals are assigned to vote in polling booths near their domiciles, where their names appear on detailed voters' rolls. Booth number 1, located in north-west Natzerat Illit, stands out amongst the town's twenty-five booths: it is the only one where Palestinian voters have an overwhelming majority. In 1988 476 out of a total of 706 voters registered in polling booth 1 were Palestinians. On some polling events Palestinians represented up to three-quarters of the qualified vote. This enables a fairly accurate extrapolation of their voting pattern over time.[7]

Table 11 and table 12 present the fluctuations in the Palestinian vote in polling booth number 1 between 1977 and 1989.

The five columns furthest to the right in table 11 and table 12 are particularly relevant, as they compare the Palestinian vote recorded in booth 1 with voting patterns in adjacent Nazareth and in Palestinian communities in Israel at large. Generally speaking, the voting pattern of Palestinian residents in booth 1 resembles trends typifying Palestinian voters countrywide. In broad strokes, a gradual shift can be discerned in the 1970s from support of Zionist parties – particularly Labour – to backing mainly the communist-led DFP, and later also PLP and DAP.

Three trends are nevertheless worth noting which are peculiar to booth 1. First – the level of support for Labour has always tended to be somewhat higher here than it was in Palestinian communities countrywide. This can be explained by the presence on the roll of Palestinian residents of Shikūn al-Akhdar – the housing estate established in the 1970s for Palestinian Labour activists, mostly from Nazareth. Some residents of this estate still harbour genuine gratitude and loyalty to Labour for their apartments. More importantly, the residents are anxious to receive long-awaited planning permission which would enable them to substantially enlarge their flats and thus improve their quality of life and increase the value of their properties. This, they feel, would not be granted by the council were they to withhold electoral support from Labour. Also, as residents of a clear and visible Palestinian core in a predominantly Israeli town, many

Table 10. *Labour's edge over Likud and the proportional weight of the eligible Palestinian vote, Natzerat Illit 1973–1989*

Campaign	Percentage voted Labour	Percentage voted Likud	Margin	Palestinian voters (eligible)	Palestinian voters as percentage of the total no. of voters
1973 K	59.6	24.5	35.1	50	0.4
1977 K	39.5	37.0	2.5	450	3.3
1981 K	46.8	39.1	7.7	800	4.9
1983 C	53.6	38.6	15.0	1100	6.4
1983 MA	56.2	43.8+	12.4	1100	6.4
1984 K	43.7	35.8	7.9	1150	6.7
1988 K	39.8	31.9	7.9	1261	7.0
1989 C	45.0	40.1*	4.9	1350	9.5**
1989 MA	53.5	46.0*	7.5	1350	9.7**

Legend: K = Knesset (parliamentary) elections
C = Local Council elections
MA = Separate mayorship ballot
+ = including independent right wing candidate (Cohen)
* = in 1989 Likud presented two separate lists of candidates. The figure represents the total for the two combined.
** = of qualified votes
Note: Pre-1988 figures for Arab voters are extrapolated from official figures for 'non-Jews'
Sources: State of Israel 1974; 1978; 1982; 1985
Natzerat Illit local elections committee 1983; 1989
DFP Natzerat Illit 1989
Bar-Gal 1986:53–4 (modified)

Procedure for the extrapolation of data presented in Tables 11 and 12.
Official publications of election results since 1981 offer no distinction between Israelis and Palestinian citizens of Israel. Prior to 1981 official publications indicated, for settlements larger than 2,000 inhabitants, the total number of voters, and the number of Israeli ('Jewish') voters. A simple subtraction thus yields the number of 'non-Jewish' voters. However in many cases this does not give an accurate figure for Palestinian voters. In Natzerat Illit, for example, the figure includes non-Jews who are not Palestinians (e.g. spouses of new immigrants, particularly from East Europe, who never completed the formalities of conversion into Judaism).

The other problem with this figure is that it pertains to Natzerat Illit as a whole, while the discussion in chapter 9 is interested mainly in polling booth number 1 and its representation of the north western part of town.

The only accurate figure regarding the respective numbers of actual votes by Israelis and by Palestinians in polling booth 1 (and, for that matter, in the rest of Natzerat Illit), are those recorded by the activists of the independent list in the 1989 local elections. Having studied the electoral roll before the election, and the sheet which carries the signatures of all actual voters at the end of polling day, the activists added up all the signatures of Palestinians (whose names generally stand out quite clearly from those of Israelis). This gave them an accurate figure of how many Palestinians actually came out to vote.

Earlier election campaigns, however, had no one doing this, so extrapolation is based on incomplete data. Let me demonstrate my extrapolation procedure by giving, as an example, my calculations with the actual figures for 1977.

The first step is to determine the number of Israelis and Palestinians entitled to vote in polling booth 1. In 1977 (ninth Knesset) there were 522 'non-Jewish' voters in Natzerat Illit (State of Israel 1978:20). This implies approximately 450 Palestinians. To determine how many of those lived (and voted) in the north-west, I took Bar-Gal (1986:53–54) as a guideline. He indicates that in 1979 58.3 per cent of the Palestinian residents of Natzerat Illit were living in north-west, and that this proportion steadily declines as more Palestinians moved to the town in subsequent years. In 1984, according to Bar-Gal, the proportion of Palestinians living in the North West declined to 28.6 per cent. Assuming the decline took place at a similar rate prior to 1979, we get for 1977 a figure of 75 per cent of the Palestinians of Natzerat Illit as residents of the north-west. This implies 337 Palestinian voters registered in polling booth 1.

With no official indication of the total number of voters per polling booth in 1977, I shall assume that the 13,371 voters registered in Natzerat Illit (State of Israel 1978:20) were evenly distributed between the twenty-two polling booths which operated that year (*ibid*:194). This yields an extrapolated figure of 607 eligible voters per polling booth. Take away 337 (eligible Palestinian voters), and we are left with 270 eligible Israeli voters.

With a turn out in Natzerat Illit of 81 per cent for the parliamentary elections (State of Israel 1978:194) – a figure I am assuming to have been the same for Palestinians and for Israelis, the total of votes actually cast in polling booth 1 would have been 492 votes – 273 Palestinians, 219 Israelis.

Labour had 34 per cent of the votes in polling booth 1 (State of Israel 1978:194), equivalent to 167 votes. I am assuming that Palestinians did not vote for right-wing and religious Jewish parties, and that Israelis did not vote for the DFP (nor for PLP and DAP when they appeared in 1984 and 1988 respectively). The total number of votes in 1977 for the right wing and religious parties, which was 191 (*ibid*:194), is thus taken away from the total Israeli vote (219), leaving 28 Israeli votes available for Labour. The balance of Labour votes (157) came from Palestinians.

For DFP (and later for PLP and DAP) rate of support amongst Palestinians, all we need is the number of votes these parties had in polling booth 1. We know these ballot papers all came from Palestinians, and all we need to do is to divide it by the number of actual Palestinian voters.

The same procedure applies for all other election campaigns represented in tables 11 and 12, with one qualification. The accurate figures produced by the independent list for 1989 indicate a significant trend: the Israeli residents of the north-west, who tend to be veterans of the town, of European origin, and fairly well to do (mostly living in private homes), had a particularly low turn-out (36.6 per cent) that year. This is not particularly surprising. Many residents were evidently tired of Labour's extended control of the local council, but nevertheless were loath to vote Likud. These being the only two alternatives, many chose to abstain. The same trend is assumed in 1984. Hence the low figures for actual Israeli voters in polling booth 1 in 1983 too.

Table 11. *Voting patterns of Palestinians in polling booth 1 – Natzerat Illit 1977–1988 (Knesset)*

| Campaign | Qualified votes for Labour | | Votes for Labour | Israeli votes for right wing and religious | Votes for Labour | | Palestinian votes for Labour (Percentage) | | Palestinian votes for DFP (percentage) | | |
	Palestinians	Israelis			Israelis	Palestinians	Booth 1 (##)	Nazareth	Booth 1	Rest of N.I	Nazareth
1977	273*	219*	183#(34%)	191(S1)	28*	157#	57.5#	20.9	34.4	60.8	69.6(S1)
1981	289*	196*	281#(58%)	107(S2)	89*	192#	66.4#	38.4#	30.2	38.3	53.2(S2)
1984	262*	246*	198 (39%)	85(S3)	161*	37*	14.1*	18.4(S3)	52.2**	43.5**	56.0(S3)**
1988	397(S6)	195	197 (33%)	104(S4)	91*	106*	26.7	11.1(S5)	48.5*#	52.5*#	54.6(S5)

Notes: * Extrapolated from official sources (see sources below) using the procedure for the extrapolation of data specified on pp. 152–3
  # Including a Palestinian list affiliated with Labour
  ** Additional Palestinian votes went to PLP: ca. 22% in booth 1; 11.2% elsewhere in Natzerat Illit; 14% in Nazareth
  ## Calculations of voting patterns amongst Palestinians in Natzerat Illit outside booth 1 in 1981 and 1984 were affected by a disproportionately low rate of participation on the part of Palestinians. My calculations for the 1981 and 1984 figures in this column thus assume a mere 50% turn-out. The situation changed in 1988, when the DFP embarked on a determined and effective door to door campaign to persuade Palestinians living in Natzerat Illit to vote
  *# Significantly, Palestinians also voted for PLP and DAP: 17.5% in booth 1; 17.4% in the rest of Natzerat Illit; 23.2% in Nazareth (S5)

Sources: S1: State of Israel 1977/78:20; :193–4
  S2: State of Israel 1981/82:19; :194–5
  S3: State of Israel 1984/85:260–1
  S4: Labour branch Natzerat Illit, mimeographed results sheet
  S5: DFP Nazareth branch, mimeographed result sheet
  S6: DFP Natzerat Illit figures

Table 12. *Voting patterns of Palestinians in polling booth 1 – Natzerat Illit 1983–1989 (municipal elections)*

	Qualified votes		Votes for Labour	Israeli votes right wing + and religious	Votes for Labour(qualified)		Percentage Palestinian votes for Labour	Palestinian voting ratio**#	Percentage votes for the independent list	
	Palestinians	Israelis			Israelis	Palestinians			Booth 1	Natzerat Illit
1983 Council	205*	110*	264(S1)	51(S1)	59**	210**	100	64.1	No run	No run
1983 Mayor	194*	110*	270(S1)	34(S1)	76**	194**	100	60.6	No run	No run
1989 Council	394(S3)	153	200(S2)	75(S2)	78	122	31.0	68.3	68.3	74.1
1989 Mayor	374#	153	437(S2)	72(S2)	76##	361	96.5	78.9	No run	No run

Notes: *Extrapolated from official sources (see sources) by the procedure for the extrapolation of data specified on pp. 152–3. Note my assumption (there) that the turn-out amongst Israelis in booth 1 in 1983 was similar to that accurately recorded by independent list activists for 1989 (36.4%)

**Extrapolated from S1 (see sources) and Bar-Gal 1986:54-3

#Assuming five Palestinian voters abstained in the mayorship ballot, and fifteen more were disqualified. These are based on unofficial assessments by polling booth attendants that the majority of the twenty disqualified votes in booth 1 had three ballot papers inside them, instead of two. Most had one for the independent list, one for Labour's list and one for Labour's candidate for mayorship

##Following on from #, the balance of the twenty disqualified votes in the mayorship ballot had to be votes cast by Israelis

**Voting ration here is qualified votes as a proportion of eligible votes

Sources: S1: Report by the local polling committee, Natzerat Illit 1983:2
S2: Report by the local polling committee, Natzerat Illit 1989:2
S3: The List for Coexistence and Peace (the independent list), mimeographed results sheet, 1989
Bar-Gal Y. (1986:54-3; 63) was used as an additional basis for extrapolation

residents of the north west attempt to display conformity with mainstream Israel, embodied locally by power-holding Labour.

The second and third points worth noting in the voting record of Palestinians in booth 1 are the outstanding success of Labour in the 1983 local election,[8] and its appalling failure in the 1984 parliamentary vote.[9] The two events are linked. Shortly before the municipal election of 1983, the local branch of the Labour party learnt that an independent group of Palestinian activists were planning to contest a seat on the council. Realizing the electoral damage such a move was likely to cause Labour, the party approached the Palestinian activists and proposed a deal along the good old lines: termination of the independent initiative and a return to a universal Palestinian vote for Labour in exchange for substantial improvements in services and infrastructure in the predominantly Palestinian residential areas in the north west. Provided, of course, Labour stayed in power.

The deal agreed, the Palestinians stood up to their commitment to the letter. They withheld the plan to feature an independent list, promptly delivered votes for Labour and became a significant factor in its decisive win in the municipal ballot of 1983. The party, on the other hand, did not pay up. Little improvement in infrastructure and resources was evident by the 1984 parliamentary elections or, for that matter, by the early 1990s. The abysmal returns for Labour in polling booth 1 in 1984 – 14.1 per cent of the Palestinian vote, Labour's lowest performance ever in this polling booth – reflects a protest vote by Palestinians against what they saw as a cynical betrayal. This disappointment was later compounded by disillusionment at Labour's abstention from statement and action against what Palestinians see as spontaneous racism in Natzerat Illit; by disappointment at Labour's policy towards the Palestinians in Israel and in the territories; by Labour's failure to regain control of central government, and by the party's participation in wall-to-wall national unity coalitions with right-wing Likud in 1984 and 1988.

The independent list
The Palestinian residents of Natzerat Illit perceive their community as a suburban offshoot of Nazareth, where their kin, professional, commercial and community connections are. Many of them relate to Nazareth as their political centre of gravity. This partly explains their long-standing indifference towards public affairs in Natzerat Illit.

The mid-1980s however saw first signs of change. In 1984, one year following the short-lived initiative of 1983 to run an independent effort in the

municipal elections, the three activists who had been behind the move
came together again and established *Lajnat ḥay al-Kūrūm* (al-Kūrūm
neighbourhood committee). With infrastructure and services consistently
poorer in al-Kūrūm than elsewhere in Natzerat Illit, and following the
1983–1984 debacle, the residents became convinced that the prevailing
power structure would never yield them an equal share of municipal
resources and services. It also demonstrated that the Palestinian residents,
if organized, could gain considerable influence in local politics.

The primary objectives of Hanna Ibrahim, Ṭalal Ḥadad and Salim
Khūri, the three founders of *Lajnat Ḥay al-Kūrūm,*[10] were essentially
municipal in nature. They wanted new roads, pavements and street lights, a
better water supply, a modern sewage system, an efficient garbage collection, playgrounds for children, better parking. Attaining these objectives
naturally required some kind of dialogue with the council. Their contact
with the council between 1984 and 1988 included communication with
various officials as well as with the mayor himself. Alas, while generally
cordial, this liaison was hardly effective. Improvement in services and
infrastructure for al-Kūrūm was slow and painstaking.

Not surprisingly, the existence of *Lajnat Ḥay al-Kūrūm* was hardly recognized by Palestinian residents of other parts of Natzerat Illit. Where
known, the committee had an image of an *ad hoc* local residential group
with a dubious tendency to collaborate with the all-Israeli council; this,
once again, in spite of the limited impact this liaison had on the situation
on the ground. The limited scope of its agenda and the inevitable resort to
negotiation with the council were enough to implicate the committee as
representing the narrow interest of a specific group rather than general
issues preoccupying Palestinians in Natzerat Illit at large.

The idea of forming an independent list to contend a seat on the municipal council re-emerged in May 1988. This time, however, the activists were
fully conscious of the need to get support from residents beyond al-Kūrūm
and its immediate environs. Indeed their first move was to place an adver-
tisement in the popular Arabic daily *'al-'Itiḥad'*, inviting 'all Arab residents of Natzerat Illit' to a general meeting.

Approximately fifty people attended the meeting, which was held in the
public playground in Ḥay al-Kūrūm. Most were residents of the neighbourhood, although a handful of men who lived in other neighbourhoods
attended too. At one point two of the visitors challenged their hosts,
arguing that *Lajnat Ḥay al-Kūrūm* had been working for the narrow interests of the neighbourhood while 'forgetting about us brothers in other
parts of town'. 'Only now', one of the critics said, 'when you realize you

need our votes to secure a seat in the council, do you suddenly remember us.' A committee spokesman responded with pacifying – if somewhat patronizing – remarks, claiming the unity and success of the whole community was more important than past grievances.

The question of securing the votes of Palestinian residents living outside al-Kūrūm and the northwest was rightly considered the make or break point for the new initiative. Salim Khūri, who gradually emerged as the central figure in the forming outfit, once said: 'We know we can get most of the votes in al-Kūrūm. After all, people know us here as neighbours, and appreciate our work. It is our potential (Palestinian) voters elsewhere that I am worried about.'

Khūri's preoccupation with this problem was understandable. Less than 40 per cent of his potential voters lived in al-Kūrūm, mainly in private houses built on land they owned. These constituents, who see their residence in Natzerat Illit as definite and long-term, are naturally more aware of their need in representation on the council than are Palestinian residents of other parts of town, most of whom live in apartment blocks and perceive themselves as temporary residents in Natzerat Illit.[11] Many of the latter in fact prefer the Palestinians to keep a low profile and refrain from self assertion – not least since anti-Palestinian provocation by Israeli extremists in Natzerat Illit (see Shipler 1986, Rabinowitz 1990, 1992a) tend to take place nearer their homes – not at the wealthier, better-established, less-visible and geographically marginal al-Kūrūm.

In December 1988, shortly after the official announcement by the Knesset that polling day for the approaching local government elections was set for 28 February 1989, members of *Lajnat Ḥay al-Kūrūm* issued a leaflet inviting all Palestinian residents of Natzerat Illit to attend a general meeting. This six paragraph text – an early and abbreviated version of a manifesto – reads as follows:

An Arab-Jewish list for the local council elections, to work for coexistence and full equality in Natzerat Illit

The mobilization of the Arab public of Natzerat Illit to work with the democratic forces in the town, is the only guarantee against racism, and will give the Arabs their rights and equality in (municipal) services.

Dear fellow Arab citizens of Natzerat Illit. Once more, and more than ever before, the need arises to have on the local council representatives of the Arab residents of Natzerat Illit and of those Jewish residents who believe in Arab-Jewish coexistence and in Arabs attaining full rights and full equality in services. The number of Jewish residents who currently believe in coexistence is small. This however must not reduce our capability, as Arab residents, to unite and elect representatives to the council who will raise our voices from within the council itself and demand our lawful rights. We have bought our homes with our own money, and we pay our taxes in full. Nevertheless the town's council practice is to deny us our rights for services, thus causing us residents to feel discriminated against. Also, we are concerned about the appearance of racist voices wishing to 'clean' the town from Arabs, in a manner not unlike the Likud's recent manifesto for the local elections in Acre, calling for 'Transfer of the Arabs'. Such policies and voices make it imperative for us to unite and work together. The racists on the one hand and the council on the other must realize that the Arabs of Natzerat Illit continue to maintain their right to stay in the town and receive services equal to all other residents. This is a line we are not going to retreat from.

Most respected Public. The Arab residents' committee of Natzerat Illit, consisting of groups of residents who believe in this way and are planning to campaign for it in a structured, serious manner, convened recently and decided to call for a general meeting of the Arab residents, in which the subject will be discussed and practical organizational steps to further the cause will be decided.

The meeting will take place on 22 December 1988, at the YMCA club in Nazareth. You are all requested to make every effort to attend the meeting and contribute to its success. Its success will be the success of the Arabs of Natzerat Illit and the success of coexistence based on mutual honour and equality.

Blessings,

The Natzerat Illit Arab residents' Committee

Significantly, the letter featured the first appearance in print of the term *Lajnat Sukan Natzerat 'Ilit al-'Arab* (The Committee of the Arab Residents of Natzerat Illit). The old connotation of a residential self-help group, as manifest in *Lajnat Hay al-Kūrūm* thus gave way to a new title in which the name of the town replaced that of the neighbourhood. The first appearance of the term 'Arab' ruptured the curtain of invisibility that had shrouded the Palestinian collective in Natzerat Illit for so long.

The demands that the council provide al-Kūrūm the services which they deserve and pay for are reinforced for the first time by a number of wider, more emotive issues: the need to unite against local Jewish racism; the need to work more actively for peaceful coexistence; the quest for honour and mutual acceptance. Palestinian solidarity and rights have twelve central citations. On the other hand equality in services, the initial *raison d'etre* of *Lajnat Hay al-Kūrūm*, while present in the text, is there mainly as abbreviated clichés, tending to end sentences rather than begin them. The text thus signifies a departure from traditional appeals to Israelis and a turning to Palestinians to mobilize around their true identity and help themselves.

The campaign unfolds

22 December 1988. 19:30: I arrive at the YMCA club of Nazareth, park the old Renault and walk self-consciously towards the main building. I have been to the place before to watch YMCA's basketball club under coach Ra'id Riziq famously beating Israeli teams on its historic way to national league division 2. The atmosphere tonight, however, is different. No commotion, no youngsters hurrying breathlessly towards the open court in the shallow valley at the eastern side of the compound, no howling cheers from two thousand spectators forming a human wall around the field. The night is quiet, action scarce. I enter the club house, feeling as though the dozen or so young men seated around the scattered tables in the lobby are all busy eyeing me, a European-looking non-native. I nod 'good evening' and vanish up the stairs to the second floor.

At the meeting hall I am relieved to find a number of acquaintances, who introduce me to those I do not know. The turnout is disappointing – less than twenty, with only two women. People are waiting, chatting and sipping juice, obviously hoping for an increased attendance. Finally, forty-five minutes after the advertised time, with attendance having crept to twenty one – the meeting gets under way.

The proceedings take place around a rectangular formation of tables. The three veteran campaigners Ḥanna Ibrahim, Salim Khūri and Ṭalal Hadad sit at the top, facing the rest. Outflanking them are two younger men, well-known members of the DFP Nazareth apparatus. The chairman is Khūri. At forty-seven, he is a heavily built, jovial man. Like most Palestinians living in Natzerat Illit he is a Christian, but unlike most, who come from Nazareth, he is a native of Kafr Kana, a village 7 kilometres north. Prior to moving to al-Kūrūm in the early 1980s he had always lived in his native village, where he still has kin and property, including a sewing workshop he owns and runs. Typical of Christian Nazarenes, his political sympathy is firmly with the DFP. However his thirty years long association with the Arab Israeli Bank (recently purchased by Bank Leumi Le-Yisrael, Israel's largest bank), has made explicit political affiliation out of the question. His position as manager of the Nazareth branch of the Arab Israeli Bank and his ongoing involvement with the Nazareth Rotary club (of which he has been president), make him a well-known figure in the Palestinian town and amongst Palestinians in Lower Galilee at large.

Khūri stands up, greets the audience and immediately invites his colleague Hanna Ibrahim to speak. Ibrahim, a lawyer, and an erstwhile supporter of the Progressive List for Peace (PLP) presents a logical, dispassionate, coherent argument. He traces the history of Lajnat Ḥay al-Kūrūm *and, conscious of the presence of the two DFP men alongside him and of the danger that the new outfit might be construed as affiliated with the DFP, goes out of his way to stress the non-partisan nature of the new initiative. 'Our objective all along', he emphasizes, 'was municipal, social and community services for Arabs in Natzerat Illit.' The effective means to get that, he asserts, is to have representation on the council. As long as we remain with no representation in local government, our rights will go unfulfilled, our needs neglected. An opening must be created to effect a change by democratic means.*

Ibrahim gives an account of a correspondence he had with mayor Ariav of Natzerat Illit in 1984, in which he raised the emotive issues of a church and burial services for the Palestinian residents of Natzerat Illit. He then reiterates the need for unity and determination, alludes to the importance of finding Israeli counterparts to join the outfit, assures the audience that the matter of leadership is of no consequence to him personally, and ends with greetings of success and health to all.

Khūri thanks Ibrahim for his speech, commenting that 'Hanna has described our objectives most accurately, and has always been with us on the right track'. A short, almost laconic speech from Ṭalal Ḥadad, a veteran and senior state welfare officer, follows. Then people are invited to raise questions, ideas and issues for discussion.

Someone raises the issue of countermanding Israeli racism in Natzerat Illit. The issue, however, is quickly pushed aside, with organizational matters taking centre stage. One thing the present company seems to be unanimous about is the need for the new list to cooperate with Israelis – either local branches of left of centre Zionist parties, or, failing that, with Israeli individuals.

This kind of cooperation has a central place in most mainstream political initiatives within the Palestinian community in Israel. Its aim is not necessarily shoulder-to-shoulder cooperation with Israeli activists or even an attempt to attract potential Israeli voters. Rather, it is a ritual designed to counter Palestinian apprehensions about projecting a militant Palestinian image. Such projections, many of them believe, might provoke the authorities, alienate Israeli individuals who are in working and friendship contacts with Palestinians, and keep away potential Palestinian voters.

While this logic is understandable and sound, the hope to find Israeli counterparts in Natzerat Illit is utterly unrealistic. Expecting Israeli politicians to cooperate with an outfit advocating self assertion for Palestinians in Natzerat Illit is like asking a Victorian vicar to endorse the local brothel.

Two middle-aged gentlemen, both known to have strong ties with the Labour party and the mayor of Natzerat Illit are present. At some point one of them suggests that 'if the aim of all this is to get municipal budgets then we are wasting our time'. The other gentleman is a well-known Muslim figure, strongly associated with the Labour apparatus, who told me not so long ago that he is 'in no agreement' with the idea of a Palestinian list in Natzerat Illit. He speaks, saying that 'interests of large families and denominations must be taken into account when names of candidates are put down for the list'.

I wonder about the incongruous presence of the two gentleman, and what their statements really mean. Do they imply that chances to get assistance from the council are slim anyway? Or are they saying there are better ways to go about it, indirectly offering brokerage? Are they here to assess the pros and cons of joining the new outfit? Is the suggestion of confessional and kinship criteria designed to sound out the chance to act as formal representative of his large family and of Muslims in Natzerat Illit at large? Be the case as it may, the comments made by the two men are unceremoniously put aside. This is the last I see of the two throughout the campaign.

A motion is upheld to confirm Salim Khūri's appointment as leader. A number of practical suggestions are made from the floor regarding the approaching campaign. A few men write donation cheques, others register as volunteers. The evening ends on a note of unity, encouragement, and anticipation.

The following week the new outfit was officially registered in the local election committee in Natzerat Illit as 'The List for Coexistence and Peace' – herewith the independent list.

Late December 1988 saw more cooperation between the independent list and the Nazareth branch of the DFP. One obvious indication came when activists elected the weekend edition of *al-'itiḥad*, the communist party daily in Arabic, as the paper where ads for public rallies would be placed. More significantly, in early January Kamal Saliḥ, an experienced full-time employee of the DFP's Nazareth branch, was loaned to act as campaign manager for the independent list. Saliḥ, who had been a leading organizer in DFP's operation in Nazareth during the recent Knesset elections of November 1988, came equipped with updated DFP computer files containing detailed lists of Palestinian voters in Natzerat Illit and their addresses.

Favourable stories about the independent list which appeared in *al-'itiḥad* in subsequent weeks provided further clues to the close relationship with DFP, consolidating the independent list's legitimacy in Palestinian circles in and around Nazareth. This link, however, was kept a secret from Israelis in Natzerat Illit, for fear of delegitimizing Israeli propaganda which might depict the independent list as a communist plot. Such depiction, it was assumed, might dissuade some Palestinian residents from supporting the independent list for fear that its success might lead to escalated tension in the town.

December 1988 and January 1989 saw persistent attempts by independent list activists to join forces with potential Israeli partners. First, Salim Khūri and Kamal Saliḥ approached the local branch of *Mapam*, (United Workers Party, a Zionist leftist party), only to learn that it had already committed itself to an alignment with Labour. Next they tried *Ratz* (Citizens' Rights Movements), though once again to no avail: the meeting with local Ratz activists, which I attended, convinced me that their views on Israeli-Palestinian relations were more akin to the intransigence of the majority of Israelis in Natzerat Illit than to the ecumenical spirit of the party's liberal leadership in Tel-Aviv. Ratz activists were quite willing to have the Palestinians cooperating – but only as individuals under the formal canopy of Ratz, not as a Palestinian collective.

Disappointingly to the Palestinian activists, it became clear that by the standards of the Israeli community of Natzerat Illit, both *Mapam* and *Ratz* already represent a dangerous tendency towards leftist extremism. An alliance with local Palestinians could shake the legitimacy of these two Zionist parties in the Israeli community and spell political suicide. By late January it was obvious that an alliance between Israeli and Palestinian activists in Natzerat Illit was not to be.

21 January 1989, 21:00 – 23:00. Election rally at the YMCA club, Nazareth. Part 1. This time the rally of the independent list is much better prepared, publicised and attended. I count seventy-three men and two women. Seating arrangements resemble those at the previous event. The atmosphere, however, is much more buoyant. There is no temptation to delay the meeting in the faint hope of late-comers. At nine o'clock, as advertised, business begins.

As in the previous event, Hanna Ibrahim speaks first. He begins with a factual history of the political initiative which brought the outfit to its present state. Then, suddenly, a shift in tone and substance:

If we succeed, it will be a historic event. al-Naṣira al-'Ulya (Arabic for Natzerat Illit, literally 'Upper Nazareth') was built as a Jewish town on land partially belonging to Arabs. Then, with the growth of al-Naṣira al-'Aṣliya (Original Nazareth),[12] more and more Arab brothers found themselves residences in al-Naṣira al-'Ulya. Then the Jews said: since this is a Jewish town, a development town, how can we let Arabs live here? But we have a right to live in the town, and to be represented on its council. Our right to be up there is a natural right, even before one takes into account the fact that we pay taxes like the Jews, and are entitled to the same services.

We are a part of a waṭan (nation), and for us this is a matter of life and death. We must have representation – regardless of whatever the mayor or anyone else says in the matter. It is our honour and the honour of our children that is at stake here. This is why we must all unite and work together. I know there are people here who are Ḥizb ('The Party', denoting the communist party, centrepiece of the DFP), and others who are al-Ḥarka (The Movement, denoting the PLP), and those who are for Labour, and Mapam. But all this must be set aside now. Only our unity will enable us to get the votes together.

Towards the end of his address Ibrahim informs the audience that Salim Khūri has recently been nominated leader of the independent list, and invites him to speak.

Khūri begins with a report to the constituency. He lists the various initiatives and action carried out by him and colleagues recently, then moves on to detail the attempts to strike a deal with potential Israeli counterparts, and the disappointing failure which ensued. As he recounts the room is dense with murmurs and soft exclamations. This is obviously a significant juncture for the congregation.

As I write this four years later it occurs to me that for Palestinian citizens of Israel the success or failure of political cooperation with Israelis carries meanings which go beyond considerations of electoral efficacy. Not every political outfit of Palestinians within Israel determines to seek this kind of unity with Israelis. Those who do, however, invite a moment of stock-taking, an assessment of their standing *vis-à-vis* the dominant majority. Not least, it is a point for reflection on decisions taken by Israelis initially construed as likely allies.

Hanna Ibrahim turns to me from the table at the top, calling on me to join and be a candidate. Is this my litmus test as ethnographer, a sign of my long-awaited approval by those I am out to study? Or am I merely chosen by default, being the only Israeli interested in and sympathetic to their cause? Do I want to join and publicly identify myself with the group the Israelis here insist should never have appeared in Natzerat Illit in the first place?

Confusion. The cool winter night is not enough to stop my face from burning. I know I cannot accept, and cannot even buy more time. I must explain, to myself as much as to these people, why I abstain. Here I go . . .

The slight diversion of my failed recruitment is over. This may be a special moment in my fieldwork, one I shall have long to ponder over. Now, however, Salim Khūri is in his stride again. I pick up my pen again and go back to my notebook.

A Change of pace

In early February the independent list's manifesto *(barnamij)* was printed and delivered to all Palestinian homes in Natzerat Illit. The document, which begins with a brief history of the independent list, goes on to pledge support for the Committee of Heads of Arab Local Authorities and its supreme Monitoring Committee – two countrywide organizations perceived by many as the senior bodies of Palestinian representatives within Israel, and whose prestige amongst Palestinians at the time emanated from the refusal of the Israeli government to recognize them (see Al-Haj and Rosenfeld 1990, chapter 5; Benziman and Mansour 1992:94; 208). The manifesto call to open local institutions and committees to Palestinians is phrased as a quest for honour. Demands for schools, youth clubs and the use of Arabic on street signposts takes precedence over issues such as the civil engineering needs of al-Kūrūm. The latter is alluded to just once, indirectly, under the vague heading of 'equal services in every part of town'.

This shift in tone and emphasis became most pronounced in the narrative employed by Salim Khūri in the election rallies he attended in the latter part of the campaign.

17 Friday, February 20:30. Salim Khūri addresses some thirty men at a rally in a private house in an all-Palestinian street at the north-western part of town. Most of his audience are residents of the area, but their particular grievances vis-à-vis *the council are absent from the leader's agenda. His speech begins:*

Friends, thank you all for coming. I would like to tell you right at the start that the question here is not one of sewage or water pipes – and you all know I live in the lowest part of the slope here, where in the summer we hardly ever get water before midnight. No, the question is our very existence in Natzerat Illit. There are people who want to throw us out of here. Hear this, for example. A few days ago I received a phone call to my office. It was a senior candidate on a right-wing local party. And he had the cheek to tell me that 'there is a solution to the problem of the Arabs in Natzerat Illit: the town should give up the entire territory of al-Kūrūm, simply surrender it to the local authority of Nazareth or of Raina'.

When I asked him what about those of us living dakhil *['inside', meaning the mixed neighbourhoods, see chapter 2 above], he said: 'well, this matter is not for us here. It is for central government to decide.' At which point I told him: 'our right to live in Natzerat Illit is just as valid as yours, and probably more. After all, most Jews bought their flats here aided by a government mortgage. We bought ours with our own money. And besides', I told him, 'the land on which this town is built is ours. It is Arab land, expropriated from their rightful owners and transferred to Natzerat Illit. So our right to be here is seven fold!' And let me tell you, friends: all political parties in this town are like this man.*

Khūri then relays an incident which took place the day before yesterday at an election rally organized by Labour at the house of a local Israeli supporter, with the Mayor as main speaker. The audience was predominantly Israeli. Khūri, who did not attend, heard the details from a friend and now conveys a selection:

There was this Jewish doctor of Indian origin, who, I think, works in a clinic in downtown Nazareth. And he stood up and challenged the mayor: 'This is the 20th century', he told the mayor, 'and you are supposed to run a modern town. How can you explain, then, that in your town there are hundreds of people living in a large area with no sewage whatsoever?'

There are murmurs of approval. People's remarks indicate they are impressed primarily by the existence in Natzerat Illit of an Israeli who is attuned to their problems, and who sympathizes with them to the point of publicly challenging the Mayor on their behalf. When Khūri cites the Mayor's reply – a claim that the new sewage system had already been completed but was not connected because some cheques paid in by residents of al-Kūrūm had bounced – the audience are enraged. Some cry 'thief', 'dog' and 'liar' at the Mayor's expense. The issue of sewage has obviously recycled itself into a feature of the Israeli–Palestinian frontier here.

Next Khūri describes the poor condition of roads in the north-west, concluding with rhetorical questions that cleverly echo Shylock's famous speech about being a Jew in Shakespeare's The Merchant of Venice*: 'It is our children who walk and play these streets', he said. 'Are not their lives considered lives? Are they not in daily danger?'*[13]

This must be where Khūri and his outfit are most effective. The pregnant transformation of local into larger solidarities is done so naturally, so effort-lessly – a metamorphosis which needs no manufacturing. For Palestinian citizens of Israel the connection between personal discrimination, municipal deprivation and national suppression is so obvious that all a politician drumming grass-root support needs do is to declare his willingness to recognize this truth and strive to expose it, hopefully en route *to have reality repaired. Surely, this is what the campaign is all about.*

What is political? who is a leader?

*21 January 1989, 21:00 – 23:00. Election rally at the YMCA club, Nazareth. Part 2. By 22:30, the main speeches of the evening are done. The floor is open for discussion, comments and suggestions. Some of the points, however, are hailed by members of the audience as 'too political'. A discussion ensues as to how political (*siyasiya*) the independent list should be. The use of 'politics', I notice, is not unlike its use in standard Israeli discourse, denoting the amalgam of existential problems associated with the Israeli–Palestinian conflict. It seems to me that for many Palestinians the distinction between 'political' and 'a-political' fits that between* ad hoc, *spontaneous associations of people trying to solve concrete and local problems ('a-political'), and more formal organizations such as established parties, whose longer-term positions and intentions inevitably refers to the Israeli–Palestinian conflict ('political').*

The argument continues until a middle-aged man stands up. He wishes to read out a poem he has just composed. The murmur stops. He reads [my translation]:

Every day of my life is a mountain,
and I walk towards its peak,
I see my days turning into summits,
into mountains who meet mountains.

God has set my fear to be my goal,
therefore I follow my path fearless.
He who is afraid of the dark,
will be a slave forever.

The impromptu poem is received with a spontaneous uproar of approval, hand-claps and proud smiles. The author beams with joy.

I approached the poet once the rally was over and asked if we could meet. The man, whom I later learnt is a high school teacher in a near-by village, and who occasionally publishes poetry in Arabic and Hebrew newspapers and journals, invited me to come and see him at his apartment in the southern section of Natzerat Illit. I came a few days later, and we talked of the particular moment he chose to read his poem at the rally. He explained that his intention had been to encourage the others not to be afraid of anything, and to have courage and resilience in becoming more 'political'. 'After all', he said, 'if you mean well and your cause is just, why should you ponder and hesitate?'

He showed me some of his earlier work, which had other orientations – invoking amorous sentiments, exalting friendship and the beauty of the world. Other Palestinians later told me of the man's political record, which included spells of active involvement with the Labour party and even with right-wing *Likud*.

This put the poem and its public reading in a new perspective. The newly found spirit of solidarity obviously had a dual effect. First, it brought together people who had previously been divided along party political lines, particularly supporters of the DFP – the majority amongst the activists and those attending – and all others. Second, the new outfit clearly had the role of 'identity laundry', whereby enthusiastic affiliation cleansed sullied reputations. This in turn enabled the newly found political community to embrace and rehabilitate those who had previously been marginal, thus spelling personal and social metamorphosis beyond specific political agendas. Surely the special place which poetry occupies in Palestinian nationalism and identity made this particular re-entry to the fold more natural and easy.

The poet and the point he made came back to me one afternoon a few weeks later, when Khūri gave me a ride in his car from Nazareth to Natzerat Illit. The car was making slow progress in the perpetual traffic jam which has become a standing feature of downtown Nazareth. There was nothing anyone could do but patiently shift from gear to neutral and back again, greet passers-by, exchange a word or two with drivers going in the opposite direction – all of which Salim did incessantly as we nudged our way uphill. Then at one point he turned to me and said:

Remember the meeting I had last month with the mayor? When he invited me to try and talk me out of our campaign? Well in that meeting he said he wanted to know whether our outfit had to do with the real problems of the community in the town. If it had to do with local issues, he said, he could try and help and we could talk. But if it had to do with politics – then there was nothing to talk about.

'Well', I said, what did you tell him? To which Khūri replied:

I said we were 'municipal', of course. After all, we are not affiliated with any political party, are we?

The mayor was quite consistent in his distinction between 'political' and 'municipal'. He is aware of course that upward of 70 per cent of votes cast by Palestinians in the November 1988 Knesset elections went to non-Zionist parties (DFP, PLP, DAP), and that if the emphasis of the municipal campaign within the Palestinian community shifted to 'political' issues, meaning the Israeli–Palestinian conflict, than he and the Labour party had very little to offer. Khūri's deliberately narrow interpretation of the term 'political', on the other hand, reflected the juggling act which he felt was necessary for his political survival in the predominantly Israeli town. He obviously believed that the 'politicization' of the independent list, while a prerequisite for electoral success amongst the Palestinian voters, had to be concealed from the eyes of the mayor and from Israelis generally, lest they wage a delegitimization campaign against it. This could have been unpleasant and, even more important, could modify the willingness of many Palestinians to support the list.

The fact that Khūri pleaded a-politicization with the mayor did not surprise me. The fact he chose to do the same with me, however, was frustrating. Surely he knew I know 'political' has more to it than formal affiliation with a registered party. He did not have to throw the book at me like that. What does he take me for, an outsider?

Challenging Israelis

Khūri's meeting with the mayor came up in another election rally. One of the mayor's objectives, said Khūri, was to dissuade the independent list from running – possibly an attempt to repeat the deal of 1983. 'He told me', Khūri said to the audience that:

it was in our best interests to work with Labour, not against it. But not only did I tell him this was nonsense, I also told him that if his party employs a smear campaign against us, we shall do all we can to persuade all our supporters to vote against him in the personal mayorship vote.[14]

The listeners were clearly amused. Smiles of content broke into gleeful bursts of laughter. People clapped occasionally. Salim's story was about a contest – a dual which carried great significance for them, and which they clearly felt he won for them.

On another public occasion he recounted a chance meeting he had a few days earlier with a local right-wing politician of relatively mild persuasion who had recently formed an *ad hoc* coalition with a person renowned for his extreme anti-Palestinian stance:

As soon as I saw him I said to him: 'you are a spineless bastard. You, who for years used to call that guy a racist pig, now join a coalition with him?' And when he replied: 'well, what can you do, this is politics', I said: 'You have thirty-five faces. Us lot, we have a single face. We don't play games or mess about.'

This exchange, portraying Khūri as a powerful and unpredictable person who speaks his mind right to the face of an authoritative Israeli, again went down well with the audience. Khūri's deliberate and well-timed switch from the first person ('I met this person') to the plural ('Us lot we have only one face') transformed the encounter from personal to collective. The connotation was obvious: 'us Palestinians' (strong and honest) versus 'you Israelis' (weak and inconsistent).

The theme of head-on collisions with Israeli politicians was one of Khūri's favourites. Once he proudly told a gathering how he called the mayor's home at midnight to complain about failed water supply to al-Kūrūm. Kamal Salih, his chief aid throughout the campaign, relayed another incident which took place at a meeting of the Regional Election Committee some weeks before polling day, when representatives of all lists came to present the committee with graphic designs for ballot papers. When the independent list presented their logo – the Hebrew letter *Kaf* (equivalent to C or K in English), an Israeli representative of one of the Zionist parties turned to Khūri and asked jokingly: 'What does this *Kaf* stand for then? Kahana?'[15]

This prompted a reaction Salih will long remember. In his words:

Salim got really angry and started shouting at the man. 'What Kahana? Why Kahana? If anybody here is Kahana it's you. You should be ashamed of yourself.' I tell you, Salim is really the man we need on the local council. He takes no notice of rank or national affiliation. He really speaks his mind out, whoever the opposition.

Khūri's relentless image was cultivated independently of his political career. He clearly sees himself as a ferocious man who makes no distinctions along status lines and who, as he put it to me once, 'always tells the truth right to a bastard's face'. He revelled in accounts of outrageous public challenges he had made to Israeli superiors in the boardroom of the bank for which he worked for nearly thirty years. One incident he was particularly proud of had taken place a few years earlier at a farewell lunch in honour of a senior executive from the head office of the bank, an Israeli whom, according to Khūri, many of the Palestinian branch managers disliked. Khūri's account of the event included this:

I waited for all the flatterers to finish their cowardly farewell speeches. Then I stood up. I said to him, right then and there at his own party, the very things which everyone else thought but never dared to utter: that he was a reckless liar, a dishonest coward. They tried to stop me going on, but I did not give in. I said it all until I finished. I gave him hell.

Another incident had taken place in the office of the managing director of the bank, and included Khūri hurling abuse 'right at the director's face'. These incidents, he said, matched his aggressive and unyielding style as secretary of the workers' union of the bank, an office he held in the 1970s. In his words: 'Workers and management alike know me well. I am someone who stands his own ground. I am afraid of no one. People prefer not to mess with me.'

I spent numerous mornings in Khūri's glass walled office at the main hall of the bank, where his unique style of management became evident. Clerks who came in or rang with requests to authorize credit for clients always had the manager's undivided attention, benefitting from quick, efficient decisions. When it came to communicating his decisions to the clerks, however, he often used an impatient, temperamental phrase or term. 'OK', he would say to a clerk, 'you tell the son of a bitch he gets away with it this time, but no more. We've had enough of his treacherous practices.' Or: 'No bloody way. You tell him I am not authorizing. If he wants to, let him come begging here himself. But first you make sure he realizes that I'm not budging.'

At first this style sounded as though the manager was taking his relations with his clients personally. My observations of him during the campaign however made his conduct at the bank look more controlled and contrived. The purpose was not merely to project managerial decisiveness and determination, although this too was useful in saving time he would have otherwise spent fending off clients' pledges and appeals. More importantly, it kept subordinates at bay. His strong expressions often suggested that the issues were elementary, and that anyone – including the clerk who brought the matter to his attention in the first place – could have guessed the right decision. And yet, since the clerks in question were not authorized to take the relevant decisions by themselves, they were repeatedly subjected to a catch: having to accept the manager's decisions unquestioningly while at the same time becoming a captive audience to his humiliating reprimands.

One of Khūri's officers in the independent list once said smilingly: 'Salim is crazy. That is his great advantage. He is afraid of no one. He is from Kafr-Kana where folk are known to be hot-blooded.' Clearly, the man's strong personality, complete with popular allusions to the ostensible connection between his birth-place and his character, were harnessed to bolster a particular political image. The public image which emerged embodied the promise which the independent list held for its constituency: level- headed, resilient, honourable representation, particularly in front of Israelis.

Polling day on 28 February went relatively smoothly in Natzerat Illit. First unofficial results arrived at the independent list's headquarters in al-Kūrūm shortly before dawn the following morning. The list, it soon transpired, had over 700 votes, so Khūri's place on the new council was virtually secured. There was a spontaneous uproar of applause, complete with claps and cheering. Soon the place resounded with loud chanting of *'Bilṭul, biParḍ, alwaḥda thiz aParḍ'* ('along and across, our unity will shake the earth'). A convoy of hooting cars left the headquarters in al-Kūrūm at four o'clock in the morning, heading for DFP's Nazareth headquarters. One of the activists later told me of his sense of pride and achievement when in the faint light of dawn he recognized around him supporters of the independent list whom he knew had never been associated with the DFP. For him it clearly signified that support for the independent list crossed partisan affiliation – a further proof of the outfit's strength and representational validity.

The break-down of support for the independent list by residential area is instructive. In polling booth number 1, covering al-Kūrūm – home of Khūri, of *Lajnat Ḥay al-Kūrūm* and cradle of the independent list itself – the list had 68.2 per cent of the ballots cast by Palestinian voters. In the rest of Natzerat Illit, where Khūri feared support would be limited, the independent list had 74.1 per cent of ballots cast by Palestinians. Obviously, the new outfit succeeded to transform the limited and local significance of the ostensibly municipal contest into an arena where more general and sweeping aspects of being Palestinian took centre stage.

The politics of honour

The independent list was essentially a municipal effort: its constituency was local, as was its sphere of influence and projections for action. This notwithstanding, the wider context of Palestinian identity and the Palestinian Israeli conflict became a major aspect of its campaign. Not an ordinary feature of campaigns in local level politics in Palestinian communities in Israel at the time, this fusion has nevertheless been known before, primarily in DFP's campaigns (Al-Haj and Rosenfeld 1990:56).[16]

The independent list's leap-frogging to the ideological terrain it eventually came to occupy cannot be seen in isolation from the specific circumstances of Natzerat Illit. Khūri and his outfit were first and foremost

Palestinians operating in a political arena solidly dominated by Israelis. Doomed to play a minor role at the best of scenarios, one of the activists' priorities was to distance themselves from 'selling' to the Israelis. Their choice of Palestinism was not primarily a programmatic statement indicating plans for action. Rather, it was a marker of allegiance signifying solidarity, integrity and loyalty. Significantly, as soon as Khūri took office as a council member, his rhetoric – now produced for Israeli members' ears – reverted to a highly pragmatic discourse restricted to local municipal affairs.

The turning point in the campaign was surely in mid-January 1989, with the final realization that collaboration with local Israeli activists was out of the question. Once this possibility evaporated, the independent list's political horizon and rhetorical manoeuvreability were substantially widened. Emancipated from the need to accommodate would-be Israeli partners, the leaders of the list transformed their strategy of discourse. Their project was now dubbed 'an historic event'; the manifesto was finally printed, pledging allegiance to organizations which embody Palestinian dissent within Israel; speakers on behalf of the list at last felt free to voice demands in lofty terms of Palestinian honour, insisting on the dignity denied to the oppressed. Salim Khūri could attribute bad roads in al-Kūrūm to Israeli disregard for Palestinian children's lives, and the idea purported by Israeli politicians to redraw municipal lines so as to exclude al-Kūrūm from Natzerat Illit could be presented as part of an evil and racist plan to transfer Palestinians from their ancestral land.

The refusal on the part of Israelis to cooperate with the independent list carried the familiar ring of rejection of Palestinian representatives and denial of their political legitimacy. Once more the legal right of Palestinian citizens to vote and to be voted for was *de facto* restricted to their own social and political milieu. Power sharing of any description was obviously out,[17] with access to what Yoav Peled dubs the common good of Israel's ethnic republic (1992) blocked even in the context of this local arena.

This conjuncture brought to the fore the key scenario of Palestinian consciousness – the sense of overarching, continuous calamity which fuses all other aspects of being Palestinian into an undeniable, subjective whole. The Palestinians' sense of being exiles on their own ancestral land was coupled with a concrete mark of being second-class citizens in a state which consistently proclaims their equal standing. Cohesive unity and self reliance thus became a logical, natural choice. Palestinism came to be a valence – an issue that the entire electorate is likely to support, and which a candidate – in this case Khūri – will strive to be identified with.

For the Palestinian residents of Natzerat Illit the turn away from the humiliations of their passive past was personified by Salim Khūri's agency. A realist, Khūri never promised over- night redemption, a final stop to discrimination or the end of bigotry in Natzerat Illit. Nor did his followers expect such miracles. His stated goal, rather, was to finally put up a struggle, thus redeeming Palestinian honour. It is in this respect that his aura as a ferocious man became so salient.

Lila Abu-Lughod's discussion of networks of honour-linked values amongst Awlad-'ali Bedouins (Abu-Lughod 1986) emphasizes the singular importance of autonomy and independence for social hierarchy. Bedouin freedom, she asserts, is closely linked to 'the strength to stand alone' and to 'freedom from domination' (1986:87). When it comes to relationships with other people, a person's freedom is won 'through tough assertiveness, fearlessness, and pride' (*ibid*).

This account is not unlike Gilsenan's description of the relationship between law and arbitrary power in the Akkar of Lebanon, where local leaders are measured by their ability to violate accepted boundaries and norms. They are, says Gilsenan, individuals who can 'go beyond the limits of others, of the ordinary, of custom and tradition' (1985:389), into realms where each of them alone is his own measure of action.

Like the Agas of the Akkar and the autonomous males of the Awlad 'ali, Salim Khūri seldom strikes. Like them, he consciously cultivates the aura of an unpredictable, brave warrior. His supporters are not coerced into his fold: they join it willingly, for a variety of pragmatic calculations but also due to their attraction to his promise 'to go beyond the limits of others'. His trademark – a relentless readiness to prick and probe Israeli figures, be they politicians, bankers or industrialists – flare up his followers' hopes.

Zeev Rosenhak (1993) has demonstrated how Israeli orientalists have tended to interpret some Palestinians' preference for the politics of honour in terms of 'traditionalism' (as opposed to modernization) and even irrationality (as opposed to soberness). As an example Rosenhak cites Jacob Landau's distinction between the 'logical' approach of some Palestinian citizens of Israel, which pushes them to accept the Israeli dominance and make the most of it in terms of economic development and educational progress; and the 'sentimental' approach of others, which prods them to reject the benefits of Israel, and could even encourage them to seek existence with less-favourable conditions in an Arab state (Landau 1969:37). Later in the same work, Rosenhak observes, Landau reformulates his distinction in terms of rationality, and applies it to party politics: those

Palestinians who support the Zionist parties are labelled rational; those siding with non-Zionist parties and movements are classified as irrational (Landau 1969:130).

Similar characterizations of the Palestinians, Rosenhak indicates, can be found in the work of Stendel (1992) who analyzes political choices within the Palestinian community in terms of 'realism' (cooperation with Zionist parties) and 'extremism' – siding with the DFP for example. This approach lies at the root of Eli Rekhes' 'radicalization thesis' (for a relatively recent version see Rekhes 1989:166–9), Ra'anan Cohen's account of the history of the communist party within Israel (1990:108–12), Aharon Layish's distinction between 'pragmatism' and 'idealism' (Layish 1989:8–9), to name but a few. In fact the distinction between 'moderates' (*metoonim*) and 'extremists' (*kitsonim*) has penetrated the Israeli public discourse of the Palestinians to the point of becoming an indispensable component of many Israelis' views of Palestinians and Arabs generally.

The tendency to depict persons who share the assumptions which underwrite your worldview as rational while rendering those who question the fundamental logic of the prevailing order as irrational extremists has obvious weaknesses and is easy to expose. Things become slightly more entangled when one is dealing with honour – an idiom which features strongly in the rhetoric of the Palestinian actors themselves and which, as I have shown, is a major preoccupation of their leadership. Honour-oriented thought and action, which the Palestinians proudly attribute to themselves, is often contrasted by Europeans with common sense, straight forward vision and a means-to-ends approach to life. Many see the linkage to honour as a remnant of what Weber called the shroud of 'magic' which dominated the human condition before the advent of redeeming rationality and its progeny, modernization.

This juxtaposition tends to isolate the obsession with honour as a particular and inferior aspect of the cosmology of orientals. People who are willing to execute an erring daughter or a sister, or who are willing to give up chances of economic progress and professional advancement just to protect a thing as vague and abstract as their honour are often eurocentrically perceived as being at odds with the notions of progress, achievement and the right of individuals to pursue happiness and personal fulfilment.

My comparison between Abu-Lughod's allusion to fearlessness and pride, Gilsenan's point of breaking norms and boundaries and the account of Khūri's calculated shows of strength stresses the similar contexts in which the three examples are imbedded. None of them, I argue, reflects free-floating 'cultural' traits, as an essentialist reading of the ethnographic detail might suggest. Rather, all three cases reflect male actors' attempts to wriggle out of the constraints of power structures which subordinate and marginalize them. Certain aspects of the problematic situation of the Awlad 'ali *vis-à-vis* the Nile valley and the Egyptian state are not unlike the situation of the Palestinian citizens of Israel. Likewise, the lords of the Akkar are not merely engaged in an attempt to subjugate and rule: they also fight a bitter, violent battle for survival in the virtually state-free country of Lebanon. Their constituents' economic livelihood and physical survival may depend on outcomes of these contests. Honour and honour-linked choices such as those exercized by Awlad-'ali chiefs, by Agas in the Akkar or by those Palestinian politicians in Israel who are ostensibly 'not for sale', emerge as efficacious strategic moves.

This interpretation is inspired by Bourdieu's treatment of male honour in Qabyle society, which he interprets as an integral and rational tool in the ever-present contest for dominance and access to resources. His description of *Nif* – male honour – includes this:

Nif – literally the nose, is very closely associated with virility . . .; the verb *qabel*, commonly used to designate the fundamental virtues of the man of honour, the man who faces, outfaces, stands up to others, looks them in the eye, knows how to receive as a host and to do his guest honour, also means to face the east *(elqibla)* and the future *(qabel)*, the male orientation par excellence.   *(1977a:15)*.

This rather 'cultural' point of departure for the interpretation of *Nif*, however, is soon augmented by Bourdieu. One of the fruitful aspects of *Outline of a Theory of Practice* is the argument that rituals of honour are everything but hollow motions, having highly pragmatic value: they determine power relations between men, and often guide the distribution of capital – symbolic or other (*ibid*:181–2). Men's relative initial standing, for example, could turn affront and riposte into prestige and power in one instance, into humiliation and loss of status in another (*ibid*:11–12). In no circumstances, however, can the eurocentric economism which dismisses preoccupation with honour as 'non-productive' and 'irrational' be justified. A similar argument, incidentally, can be made of even the most horrific manifestations of male preoccupation with family honour. A Bedouin man who, for example, does not act violently once his daughter or sister is believed to have committed adultery, is seen as lacking control over his family. This in turn might bring about loss of respect and of cooperation from agnates and others – a development which may have dire consequences for the most pragmatic aspects of his and his dependents' lives (see Stewart 1994).

Conversely, the long-term chances of Palestinian politicians who forget their honour and 'sell' votes to Zionist parties and who obviously get something out of the exchange are not necessarily rosy. First, future regrouping and restructuring of the electorate is likely to become exceedingly difficult. If the only things to be gained are tangibles, the distribution of the spoils is likely to become a central, rapturous issue. Second, even if unity within the group can somehow be maintained, manipulation by the dominant party becomes much easier. The cases of the Bedouins and the Druze in northern Israel, whose coopted leadership consistently opts for favours from the Israeli state in exchange for value-free support, is one lucid example. There, the community as well as leadership must periodically face an ungainly truth, namely that they have neither progress nor dignity. Likewise, the events of 1983 and 1984 in Natzerat Illit demonstrated to the Palestinian residents how tenuous and untrustworthy promises for progress and resources in exchange for votes can be. Their choice of 'honour' can thus be seen as calculated and effective in the long run.

It would thus appear that by electing representatives who remain 'ideological', 'honourable', 'political' – who are, essentially, elected so as to 'be' rather than 'do' – minorities keep more options open for the future. In the Arab world, just as elsewhere, honour and its attendant status are solid vehicles for future progress. There is little logic in wasting them.

Salim Khūri's emphasis on self-sufficiency and independence matched Palestinians' craving for a redefinition of their ties with the dominating Israelis and the state. His promise had a clear main text which grew progressively less technical and local, more expressive and 'Palestinian' as the campaign developed. The straight forward means-to-ends approach which typified the work of al-Kūrūm's committee thus gradually gave way to core symbols of the national predicament: dispossession, occupation, inequality, discrimination.

The paradox whereby Palestinians' participation in party politics in Israel works to marginalize the actors rather than empower them cannot be solved without a major structural change in Israel – a task which lies beyond the scope of local-level politics in Natzerat Illit or anywhere else. It is, however, temporarily mitigated through the selection of a ferocious envoy and the emphasis on bigger issues which at least some of the activists are willing to define as properly 'political'. Khūri, who was pragmatic enough to look for Israeli partners, was nevertheless resolute enough to stand alone when collaboration failed to materialize. From this point on he efficaciously personified the linkage between local experience and the Palestinian predicament at large.

Khūri's voters have displayed very limited interest in his performance as a member of the council since his 1989 election. He himself has often complained that his trials and tribulations in the council tend to go unnoticed by his fellow Palestinians, lamenting that he has no one to answer or report to. And yet, while few people would claim his term in office made substantial difference in the life of Palestinian residents in Natzerat Illit, the November 1993 local elections which had him running for a second term of office saw a slight increase in the level of support his list received.[18] His role of 'being' remained important, his scant achievements during his first term in office notwithstanding.

This indifference on the part of Palestinian voters is determined by the structural context which more or less preempts their chances to attain real power sharing. Moreover if, as I have argued, the mission of Palestinian delegates is simply 'being there', asserting autonomy, independence and pride, then records of actual achievements should even be avoided: they always carry the implication of dishonourable 'selling'.

Salim Khūri' – middle-aged, well-educated, economically independent, disassociated from the Zionist parties – is typical of the second generation of Palestinian politicians in Israel. His stances and strategies are of the type exemplified by members of Knesset for DFP, PLP and DAP. Like him, they were elected by Palestinians who see it as pointless and degrading to go on casting votes in favour of the Zionist parties, whose rigid Israeli dominated structures consistently marginalize Palestinians, candidates and voters alike. Like him, their presence in the Knesset does not go beyond vocal protest – they are not invited by either Labour or Likud to join a coalition even when their parliamentary strength could tip the coalition balance. Like him, they lament the lack of voters' interest in their performance once in office.

Elected politicians in many democracies often base campaigns – indeed careers – on the coincidence of personal disposition with rhetoric of cherished aspects of identity. A convincing concurrence of this nature can at times prove more attractive for prospective voters than a splendid record of achievement. People may back a contender whose policies could prove to work against the interests of their sector or class, providing the candidate convincingly portrays himself or herself as an authentic interlocutor of the people's past. The roles of keeper of old flames, guardian of group cohesion and *bona fide* pathfinder towards the people's destiny are easily fused.

A more general distinction emerges between political performance under normal and abnormal democratic conditions – the Palestinian citizens in Israel clearly presenting a case for the latter. Abnormal situations, where meaningful incorporation into the system is problematic, may push for ideologies which emphasize collective identity, the past, and group allegiance along primordial features and affinities, and for those leaders who are perceived as representing authentic linkage to such values. Liberal democracies on the whole tend to tolerate such ideologies as bases for political affiliations.

However only with genuine participation in the polity, which in the case of Palestinians in Israel is hardly in sight, may the emphasis switch to ideologies and genuine independent candidates whose promise is primarily to get things done. This could in turn engender political unity of the kind which has so far alluded the Palestinian citizens of Israel.[19]

Until then, the choice of Palestinian citizens of Israel remains between old style 'selling' through vote-block brokers, which regained ground in the June 1992 Knesset election with the return of Palestinians to electoral support of Zionist parties;[20] and 'honourable' politics such as vintage DFP or the independent list in Natzerat Illit. The choice, I argue finally, is not all that dramatic: both cases are second- and third-rate solutions for those doomed to view liberal democracy from its margins – those forced to sit it out until the eurocentre offers them some form of meaningful inclusion.

Resistance revisited

Kaplan and Kelly, seeking to go beyond Gramsci's basic dichotomy between unconcsious resistance and alienated ideology, suggest that:

> Emerging in between are different kinds of responsible agents. We see political terrain populated not only by unconscious resistors and alienated ideologues, but also by agents (such as union leaders and religious prophets) who challenge existing and permeable structures of domination, with varying scope of intention and facing varying modes of danger and levels of risk . . . In colonial societies, especially, the routinization of a ruling order, however productive, is inevitably vulnerable from many angles. (1994:127).

Ra'id Riziq, Nawaf Sa'adawi and Salim Khūri, none of whom can be slotted comfortably into one of Gramsci's extremes, are agents who, to use Kaplan and Kelly's terms, act within the grammar of the Israeli hegemony, or on its margins. The agency of Salim Khūri, who thrives on the image of a man able and willing to challenge the going hierarchy, at least with words and personal confrontation, is particularly intriguing in this context. After all, his popularity amongst the Palestinians owes much to his aura as a man able and willing to defy Israelis who are senior to him and come up trumps.

Gramsci fondly wanted to believe that resistance, while unconscious and restricted to the subaltern classes, is a shadow cast by future revolution or at least by future upsets to the hegemony. This rather romanticized view was too strong a temptation for anthropologists, some of whom adopted it uncritically.

Thus Peteet (1994) implies that the success of Palestinian males in overturning the meaning of beatings by Israeli soldiers from humiliation and possibly feminization into masculine honour, had a real impact on the turn of political events on the ground. This argument, interesting and far-reaching theoretically for the study of ritual, can neither be proved or disproved. My claim here is less ambitious, and focuses on the capacity of temporary role and status reversal to help those on the receiving end of power structures to carry on within the structure, rather than strive to overthrow it. To put it bluntly, I see resistance as a paradoxic vehicle of cooptation.

The argument does carry a Gluckmanian functionalist trait: Palestinians construct rituals and interactions which put them in positions of power *vis-à-vis* Israelis merely to keep themselves going within the system. Much like Jean Rouch's Africans, filmed going berserk in shanty towns on Saturday only to go back to work for European colonialists on Monday, thus reaffirming the imperialist order. Nevertheless, I hope the political context of this study of Palestinians inside Israel productively ruptures the shell of equilibrium functionalism, pointing at a reality of politics and surreptitious cooptation most orientalist approaches to Israel refuse to acknowledge.

Palestinians within Israel need strategies to help them rationalize their servitude. Precisely because their situation is endurable, in some respects even comfortable, they seek – and find – solutions which give them strength to cope with their imperfect lives and to persist. Perhaps the state does consciously encourage occasions for contained resistance as a twisted element of cooptation and control; but then again, perhaps it is not as sophisticated and thorough in its endeavours. Importantly, the evolvement of such situations lends the system stability and strength by weakening the willingness of Palestinians to look for drastic change.

Thus, analysis of beatings of young males in the Intifada as constructive passage to manhood, has little to do with the collective effort to liberate the nation. Where hegemony has collapsed, and where the going situation is revolt, resistance is no longer relevant, having lost its prime place in the hub of people's struggle for the nation's destiny. It has everything to do, on the other hand, with the ability of individuals to gain a dignified re-entry to the community, even when their manhood has been tainted and humiliated.

10

Conclusion

Sa'id Al Mutasha'il, the Palestinian hero of Emil Ḥabibi's novel *The Pessopsimist* (1974), has a troubled, tragic life. A native of Haifa who fled to Lebanon during the 1948 war, the young Sa'id crosses the border back to his homeland when the hostilities are over and is quickly found out and apprehended by the Israeli authorities. To escape expulsion, win legitimate status, make a living and keep alive the fantasy of reunification with his schooldays' sweetheart whom Israel had chased to Jordan, Sa'id becomes a collaborator. The omnipresent agents of the government assign to him the hopeless task of spying on the communist party, depicted in the book as the only option available to Palestinian citizens of Israel who wish to avoid total loss of honour and integrity under the new regime.

Sa'id works for the government for twenty years. He develops perfect identification with his new role, coupled with complete submission to his ungrateful supervisors. At one point his years of faithful service are all forgotten; a white flag he hoists on top of his house in Haifa as a sign of loyalty to Israel is interpreted as incitement to a Palestinian rebellion. He is thrown in jail, where, to begin with, he is beaten and humiliated. Then his old resourcefulness saves the day again; he expresses gratitude and admiration to his oppressors for their generosity and care and is immediately promoted to become the warden's chief informer.

In another episode his wife and son, having turned anti-Israeli freedom fighters behind his back, are hunted by the security forces and disappear forever in an underwater cave. Sa'id walks away accompanied by his secret service boss, his erstwhile operator. With the patron's friendly hand around his shoulders, the two renew their bond of old: more false promises by the Israeli agent, more unrealistic hopes for the Palestinian collaborator. And so the life of Sa'id El Mutasha'il the pessopsimist goes on.

This brilliant fantasy – arguably the high point of Ḥabibi's long career as author, columnist, ideologue and politician[1] – is an allegory on the Palestinian predicament written from within. Wry, reflexive and sophisticated, it depicts Palestinian citizens of Israel at best as spineless and confused, at worst as a treacherous lot, existing on the verge of degradation and contempt. Sa'id the pessoptimist epitomizes immoral acquiescence, physical survival at the cost of personal and collective integrity. Injustice, suffering, confused identity and shame make a dramatic backdrop to his tormented psyche. Sa'id's reflexive capability and acute awareness of the irony and tragedy of his own impasse and of life for Palestinians in Israel at large, while an important aspect of the story, cannot turn the gloomy picture upside down.

Ḥabibi, winner of the 1992 Israel prize for literature (amidst protests from Israeli right-wing politicians and controversy in literary circles in the Arab world), calls everybody's bluff. His readers can no longer credit Israel with bringing western progress and modernity to Palestinians yearning to be redeemed from oriental backwardness. His blow by blow account of the mental pressures experienced by the Palestinian citizens of Israel exposes the rhetoric of Arab nations – high words on liberating Palestine and reinstating Arab honour – as irrelevant and hollow. His narrative pushes western readers to recognize their ignorance of and indifference to the Palestinian tragedy. Above all, Ḥabibi forces his fellow Palestinians to face the role they play in their own subservience.

Twenty years on, Ḥabibi's caricature remains a vivid illustration of the predicament of the Palestinian citizens of Israel. It elucidates the strange, tormented life of people trapped on their ancestral land, doomed to be controlled and dominated by an alien, often hostile culture and society.

Don Handleman recently alluded to conflicts between citizenship and nationality in Israel (1994). The prominence of Jewishness – the essentialist precondition for belonging to the Israeli nation (*le'om*) – contradicts the Israeli myth of egalitarian citizenship and overrides it, pushing Israel's non-Jewish citizens 'to the margins of the state and beyond' (1994:449). Indirectly bolstered by the ethos of ethnicity within the Jewish fold, this hierarchizing structure of centred Jewish hegemony consistently denies Palestinians a dignified entry into the Israeli mainstream.

Built on confiscated Palestinian land, Natzerat Illit was established primarily to assert an Israeli presence in the face of Nazareth – the largest and most important Palestinian centre inside Israel since 1948. Obtrusively visible for residents of neighbouring Nazareth, the 'Shikūn' is a standing reminder of the oximoronic nature of Palestinian life in Israel.

The very presence of Natzerat Illit and the politico-historic meaning of its growth and its persistence, problematize the willingness of Palestinians to move there. Their choice, like those made by Sa'id al-Mutasha'il, is highly charged and burdened. Natzerat Illit is a site where the dual subjectivities depicted by Ḥabibi and Handelman are forced together – an arena where the pessopsimism of Palestinian citizens and the inherent exclusivism of Israelis clash.

This book does indicate that Palestinians and Israelis can live in relatively peaceful neighbourhoods even in a place like Natzerat Illit. It also suggests, however, that this is but a small part of the picture. There is no place in Natzerat Illit for a Palestinian collective, neither is there likely to be such space elsewhere in Israel as long as Israelis experience themselves as citizens and agents of 'a Jewish state'.

The three Palestinian 'heroes' of my ethnography – coach Riziq, doctor Sa'adawi and politician Khūri – bring up some of the questions raised by Michael Mann's work on the relationship between the western working classes and liberal democracy (1970, 1973). Subordinates within the Israeli system that marginalizes Palestinians and discriminates against them, the three nevertheless subscribe wholeheartedly to values which are becoming major tenets of Israeli state and society. The three men and their careers are champions of meritocracy, professionalism, hard work, universalistic pluralism, freedom of individual choice, representational democracy and equal opportunity. The liberal revolution which Israel is undergoing, of which the 1992 constitutional law of human dignity and freedom is a corner-stone, makes the three men's agency and rhetorics into shining examples of the individualized, non-prescriptive society Israel purports to be as yet another western liberal democracy.

Mann (1970) argues that it is the lack of cohesion within the working classes and, even more so, inconsistencies within each individual member, that frustrates subordinate groups from organizing to overthrow the structure which marginalizes them. Such dynamics are surely relevant to an analysis of options Palestinian individuals are facing as the Israeli system gradually opens up to them (see Smooha 1992). In many ways, the budding structure of Israeli liberalism, with its ability to reduce 'big' issues to personal events, thus flattening and depoliticizing them, could prove even more effective in keeping the Palestinians at bay than was Israeli collectivism. Put differently, temporary upsets in the form of inclusion and cooptation of individuals like Riziq, Sa'adawi and Khūri, could form the perfect legitimizing cover for indefinite exclusion of the Palestinians.

The three successful men are, in many ways, allegorical to the

Palestinians in Natzerat Illit at large – a community which uses economic purchase power to seek, and generally find, inclusion in an Israeli town. The fact that an overwhelming majority in the community are Christians is no coincidence of course. Twice a minority – within Israel as Palestinians, within the Palestinian fold as non-Muslims – the Palestinian Christians are natural candidates for an unconditional embrace of liberalism.

The argument, however, can and must be generalized from Christians to the Palestinian citizens of Israel at large, and possibly to minorities in liberal democracies and democratizing states elsewhere. The blue-collar workers in Mann's analysis, who subscribe to values such as 'hard work (and not luck or influence) is how to get on' (1970:428), overlook their own structural disadvantage compared to other potential hard-workers. Similarly, members of minorities who are offered chances to develop individually may easily identify with values underlying the very system which denies collective standing from their people.

The peace treaty between Israel and Jordan and the progression of agreements between Israel and Arafat's PLO are obviously encouraging for the Palestinian citizens of Israel. If nothing else, these processes relieve the sense of guilt at having a relatively peaceful existence under Israeli rule. At the same time, however, these developments raise serious problems regarding the position of the Palestinian citizens of Israel *vis-à-vis* both Israel and the future Palestinian state.

What precisely will ever signify the conclusion of the peace process? Once peace is here, is it realistic to hope that Israel can ever be a welcome part of the Middle East? Will the Jewish majority persist in seeing the state as 'Jewish'? Will Israeliness or, at the very least, citizenship, be open to negotiation and redefinition so as to include non-Jews? When the state of war – the chief excuse behind decades of discrimination against the Palestinians inside Israel – is over, will all citizens finally become equal? Will Palestinians be allowed to lease state land and have equal water allocation? Will there be affirmative action on capital investment, industry, welfare and education in Palestinian towns and villages? Will government and other public sector jobs be equally obtainable by Palestinian men and women as they are by Israelis?

Alternatively, is there a danger that once external problems between Israel and the Arabs are resolved, mainstream Israel might lose interest and patience with Palestinians within? Could the manoeuvrability and bargaining power of Palestinians in party politics in Israel be eroded once there is peace?

What will be the fate of 1948 refugees still in camps in Lebanon, Syria and Jordan, whose case is yet to find representation in the current process? What of the internal refugees displaced in 1948 and settled since in other Palestinian communities inside Israel? Could they expect remuneration? Will they be allowed to return to towns, villages and properties they had been chased from? What of half a million acres or so confiscated from Palestinian citizens in Israel between the 1950s and the 1970s? Will there be recompense to Palestinians evicted from their homes and land in the early 1950s, long after the hostilities were over?

Although these problems are complex and comprehensive, answers are not in sight. Liberalism as a mechanism for selective inclusion could suggest that real solutions to the Palestinian national problem elsewhere[2] may push even more Palestinian citizens of Israel to seek the benefits of liberalizing Israel. The tension between individual welfare and collective justice will be exacerbated.

Zionism and its ideology have long served as shields protecting armies of exclusionary Israeli institutions and practices, a combination which solidified Israel as a bastion of euro-centrically defined essentialist values. To gain political consequence, new ways of conceptualizing Israel must rupture the narrow definitions of Israeliness. One component of this deconstruction is a reexamination of boundaries and of internal schisms – within the state as well as within the Jewish and the Palestinian peoples.

The term post-Zionism is becoming more acceptable in Israeli public life. While more Israelis no longer associate it with the apocalyptic demise of Israel, the debate regarding the vocabulary and meaning of the idiom is just beginning (Cohen 1995). An idiom the current strength of which lies mainly in its ambiguity, post-Zionism, once detailed and operationalized, could be of theoretical and political use.

Ella Shohat's collapse of the 'Jewish–Arab' and 'Ashkenazi–Sephardi' schisms into a redefinition of Israel along first world–third world lines (1989) is an important contribution to the reevaluation of boundaries. The notion of diaspora and its place in the construction of collective self in Israel may be another.

Two relevant diasporas – the older Jewish one and the more recent Palestinian one – fell prey to systematic silencing by Zionist and Israeli narratives of history (Raz-Krakotzkin 1993). Blindfolding itself to the centrality of the diaspora and of diasporism (Clifford 1994:304) to Jewish history, Zionism rapidly manoeuvred itself to occupy the privileged position at the pinnacle of linear Jewish history (Boyarin and Boyarin 1993), assuming the existence of the state of Israel to be the ultimately 'right' conclusion to an inherently just course of history. Accordingly, most

Israelis still see their residence in Israel as a calling – a historic destiny in its own right. As James Clifford's summary of the Boyarins implies, the political use of such ahistoricism was most convenient for the budding Israeli project (1994:308).

Much has been said and written about the poverty of cultural and spiritual life in Israel compared with Jewish life in the diaspora – a point which is as relevant as questions of inclusion and exclusion. When it came to Israel, Zionism substituted the Jewish diasporic yearning for assimilation and inclusion with vehement displacement and banishment of those who may be of the place, but are not of the race.

Sadly, this had another implication. The first generations of Israelis found no better definition for themselves and for their project than in consistent alienation from and animosity against the Arabs and the East. The promise of orientalism and its powerful tropes was irresistible, becoming second nature to Zionism, Israel and Israelis. Not surprisingly, it remains deeply imbedded and highly influential in Israeli media, politics and culture.

The point of departure of Ian Lustick's interesting article on the politics of binationalism (1989) is that political life, even in Israel, has a pragmatic logic built into it. The Israelis, Lustick argues, are quite unwilling to give up Zionism as a conceptual logic. This intransigence notwithstanding, other, less-ideologized aspects of the situation could push things in counter-intuitive directions. The fierce electoral competition between Labour and Likud every four years could breed a situation in which the Palestinian citizens of Israel (just like the ultra-orthodox Jews) attain handsome achievements from either of the two parties. This road, Lustick argues, could theoretically lead to forms of power sharing and bi-nationalism[3] – without a major shift in formally agreed consensus or even policy.

Lustick's notion, restricted to the pragmatic and calculated nature of coalition politics, can be expanded and generalized using the ethnography of Natzerat Illit. If structural borders can indeed be moved solely through pragmatic agency on the part of leading actors, with no declared shifts in the consensus, (Rabin's shift towards negotiation with the PLO since 1992 is one clear case), then the very same can happen in less conspicuous arenas, removed from public gaze. This, in a nut shell, is my main argument regarding individual agency of Israelis in Natzerat Illit. Individual actions such as selling an apartment to a Palestinian, being respectful patients of a Palestinian doctor or sharing seats on the local council with a Palestinian cannot possibly be interpreted in terms of actors' personal beliefs or their rationalizations of consensual convictions.

These actions and many others – incremental, gradual, slow-moving, hardly visible – must not be analyzed as puzzling or irregular segments of reality. More often than not, they are more tangible 'realities' than the conventional formulations they seem to contradict.

Perhaps this is where anthropology could make its long overdue contribution to the study of Israel, its Palestinian citizens, and to research on deeply divided states and nations generally. If, as I argue, change can be detected in choices made by individuals, *in situ*, then it is high time to shift our scrutiny from formal politics and leaders, who are inevitably tied down to pre-existing, often over-burdened formulations. Once we redirect the spotlight, the role of ethnography as an investigative tool with powers of analysis and of prediction can no longer be ignored.

My sojourn in Natzerat Illit did not change my views on Palestinians or otherwise draw me nearer the perspective shared by so many of the Israeli residents. It did, however, teach me something about the latters' point of view. On one occasion I said to an Israeli neighbour that to the best of my knowledge Palestinian citizens are entitled to choose their place of residence in Israel without restriction. My implication was that the opposing view, to which he openly subscribed, was bigoted and dangerous. His honest reaction was one the likes of which all anthropologists should be reminded of at least once during fieldwork: 'You', he said, 'can talk like this because you don't intend to spend your life here. We and our children are the ones who'll bear the brunt when our town is taken over by the Arabs.'

My judgement that such a scenario was and still is utterly unlikely is beside the point now just as it was then. The man obviously believes that full and perfect fit between Judaism, Israeli nationalism, the state and its control of territory, the nature and identity of his local community and a unified and linear 'Israeli' or 'Jewish' history is not only feasible, but well worth living, even suffering, for.

The story of Natzerat Illit as I have tried to tell it indicates that there is nothing 'cultural' or otherwise unique about intransigience in the northern new town. Media depictions from the early 1980s notwithstanding, Natzerat Illit is not a freak conglomeration of extremist, blood-thirsty settlers out to 'get the Arabs'. On the contrary, it is a normal Israeli town with ordinary distributions of opinions, tropes, ideologies, commitment and agency. What does stand out is what the Israeli residents see as a uniquely tense frontier situation, akin perhaps to an emergency zone, if not disaster area. Obviously shaped by an uncritical acceptance of hegemonic Israeli narratives, beliefs and fears, these sentiments colour constructs of reality and strategies of agency for Israelis.

Gideon Aran's recent work on zealots, based on the case of the extreme religious right in settlements on the West Bank suggests a similar theme. His convincing readiness to see zealotry and fanatic violence not as attributes of marginal freak groups but as imbedded in widespread values, attitudes and norms suggests, disturbingly, that what we tend to label as extremism is often part and parcel of the mainstream culture (Gideon Aran, personal communication, November 1994).

Having been exposed to aspects of both the Israeli and the Palestinian sides of Natzerat Illit, and having felt the empathy and solidarity that came to me from both terrains, I have tried to convey a picture which is complex and often paradoxic. My concerns for the relations between Israelis and Palestinians are not the notions of a detached observer, but of an actor. It is precisely this commitment which compels me to take the Israeli side more seriously and less judgementally. For good or bad – and my critique of it, I hope, is neither shy nor coy – the Israeli side is indispensible to the equation. It is a portion of the problem one must not ignore when looking for solutions.

Notes

1 The Ḥaj, the mayor and the deputy prime minister

1 My spelling and pronunciation of the town's name – 'Natzerat Illit' is a transliteration of its official Hebrew name. *Natzerat* is the official Hebrew appellation of the neighbouring old Palestinian town *al-Naṣira*, known in English as *Nazareth*; *Illit* is Hebrew for 'upper'. It should be noted however that Israeli maps, signposts and documents in English carry the town's name in a variety of forms, including *Upper Nazareth, Nazareth Illit* and *Natzeret Illit*. Writers in English use various forms too, most frequent of which is *Upper Nazareth* – an unusual attempt to transliterate the Hebrew meaning of the name. The result is a term hardly ever uttered in daily use.

The Israeli inhabitants of Natzerat Illit are abhorred whenever they encounter the erroneous suggestion that their town and adjacent Nazareth are one and the same. Curiously, however, many of them refer to their town as simply *Natzeret* – the folk term most often used by Israelis for neighbouring Nazareth. In recent years they tend to use *Natzeret Illit* more often.

The Palestinian residents of the area, including those residing in Natzerat Illit, use other appellations for it. One most frequently used is *al-Shikūn* – 'The housing estate'. *Al- Naṣira al-ʾūlya* – 'Upper Nazareth' – is also used sometimes, as is *Natzeret Illit*.

2 Literally, Karm Ṭabariya means the field of Tiberias. I have not succeeded in tracing the origins of the name.

3 Strictly speaking *karm* means orchard. The term, however, is used also for other types of agricultural plots – in this case a cereal farm. *Ḍaman* is a seasonal leasing arrangement by which an owner leases land to sharecroppers for a proportion of the yield. The contract can be extended for several seasons.

4 The map, first surveyed by the British in 1930 and revised in 1946, provides good relief detail and fairly reliable information regarding buildings, orchards, vineyards and plantations. Palestinian names of places, however, are sometimes carelessly noted. For example, cereal growing fields (including the Haj's Karm Ṭabariya), which lacked landmarks such as trees or buildings, are absent.

5 Thirty-one *Dunams* is approximately seven and a half acres. 140 kells is an impressive 8,400 kilos – 270 kilos per *dunam*, 1.2 tonnes per acre.

6 Tawfiq Zayad – poet, mayor of Nazareth between 1976 and his death in 1994 in a road accident, was also a member of Knesset for the communist-led Democratic Front for Peace and Equality (Arabic: *Al-Jabha* – the front).

7 *Shikūn* became synonymous with one of Israel's most striking urban land-scapes since the 1950s: rows of apartment blocks hastily designed and built for immigrants – an apt description of the physical appearance of many parts of Natzerat Illit. Like most peripheral new towns in Israel, the town still struggles with this problematic architectural heritage, so reminiscent of tenements in East European and Third World metropoli, or, for that matter, of poorer sections in the inner cities of the West.

8 The first stage consisted of having Israelis settle in properties in old Palestinian towns such as Baisan, Acre, Tiberias or Safad; the second stage saw the construction of transition camps (*Ma'abarot*) for Jewish new immigrants in areas where cheap labour was needed for intensive agriculture and unskilled jobs in industry; the third stage was the establishment of three new towns – Natzerat Illit, Carmiel and Ma'alot in three areas which remained predominantly Palestinian despite the 1948 war and the Palestinian exodus.

9 See for examples Matras (1973); Weintraub and Kraus (1982); Ben-Zadok and Goldberg (1984).

10 Only approximately 15 per cent of the current population are Israeli born, a figure which was even lower at 6.7 per cent in 1983 (State of Israel 1984).

11 I do not consider Jerusalem, where Jewish and Palestinian residency has been mixed for centuries, on a par with the other mixed towns in Israel. Its present demographic proportions, while reminiscent of the situation prior to the war of 1948, is nevertheless a result of the 1967 war, whereby the eastern city, inhabited by Palestinians only, was taken from the Jordanians by the Israeli army to be annexed to the western (Israeli) city. The future of this area is yet to be determined in negotiations between Israel and the Palestinians.

12 Elsewhere (Rabinowitz, in preparation) I develop the concept of trapped minority more fully, and show its applicability to other political contexts.

13 The Mayor quotes from a popular Israeli song glorifying the 1948 effort to hold on to line-of-fire military outposts, some sites of which were later to become peripheral new towns.

14 Josephus began as leader in the Jewish rebellion of AD 66–73 against the Romans. Initially commander in chief of the rebellion in Galilee, he was taken prisoner by the Romans. His historical accounts, which remain the most detailed versions of the tumultuous period, were written in Rome, where he was kept as a privileged prisoner.

15 Representative examples of studies of the political sphere include Landau (1969, 1971, 1993); Harrari (1974); R. Cohen (1985, 1990); Rekhes (1986); Al-Haj and Rosenfeld (1990); Smooha (1989a, 1989b); Reiter and Aharoni (1992); Benziman and Mansour (1992); studies of the economic sphere have included Ben-Porat (1966); Haidar (1987); Portugali (1993); Semyonov and Lewin-Epstein (1987).

16 A. Cohen (1965); Marx (1967); Nakhleh (1973); Kana'na (1976); Ginat (1975); Kressel (1976); Oppenheimer (1979); and Stewart (1994) – a list including works on Bedouin and Druze communities as well – are the main and, astonishingly, most recent ones.

17 See for example Appadurai (1988); Rosaldo (1988); Gupta and Ferguson (1992); Malkki (1992); Rodman (1992); Clifford (1994).

18 A recent article by Gil Eyal (1993), analyzes the ways in which Israeli orientalists have used the concept of 'The Arab Village' – replete with stereotypical assertions on the 'primordial', 'primitive' 'chaotic' nature of the place – not only for descriptive purposes but also to sustain control over the rural Palestinian population.

19 See Lustick (1980); Smooha (1988, 1989a); Semyonov and Lewin-Epstein (1987); Haidar (1987).

20 'Development Area b' denotes a high rating on the central government's scale of development priority. Natzerat Illit's rating would be augmented to top priority 'a' in 1992.

21 One area where information was actively withheld was local municipal appraisals of the number of Palestinian inhabitants in Natzerat Illit. A local official once explained that it is council policy that such numbers are best kept secret. When such quotes were released, they tended to be unrealistically low. Thus the graphic representation in Iris Graicer's chart of Palestinian households in Natzerat Illit, based on 'Natzerat Illit Municipality, Register of Inhabitants' (1992:52), suggests that the number of Palestinians residing in the town in 1985 was only 1,700; this while her own narrative, as well as estimates by Israel Central Bureau of Statistics, indicates at least 3,000.

2 Tale of two cities

1 Lamdan and Ronen's (1983) review of the prehistoric literature indicates a number of sites in Lower Galilee where remnants of the Ascheulian culture (lower Palaeolithic) have been found.

2 For a detailed account see Morris (1987).

3 Henry Rosenfeld (1964) presents an early account of the proletarization process of the Palestinian citizens of Israel.

4 For an overview of the phenomenon of internal refugees – Palestinians who were displaced in 1948 but who remained in Israel and moved to build themselves new lives in other Palestinian communities – see Al-Haj (1986).

5 Some of the 15,000 *dunams* were torn off the municipal boundaries of neighbouring villages Raina and 'Ain Mahil. Most of the land, however, was formerly in a municipal no-man's land. The figure of 1,200 *dunams* taken from Nazareth to be included in Natzerat Illit is cited also by Sabri Jiryas (Jiryas 1966:81).

6 Saturated construction is the term used by Israeli planners to indicate intensive use of land for the construction of housing estates.

7 *Kirya* is biblical Hebrew for town. The term was used between the 1930s and 1950s as a component in names of new urban centres established by Zionism such as Kiryat Ata, Kiryat Haim, Kiryat Motzkin, Kiryat Gat and others. It was later taken up by the religious establishments, to be included in names of new settlements and neighbourhoods (e.g. Kiryat Arba near Hebron).

8 For details of the early years of Natzerat Illit see Garbuz (1973).

9 This, incidentally, happened twice more in the 1980s and 1990s, with yet more residential compounds – some erected to house new immigrants from the crumbling Soviet Union – encircling industrial parks which used to outlie the town to the east and north respectively.

10 The distinction in Hebrew between commercial centre (*Merkaz Misḥari*) and shopping centre (*Merkaz Keniyot*) is quite clear. The former rings of the 1950s. The latter connotes the 1990s.

11 This situation, while highly irregular in Israel proper, is routine in the territories occupied by Israel after the 1967 war. Israeli sensitivity to this reality and to its implication to the security of travellers at the time prompted extensive use of 'by passes': new roads designed specifically to detour Palestinian communities. The military term for such roads – *kvish okef* ('bypass road'), followed by the name of the town it circumnavigates – has since become a feature of standard spoken Hebrew. Thus the main road leading to Natzerat Illit, which by passes Nazareth, is sometimes called *Okef Natzeret* (bypassing Nazareth).

12 Representing less than 5 per cent of the total area of the town, al-Kūrūm remains the only part of Natzerat Illit where land is privately owned. Land elsewhere in town, as in upward of 90 per cent of Israel at large, is owned by the Jewish National Fund and administered by the Israel Land Administration.

13 The trend was reversed only as late as 1990, with the arrival of yet another, larger than ever wave of immigrants, this time from the crumbling Soviet Union. Estimates for persons arriving in Natzerat Illit ran at 7,000 by mid-1991, and nearly 10,000 by the end of 1992. This recent arrival has had a relaxing impact on the way Israelis in Natzerat Illit perceive their relationship with Palestinians.

14 Villages elsewhere in Galilee accounted for 15 per cent, and only 7.7 per cent were natives of Natzerat Illit (my survey, 1989).

15 The 1983 census (State of Israel 1985) indicates that 65 per cent of the Palestinian residents of Natzerat Illit at the time were Christians. My own survey of 1989 indicates that by that time the proportion rose to 85 per cent, with 15 per cent Muslims and a handful of Druze, Armenian and Circassian Muslim families. It should be noted, however, that the 1989 figure may be exaggerated upwards due to a methodological constraint. The questionnaire was distributed by paid assistants, all of whom were activists of the local branch of the Democratic Front for Peace and Equality (DFP). The households where they had positive cooperation with the questionnaire may have been those of supporters and sympathizers of the DFP. Since support for DFP amongst Christians in the Nazareth area tends to be considerably higher than amongst the Muslims, there may have been a case of over-representation in the survey of Christian households.

16 My survey of 1989.

17 The 1983 Population and Household census carried out by the state indicates that over 60 per cent of Palestinian households in Natzerat Illit had waged labour as their chief source of livelihood. The balance were self-employed or unemployed in equal proportions. Unemployment ratio in 1989 however shrank to 3.9 per cent (my survey of 1989) – a figure dramatically lower than the ratio for Nazareth as well as for Israelis in Natzerat Illit.

18 The 1983 Population and Household census indicates that the average number of persons per room was higher in 1983 amongst Palestinians – 1.41 – than amongst Israelis in Natzerat Illit – 0.94. Average size of residence in 1989 however was a high 96 square metres (my survey of 1989).

19 The 1983 Population and Household census indicates that the 1983 level of income per Palestinian person in Natzerat Illit represented only two-thirds of the income per Israeli person in the town. This does not necessarily mean poorer Palestinians and richer Israelis. Rather, it reflects the demographic structure of the Palestinian community at the time, with a larger number of children and a smaller number of earners compared to Israeli families.

20 The 1983 Population and Household census indicates that in 1983, 49.8 per cent of Palestinian households in Natzerat Illit owned cars, a proportion which rose to 52.5 per cent in 1989 (my survey). In 1989 over 80 per cent of households had telephones (*ibid*).

21 Yifrah Zilberman, personal communication, 1992.

22 Ninety-six out of 166 valid cases in my survey of 1989.

23 My survey of 1989 indicates that 47.4 per cent of the Palestinian residents of Natzerat Illit at the time (79 out of 168 valid cases) saw their sojourn in the town as temporary, indicating they were planning to stay only as long as it would take them to buy or build in a Palestinian community. This was particularly pronounced amongst residents of the mixed neighbourhoods, much less so with residents of al-Kūrūm.

24 Operating under the law of communal property, voluntary committees which manage the joint estate are in effect the only formal manifestation of the residential compound. Palestinians I knew who participated in such committees or in residents' assemblies in mixed blocks tended to play down their presence, involvement and affiliation, a level of performance which seemed to suit the Israeli residents.

25 Seventy out of 166 valid cases in my survey of 1989 had Palestinian families living in buildings where the majority of apartments were occupied by Palestinians, or where the number of apartments occupied by Palestinians was equal to the number of apartments occupied by Israelis. Three buildings, each with twenty-four apartments, had no Israeli families, only Palestinian.

26 The 1988 voters roll (State of Israel 1988) indicates that only thirty-five Palestinian families in Natzerat Illit had more than twenty-five listed voters. Out of the thirty-five, only thirteen families had the majority of members living in residential clusters – all of which were located in al-Kūrūm. No such cluster was to be found in the mixed residential quarters. (See also Bar-Gal 1986:58–60.)

27 An alternative appellation is *Arab tamanye waarba'in* – the Arabs of forty-eight, meaning those who came under Israeli rule following the 1948 hostilities and the establishment of the state of Israel. The use of *Arab* instead of *Falastiniyun* (Palestinians) is intriguing. It may reflect the dubious status, in the eyes of Palestinians outside Israel, of the Palestinian citizens of Israel, often regarded in the Arab world as having lost authenticity and moral standing through their ongoing and seemingly successful liaison with Israel and Israelis. Alternatively, it could signify an all-encompassing Arab unity against Israel. The Arab world is divided in two: all Arabs who live outside Israel, and those who live inside. A third option is to look at *Arab* in its less politicised context, meaning simply 'people', sometimes restricted to a residential group. Another label for the Palestinian citizens of Israel sometimes employed by Palestinians

in the territories is '*Arab al-Shamenet* (Grossman 1992:32). *Shamenet* is the Hebrew word for cream, suggesting that this segment of the Palestinian people has had an easy, cushioned life under Israel and its spoils, while other Palestinians experienced cruel hardship.

28 A complex of seven cinema halls was inaugurated in Natzerat Illit in 1993, as part of a newly constructed mall. Its popularity, at least in the initial stages of its operation, has been limited.

29 Israeli women who had been swimming there before began avoiding these occasions, claiming they felt uneasy in the presence of 'so many Arab men undressing us with their eyes'.

3 To sell or not to sell

1 The idea conceived in 1990 by Palestinian activists to replay the *Exodus* scene by seeking entrance to Haifa harbour on board a ship of returnees is one graphic example of the way Palestinians generate a discourse of return which duplicates its Zionist equivalent.

2 '*Lo lebitsū'a be'ezor pitūah Alef ūveit.*'

3 Officially handled by the Custodian of Properties of Absentees (*Haapotropūs al nikhsey nifkadim*), rights in properties which had previously belonged to Palestinians were often transferred to other agencies, for public use or, as in the case of Amidar, for residential use by immigrants.

4 These derelict and largely empty blocks were the chief housing reserve at the eve of the 1990–1901 wave of immigration from the crumbling Soviet Union. A hasty though most efficient renovation operation organized by the municipality had hundreds of rundown empty apartments rapidly prepared and made available to immigrants.

5 The notion that 'a strong Israel is essential for the security of Jews wherever they are' is a familiar rhetoric in Israeli public life. The involvement of the IDF in the mass transport of Jews from the Yemen in 1949–1950, from Ethiopia in 1991, or the role it played in the freeing of the Air France passengers held hostage in Entebbe, Uganda, in 1976, as congruent with the popular perception of the IDF as the army of the Jewish people.

6 See Lissak and Kimmerling (1984); Horowitz and Kimmerling (1974); Ben-Ari (1989:383–90); Lieblich (1987:10–14).

7 There are of course other examples within Zionism of pragmatic politics turned ideology. The very question of a territory to host the future Jewish homeland – a fundamental issue which was pending for the best part of a decade after Herzl's first Zionist congress of 1897 – is one example. Locations such as Uganda (see Heyman 1970) or the Northern Sinai were considered as feasible options. Only later did Zion/Palestine/Eretz-Yisrael emerge as an integral, obligatory and central ingredient for every ideological stream within the Jewish and Zionist world.

8 The ritual in which Israeli school children give weekly petty-cash donations to the 'blue box' of *Keren Hayesod* for the purpose of 'redeeming the land' is one graphic illustration of many.

9 The 800 or so Palestinian households in Natzerat Illit include approximately 500 flats bought from Israelis and 200 more rented from them (the rest being

residences built by Palestinians on privately owned land). 500 flats purchased at $20,000 each represent over a decade some $10 million. 200 rented properties at $70 a month represent $168,000 per annum, or $1.68 million for the decade (assuming the number of rented apartments was initially high in proportion, keeping a constant of approximately 200 rentals annually throughout the decade). Rates for all 800 Palestinian households, at about $400 per annum each, represent $320,000 per annum for the second half of the decade, and approximately half that annual sum for the first half of the decade – a total of $2.4 million over the decade. The grand total of income generated by Palestinians buying, renting and paying rates alone is thus $14.08 million.

10 The emphasis on action rather than rhetoric is clearly represented in two further idioms – *ūvdot bashetah* (literally facts on the ground, normally pertaining to settlement or other forms of physical presence); and *bitsū'ist* (literally 'actionist'), meaning someone with a proven record of efficient creation of *ūvdot bashetah*.

11 The PLU versus PLO dichotomy is my own application into this context of idioms I first encountered amongst middle-class British Jews who used it to distinguish persons who were Jewish ('PLU') from all others. A pun based on the similarities in English between the two idioms, it cannot feature as such as part of Hebrew discourse.

4 Differentiated space

1 Nazareth, for example, has very few estate agents. Palestinians I spoke with were often suspicious not only of practitioners, but also of those who turn to them as clients. The implication was that proper transactions should take place between people who know each other well, preferably between kin.

2 *Moshavim* are rural settlements which resemble villages, with individuals owning at least some of the means of production. Using publicly owned land, however, they are by definition part of the national settlement effort. They broadly fall into two categories – *moshavim shitufiyim* where means of production are held as common property, and *moshavey ovdim* where only marketing and purchases are done collectively.

3 The use of the term herewith is interchangeable with settlement (*sic*).

5 The limits of liberal education

1 See for example the testimony of 'Abd-al-Wahab Darawsha (Rabinowitz 1988) regarding the daily hike to school from Iksal to Nazareth.

2 At the beginning of each academic year school principals in Nazareth list those students who are residents of Natzerat Illit. The lists are submitted to the education department at the council, which passes them on to the education department of Natzerat Illit. The Israeli officials then buy season tickets from the local bus company in the number required, pass them back to their opposite numbers in Nazareth, who distribute them to the children through the schools. This is one of the few channels of cooperation between the education departments of the two towns, or, for that matter, between the two municipalities in general.

3 Performance of Palestinian students in Israeli universities depends a lot on

proficiency in Hebrew, the idiom of instruction. Palestinians who attend Israeli secondary schools thus have a meaningful advantage on those who don't.

4 Marriages between Israeli men and Palestinian women are rare in Israel, with Natzerat Illit no exception. I estimate the number of mixed couples in Natzerat Illit – all of them Palestinian men and Israeli women – to be between five and ten.

5 It carried on as an all-Israeli school for a number of years, then was phased out until its final dissolution in 1987 – not least because of dwindling demand in an aging part of town. In the late 1980s the building was serving as headquarters for the regional fire brigade.

6 The two Israeli head-teachers in the nursery schools established for Palestinian toddlers in 1980 in the northern part of town have since been replaced by Palestinian teachers.

7 Likewise, as Michael Herzfeld pointed out (personal communication, 1995) Greeks pay praise Turkish food (but little else), Europeans pay tribute to Egyptian hospitality etc.

8 Nursery school staff are not allowed by law to collect and manage such funds, and must have a voluntary committee of parents to manage them.

9 Dates for holidays in Israel are determined by the Jewish calendar, and thus may shift along the western calendar from year to year.

10 Natzerat Illit, like most communities in Israel, has at least one other public event staged in the late afternoon of Remembrance Day. Held near the main memorial for residents of the town who had been killed in wars, it is a smaller, more solemn event, most often attended by the families of fallen men.

11 For an exposition of the centrality of the idiom of blood for states and nations see Herzfeld 1993:23–5.

12 In 1988–1989 only five of the thirty-five children attending Na'ila's nursery were Muslim.

6 Reflexivity and liberalism

1 This approach has been a feature of parties who lean on votes cast by Israel's Palestinian citizens in Israeli since the 1950s such as the Israeli communist party and, in the 1980s, the Progressive List for Peace. (See Rekhes 1986; R. Cohen 1990:112; Reiter and Aharoni 1992:17–18.)

2 A session organized by the American Ethnological Society as part of the American Anthropological Association annual convention on 20 November 1993, entitled 'Twice Strangers: Jewish Fieldworkers in the Christian West' was dedicated to dilemmas of Jewish ethnographers doing field work in Catholic communities such as Spain, Mexico, Peru and Poland. Some of the researchers were preoccupied with being exposed, as Jewish persons, to a rural community which held the Jews responsible for the death of Jesus. Some of the contributions to the session carried reminders of my own situation in Natzerat Illit. (see Behar 1993; Friedlander 1993; Kugelmass 1993; Orlove 1993.)

3 A selection of anthropological works favouring reflexivity includes Rabinow (1977); Clifford and Marcus (1986); Marcus and Fisher (1986) Crapanzano (1987); Clifford (1988); Rosaldo (1989).

4 Works in this vein include Abu-Lughod (1986); Dominguez (1989); Lavie (1990); Ben-Ari (1989); Swedenburg (1989); Shokeid (1992); Kunda (1992).

5 Works critical of this trend in anthropology include Sangren (1988); Roth (1989) and, in a milder tone, Tedlock (1991).
6 An incomplete list includes Rosenfeld (1958, 1964, 1968); Marx (1967); Landau (1969, 1993); Peres (1970); Kressel (1976); Ginat (1975, 1982); Semyonov and Lewin-Epstein (1987); Morris (1987); Smooha (1988, 1989a, 1992); Rekhes (1986, 1993); Cohen R. (1990); Reiter and Aharoni (1992).

7 Hospitality and the engendering of space

1 The village of Saffuriya, some 8 kilometres west of Nazareth, was demolished by the IDF in 1948. Many of its inhabitants initially fled to Lebanon, their land consequently seized by the state and allocated to a new *moshav*, Tsipory, situated in and around the ruins. A considerable proportion of ex-Saffuriates and their descendants now live in Nazareth, in a neighbourhood called Saffurya.
2 In retrospect some of these assaults are better analyzed as attempts by local Palestinians to protect their rights in conveyance.
3 The construction of a new central bus station in the southern part of Natzerat Illit in the early 1990s has brought about changes in routes. Before, with no central bus station, the Haifa bus, like other intercity lines originating in Natzerat Illit, picked up passengers all over Natzerat Illit before heading to Nazareth and Haifa.
4 The intercity buses which run from Natzerat Illit through Nazareth do not set passengers down in Nazareth. Passengers who want to go from Natzerat Illit to Nazareth must use the local lines.
5 Since none of the bus lines serve al-Kūrūm, the issue of crossing over from 'Israeli' to 'Palestinian' turf within Natzerat Illit does not arise.
6 Works cited by Abu-Lughod have been supplemented since with studies such as Scott (1990); Taussig (1990) on The Americas; Kelly (1991) and Kaplan and Kelly (1994) on Fiji; Comaroff and Comaroff (1991) on South Africa; and Peteet (1994) on Palestinians. The University of Chicago Press and *American Ethnologist* have been particularly instrumental in carrying the debate (note the references cited).
7 For a discussion of Gramsci's eurocentric skew see Kaplan and Kelly (1994:126–7).

8 Risk, rationality and trust.

1 Following the 1990 season *Hapoel Natzerat Illit* was promoted to the third division. In 1991 it competed for promotion to the second, eventually losing by a narrow margin. Playing in the third division until 1995, when it was demoted to the fourth, HNI remains Natzerat Illit's only competitive basketball team, and one of the town's chief sporting representatives.
2 Competitive sport in Israel is controlled by politically oriented sports federations. *Hapoel* is the biggest federation. Others are *Maccabbi* (historically affiliated with the liberal party, now part of the-right wing Likud coalition); *Betar*, affiliated with the right-wing party *Ḥerut*, and *Elitzūr*, associated with the national religious party *Mafdal*.
3 Migdal Haemek is an Israeli new town established approximately 6 kilometres south west of Natzerat Illit, on the site of the large Palestinian village Mjaidal, destroyed in 1948 and reduced to rubble shortly after.

 4 Investigations in Britain and abroad have since established unequivocally that the PLO was not involved in either planning or executing the operation.

 5 Most sports in Israel are played in seasons which correspond with the academic calendar, beginning in September or October and ending in May or June. Summer months are used for rest, regrouping and preparations for the coming season.

 6 Palestinian coaches have not ascended to significant heights in any of Israel's main sporting establishments. Two outstanding examples are the rather marginal sports of weightlifting and boxing, which are considerably more popular amongst Palestinians than they are amongst Israelis, and where Palestinian coaches and managers have made their mark. The head coach of the Israeli national team in 1991, for example, was a Palestinian.

 7 Riziq's proficiency in the production of such parlance was probably acquired during his academic training at Israel's main sports academy, the Wingate Institute (named after the British Colonel Charles Ord Wingate). The institute trains students to use curt, military-like speech when issuing exercise demands to trainees and students.

 8 Although this conversation, like all others he ever had with players of HNI, was conducted in Hebrew, the term sick-note was said in English. Although Israeli army jargon still retains a few British Army phrases (e.g. pass, afterduty), sick-note is not one of them. The player seemed to take a while to realize the meaning.

 9 See Horowitz and Kimmerling (1974); Katriel (1986:30–1); Ben-Ari (1989); Helman (1993); Kimmerling (1993).

10 Riziq coached another team – a youth team in Nazareth – on alternate nights.

11 In April 1995, when I read the final draft of this chapter to Ra'id, he was even more emphatic. He said: 'When I began coaching at the YMCA, it was a different world, in terms of my demand and my insistence that I get my way. One time, when I discovered that management had failed to provide the players with pen and paper to take down my brief, I made a fuss and got what I had asked for. I tell you, I was as harsh with management as I was with the players.'

12 The nationwide crisis of the *Hapoel* sports federation in the late 1980s brought about a similar solution in many branches. Locally organized voluntary associations were often invited to take over the responsibility for senior competitive teams, sometimes even of youth activities. Relinquishing some control over potential foci of public interest, local workers' councils thus nevertheless freed themselves from crippling debts and a considerable workload for their officials.

13 Since Sa'adawi is presently not affiliated with KHK, where Brakha and her family are insured, her visit to him had to be paid for privately. The selection of specialists in Natzerat Illit being as poor as it is, her alternatives of Israeli specialists would have had to be further afield, in Haifa or Afula.

14 Hughes (1945) goes on to indicate that the common solution in the USA seems to be voluntary segregation by which, for example, women lawyers represent women clients and black personnel managers 'act only in reference to negro employees' (Hughes 1945:355).

15 See Peres and Levy (1969); Peres (1971); Robin (1972); Levy and Guttmann (1976); Zemach (1980); Bizman and Amir (1982); Smooha (1988, 1989a, 1992).

16 These findings, with their emphasis on intention rather than attributes, suggest

certain modification of Said's assertion that the Zionist view of Palestinians – which he sees as an amplification of the Western view of the orient – portrays the Palestinians as equally vicious and stupid (Said 1980:26).

17 A headline in *Yediot Aharonot* of 16 July 1991, which deals with an assault by a Palestinian, reads: 'He ran with the axe, waved it about and assaulted as if possessed by a craze.' Such characterizations are common place in cases of Palestinians attacking Israelis, but hardly feature when Israelis use violence against Palestinians.

18 There are of course cultural and historical variations. An impressionistic view of mainstream Israel, for example, would suggest that physicians, judges, professional soldiers and civil engineers enjoy a fair amount of popular trust. Advocates, clergymen, academics and media people, on the other hand, are not as fortunate.

19 Theoretical discussions of the main issues related to trust can be found in Blau (1964, 1968); Deutch (1962); Garfinkel (1963, 1967); Henslin (1972); Holzner (1973); Luhmann (1979, 1988), Barber (1983); Lewis and Weigart (1985a, 1985b); Zucker (1986); Shapiro (1987); Roniger (1990).

20 For non-Arabic speakers such as HNI players, Ra'id Riziq's real name is somewhat awkward to grasp: both parts could denote either a family name or a forename. In fact most players were unclear as to which was what. Some addressed him and referred to him only by his surname Riziq, thinking they were using his given name.

9 In search of genuine representation: the independent list

1 See Shim'oni (1947:176–7); Cohen (1965); Rosenfeld (1968:248); Lustick (1980:199–207); Kimmerling and Migdal (1993:18–20).

2 See Marx (1967); Baer (1980); R. Cohen (1990:91–6); Benziman and Mansour (1992:184).

3 The 1992 parliamentary elections saw many Palestinians regress to the old pattern of electoral support of Zionist parties in return for promises of tangible benefits – more like the politics of 'doing'. The present discussion, however, looks more closely at trends and processes characterizing the earlier phase, in which Palestinian consciousness and the politics of 'being' seemed to play a more decisive role, a trend which resurfaced in the 1996 elections.

4 For an earlier critique of this approach see Smooha (1989a:62–3).

5 Abu-Lughod (1989:41) and Comaroff (1985) offer critiques of this conventional dichotomy.

6 Writers on patronage include Peters (1968); Boissevain (1977); Rassam (1977); Littlewood (1981); Zuckerman (1977:65). For the Palestinian case see Rosenfeld (1968:248); Asad (1975:252–6); Lustick (1980:199–207).

7 For a detailed account of the arithmetics of extrapolation see pp. 152–3.

8 Returns in polling booth 1 included, in the 1983 local elections, an unprecedented 100 per cent of actual Palestinian votes for Labour in both the council and the mayorship votes.

9 The 1984 parliamentary election saw Labour securing only 14.1 per cent of Palestinian votes in polling booth 1 – its lowest return ever and way below its second worst result (26.7 per cent in 1988). Labour's previous performance in

polling booth 1 had been 66.4 per cent of the Palestinian vote in 1981 and 57.5 per cent in 1977 – substantially above its average return in Palestinian communities countrywide.

10 Like Ra'id Riziq, Salim Khūri, to whom I read a transliteration of this chapter, agreed to appear here in his real name. The names of other persons mentioned in this chapter have been disguised.

11 My survey of 1989 indicates that more than 50 per cent of Palestinians occupying apartments in the mixed parts of Natzerat Illit plan to move out of the town as soon as they can afford buying or building in adjacent Nazareth or elsewhere in a Palestinian community. In contrast, only 8.8 per cent of Palestinians living in private houses in Natzerat Illit – most of them naturally in al-Kūrūm – hope to move away.

12 *Al-Nasira al-'Asliya* is Arabic for 'original' Nazareth. Known simply as *al-Nasira*, (colloquially as *Nasira*) the Palestinian town is hardly ever referred to as *al-Nasira al-Asliya*. In the present context the term was probably invoked in juxtaposition to *al-Nasira al-'Ulya* – Arabic for Natzerat Illit ('upper Nazareth').

13 A similar and more dramatic reference to Shylock's speech was made in *Avanti Popolo*, an Israeli feature film produced in the late 1980s. It features two Egyptian soldiers fleeing in the Sinai desert during or immediately after the 1967 war, who are caught by Israeli soldiers. The Egyptians are thirsty and hungry, and beg the Israeli soldiers for their lives and for a drink of water. In the course of their petition one of them quotes Shylock's dramatic speech about his essential humanity despite being a Jew. This creates a comic reversal of roles, whereby an Egyptian plays the diaspora Jew begging to be treated fairly, while Israeli Jews are in the powerful position of being appealed to. An added twist is that the Israelis are totally ignorant of the text they hear or of its original meaning in Shakespeare's work.

14 While seats on local councils are contested by lists of candidates – often representing established political parties or associated with them – mayorships are contested by individuals. Votes for both contests are cast at the polling booth on the same occasion.

15 The intended joke was based on the unlikely proposition that a list of candidates purporting to represent the Palestinian residents should be identified in any way with *Kach*, the racist party headed at the time by the late Meir Kahana, which advocates expulsion of all Palestinians from the Jewish state.

16 Al Haj and Rosenfeld specify Shafa'amar since 1978 Ṭamra in 1980, Nazareth since 1976 and Ūm al-Faḥim since 1978 as outstanding instances in which national issues were introduced to local arenas (Al-Haj and Rosenfeld 1990:73–86). The 1993 local election campaign saw national and international politics introduced to many towns and villages. Many candidates took great pains to demonstrate their loyalty to and close relationship with PLO headquarters in Tunis. Photographs of candidates with Yassir Arafat and his aides in Tunis became common currency in posters on billboards during the campaign.

17 That Palestinians are practically non-participants in coalition politics in Israel, despite the official one person one vote system, was illustrated in March 1990,

July 1993 and November 1993. On all three occasions the Labour party declined to form ruling coalitions with members of parties where popular support is based on Palestinians.

18 The 807 votes his list received were enough to secure his place on the local council for the second time running.

19 Linda Layne's account of the electoral behaviour of the Balga Bedouin in the Jordanian Parliamentary by-elections of 1984 (1987) presents an interesting contrast. Unlike the Palestinians in Israel and, for that matter, in Jordan, the Bedouins in Jordan are comfortably integrated into the state and its institutions. This emancipates them from the need to mobilize around their Bedouin identity and tribal leaders, in turn enabling them to avoid 'tribalism' in their electoral performance. This, Layne argues, was demonstrated in the regional by-elections of 1984, in which the Bedouins voted more or less like other parts of the population. This refuted apprehensions by metropolitan Jordanians that the Bedouins' tribal allegiances as tribesmen might endanger the state and its cohesion.

20 Palestinian votes for Zionist parties, which was at an all-time low in 1988 with 42 per cent, rose to approximately 53 per cent in 1992.

10 Conclusion

1 Between 1953 and 1972 Emil Habibi served as a member of Knesset for the communist party.

2 That is, a Palestinian state which does not prove to be a protégé state, a kind of Palestinian Bantustan under the military and economic mantle of Israel.

3 The headway made by the communist-led DFP and by DAP by lending the Labour party their unconditional coalition support during 1992–1996, a critical period for the process of negotiations between Israel and the Palestinians, is a perfect example of such eventualities.

References

Abu-Lughod, Lila (1986) *Veiled Sentiments.* Berkeley: University of California Press
  (1989) The Romance of Resistance: Tracing Transformations of Power through Bedouin Women. *American Ethnologist* vol. 17:41–55
Al-Haj, Majid (1986) Adjustment Patterns of the Arab Internal Refugees in Israel. *International Migration* vol. 24, no. 3:651–74
Al-Haj, Majid and Henry Rosenfeld, (1990) *Arab Local Government in Israel.* Givat Haviva: The Institute of Arab Studies (in Hebrew)
Al Hamishmar (Daily paper) (1983) We Herewith Pledge not to Sell an Apartment to any Member of the Minorities. By Omri Mishor. 17 March:3 (in Hebrew)
  (1984) Natzerat Illit – the Real Side of the Coin. By Omri Mishori. 11 January:3–4 (in Hebrew)
Anderson, Benedict (1983) *Imagined Communities.* London: Verso
Anzaldua, Gloria (1987) *Borderlands La Frontera: The New Mestiza.* San Francisco: Spinsters/Aunt Lute Books
Asad, Talal (1975) Anthropological Texts and Ideological Problems: An Analysis of Cohen on Arab villages in Israel. *Economy and Society* vol. 4:251–81
Appadurai, Arjun (1988) Introduction: Place and Voice in Anthropological Theory. *Cultural Anthropology* vol. 3:16–20
Baer, Gideon (1980) The Office and Function of the Village Mukhtar, in Yoel S. Migdal (ed.) *Palestinian Society and Politics.* Princeton, NJ: Princeton University Press
Barber, B. (1983) *The Logic and Limits of Trust.* New Brunswick, NJ: Rutgers University Press
Bar-Gal, Y. (1986) Penetration and colonization of Palestinians in Natzerat Illit – Early Evidence, in A. Sofer (ed.) *Residential and Internal Migration Patterns among the Palestinians of Israel.* Haifa, University of Haifa (in Hebrew)
Barrett, Stanley (1984) *The Rebirth of Anthropological Theory.* Toronto: Toronto University Press
Befu, H. (1977) Social Exchange. *Annual Review of Anthropology* vol. 6:255–281
Behar, Ruth (1993) What the Anthropologist Can't Tell. Paper presented at the American Ethnological invited session on Twice Strangers: Jewish Fieldworkers in the Christian West. American Anthropological Association annual meeting, Washington DC 20 November 1993

Beinin, J. (1990) *Was the Red Flag Flying There? Marxist Politics and the Arab-Israeli Conflict in Egypt and Israel, 1948–1965*. Berkeley, CA: California University Press

Ben-Ari, Eyal (1989) Masks and Soldiering: The Israeli Army and the Palestinian Uprising. *Cultural Anthropology* vol. 4 no. 4:371–89

Ben-Ari, Eyal and Yoram Bilu (1987) Saints' Sanctuaries in Israeli Development Towns: On a Mechanism of Urban Transformation. *Urban Anthropology* vol. 16, no. 2:243–72

Ben-Arieh, Yehoshua and Miram Oren (1983) The Settlements of Galilee at the Eve of the Zionist Settlement Project, in Shemueli, Sofer and Keliot (eds.) *The Lands of Galilee* vol. I:315–52

Ben-Artzi, Y. and M. Shoshani, (1986) The Palestinians of Haifa 1972–1983: Demographic and Spatial Changes, in A. Sofer (ed.) *Residential and Internal Migration Patterns among Palestinians of Israel*. Haifa: University of Haifa

Ben-Porat, Yoram (1966) *The Arab Labour Force in Israel*. Jerusalem: The Maurice Falk Institute

Ben-Zadok, E. and G. Goldberg (1984) Voting patterns of Oriental Jews in Development Towns. *Jerusalem Quarterly* vol. 32:16– 27

Benziman, Uzi and Attallah Mansour (1992) *Subtenants*. Jerusalem: Keter (in Hebrew)

Betts, R.B. (1979) *Christians in the Arab East*. London: SPCK

Bishara, Azmi (1992) Between Place and Space. *Studio*, no. 37:6–9 (in Hebrew)
    (1993) On the question of the Palestinian Minority in Israel. *Teorya Uvikoret* vol. 1 no. 3:7–20

Bizman, A., and Yehuda Amir (1982) Mutual perceptions of Arabs and Jews in Israel. *Journal of Cross-Cultural Psychology* vol. 13:461–9

Blau, P.M. (1964) *Exchange and Power in Social Life*. New York: Wiley
    (1968) Social Exchange, in *International Encyclopedia of the Social Sciences* vol. VII, New York: Macmillan and Free Press

Bloch, Maurice, and Jonathan Perry (1989) Introduction to *Money and the Morality of Exchange*. Cambridge: Cambridge University Press

Boissevain, J. (1977) When the Saints Go Marching Out: Reflections on the Decline of Patronage in Malta, in E. Gellner, and J. Waterbury (eds.) *Patrons and Clients*. London: Duckworth

Bonacich, Edna (1980) *The Economic Basis of Ethnic Solidarity*. Berkeley: University of California Press

Bourdieu, Pierre (1977) *Outline of a Theory of Practice*. Cambridge: Cambridge University Press
    (1977) The Economics of Linguistic Exchange. *Social Sciences Information* no. 16:645–68

Bourdieu, P. and J. C. Passeron (1977) *Reproduction in Education, Society and Culture*. London: Sage

Boyarin, Jonathan (1992) Ruins on the Way to Jerusalem. *Studio* vol 37:10–11 (in Hebrew)

Boyarin, Daniel, and Jonathan Boyarin (1993) Diaspora: Generational Ground of Jewish Identity. *Critical Inquiry* vol. 19(4):693–725

Brogger, Jan (n.d.) *Pre-Bureaucratic Europeans: A Study of a Portuguese Fishing Community*. Oslo: Norwegian University Press

Campbell, A. and H. Schuman (1968) *Racial Attitudes in Fifteen American Cities*. New York: Praeger

Clifford, James (1988) *The Predicament of Culture*. Cambridge, MA: Harvard University Press

(1994) Diasporas. *Cultural Anthropology* vol.9 no. 3:302–38

Clifford, James and George E. Marcus (1986) *Writing Culture: The Poetics and Politics of Ethnography*. Berkeley: University of California Press

Cohen, Abner (1965) *Arab Border Villages in Israel: a Study of Continuity and Change in Social Organization*. Manchester: Manchester University Press

Cohen, Adir (1987) *The Image of the Arab in Israeli Children's Literature*. Haifa: University of Haifa (in Hebrew)

Cohen, E.G. (1982) Expectation States and Interracial Interaction in School Settings. *Annual Review of Sociology* vol. 6:479–500

(1984) The Desegregated School: Problems in Status, Power and Interethnic Climate, in N. Miller and M. B. Brewer (eds.) *Groups in Contact*. London: Academic Press

Cohen, Eric (1995) Israel as a Post-Zionist Society *Israel Affairs* vol. 1, no. 3:203–14

Cohen, Ra'anan (1985) *Processes in the Political Organization and Voting Patterns of Arabs in Israel 1973–1984*. MA Thesis, Tel-Aviv University (in Hebrew)

(1990) *Complexity of Loyalties. Society and Politics: the Arab Sector in Israel*. Tel-Aviv: Am-Oved (in Hebrew)

Comaroff, Jean (1985) *Body of Power, Spirit of Resistance*. Chicago: Chicago University Press

Comaroff, Jean, and John Comaroff (1991) *Of Revelation and Revolution: Christianity, Colonialism and Consciousness in South Africa* vol. 1. Chicago: University of Chicago Press

Crapanzano, Vincent (1987) Editorial. *Cultural Anthropology* vol. 2 (2):179–89

Davar (Daily paper) (1982) A Storm in a Cup of Dirty Water. By Yitzhak Meridor and Muhamad Halaila. 22 October:19 (in Hebrew)

Dawes, R.M (1980) Social dilemmas. *Annual Review of Psychology* vol. 31:169–93

Deutch, M. (1962) Cooperation and trust: some theoretical notes, in *Nebraska Symposium on Motivation*. Lincoln: University of Nebraska Press

Dominguez, Virginia (1989) *People as Subject, People as Object*. Madison: Wisconsin University Press

Ekeh, P. (1974) *Social Exchange Theory, The Two Traditions*. Cambridge, MA: Harvard University Press

Elliot, W.A. (1986) *Us and Them: a Study of Group Consciousness*. Aberdeen: Aberdeen University Press

Eyal, Gil (1993) Between East and West: the Discourse of 'The Arab Village' in Israel. *Theory and Criticism* no. 3:39–56 (in Hebrew)

Falah, Ghazi (1991) Israeli Judaization Policy in Galilee. *Journal of Palestine Studies* vol. 20 no. 4:69–85

Festinger, Leon (1957) *A Theory of Cognitive Dissonance*. Stanford, CA: Stanford University Press

Foucault, Michel (1972) *The Archaeology of Knowledge.* London: Tavistock
    (1978) *The History of Sexuality* vol. I: An Introduction. New York: Random
    House
    (1980) *Power/Knowledge.* Colin Gordon (ed.) New York: Pantheon
Friedlander, Judith N. (1993) Christians, Jews, the Marranos and Me: In Mexico
    and Lithuania. Paper presented at the American Ethnological invited session
    on Twice Strangers: Jewish Fieldworkers in the Christian West. American
    Anthropological Association annual meeting, Washington DC 20 November
    1993
Gambetta, Diego (1988) Mafia: the Price of Distrust, in D. Gambetta (ed.) *Trust.*
    Cambridge: Cambridge University Press
GAP (1987) (Group for the Advancement of Psychiatry, Committee on
    International Relations). *Us and Them: the Psychology of Ethnonationals.*
    New York: Brunner-Mazel
Garbuz, Y. (1973) Natzerat Illit – Socio-Economic Development. *Shikun Uvniya*
    vol. 38 (in Hebrew)
Garfinkel, H. (1963) A Conception of, and Experiments With 'Trust' as a
    Condition of Stable Concerted Actions, in O.J. Harvey. (ed.) *Motivation and
    Social Interaction: Cognitive Determinants.* New York: Ronald
    (1967) *Studies in Ethnomethodology.* Englewood Cliffs, NJ: Prentice-Hall
Gehrke, N. J. (1979) Rituals of the Hidden Curriculum in Y. Yamomoto (ed.)
    Children in Time and Space. New York: Teachers College Press:103–27
Geertz, Clifford (1973) *The Interpretation of Culture.* New York: Basic Books
Gilsenan, M. (1985) Law, Arbitrariness and the Power of the Lords of North
    Lebanon. *History and Anthropology* vol. 1:381–400. Harwood Academic
    Publishers, UK
Ginat, Yosef (1975) *A Rural Arab Community in Israel - Marriage Patterns and
    Women's Status.* PhD dissertation, University of Utah, Salt Lake City
    (1982) *Women in Muslim Rural Society – Status and Role in Family and
    Community.* New Brunswick, NJ: Transaction Books
Goode, William (1969) The Theoretical Limits of Professionalism, in A. Etzioni,
    (ed.) *The Semi-Professions and their Organizations.* New York: Free Press
Graicer, Iris (1992) Spatial Integration of Arab Migrants in a Jewish New Town.
    Professional Geographer vol. 44, no. 1:45– 56
Gramsci, Antonio (1971) *Selections from the Prison Notebooks of Antonio
    Gramsci.* London: Lawrence and Wishart
Grinberg, Lev (1991) *Split Corporatism in Israel.* Albany: State University of New
    York Press
Grossman, David (1992) *Present Absentees.* Tel-Aviv: Hakibbutz Hameukhad (in
    Hebrew)
Gupta, Akhil and James Ferguson (1992) Beyond 'Culture': Space, Identity and
    the Politics of Difference. *Cultural Anthroplogy* vol. 7 no. 1:6–23
Gurr, T. (1993) *Minorities at Risk.* American Institute of Peace Studies,
    Washington DC
Haaretz (Daily paper) (1978) Natzerat Illit: in the Shadow of the Coup, by
    Attlalah Mansour, 17 September:10 (in Hebrew)

(1981) New Natzerat Comes of Age, by Attallah Mansour, 9 November:10 (in Hebrew)

(1983) Back to the Ghettoes, by Attallah Mansour, 28 August:9 (in Hebrew)

(1991) Piece by Yehudit Greenblat reporting statements in a public meeting the previous day in Tel-Aviv, 17 February (in Hebrew)

Ḥabibi, Emil (1974) *The Miraculous Chronicle of the Disappearance of Sa'id Abū A-Nakhas Al Mutashail.* Haifa: Arabesque (Arabic). (Hebrew version: *The Opsimist* Haifa: Mifras, 1984)

Haidar, Aziz (1987) *The Palestinians in Israel Social Science Writings.* Washington DC: International Center for Research and Public Policy

Handelman, Don (1994) Conflicts Between Ethnicity and Citizenship in Israel. *Poetics Today* vol. 15, no. 4

Handelman, Don and Lea Shamgar-Handelman (1990) Holiday Celebrations in Israeli Kindergartens, in Don Handelman, *Models and Mirrors: Towards an Anthropology of Public Events.* Cambridge: Cambridge University Press

Harrari, Y. (1974) *The Arabs in Israel, 1973: Facts and Figures.* Giv'at Haviva: Centre for Arab Studies

Hart, Keith (1988) Kinship, Contract and Trust: The Economic Organization of Migrants in an African City Slum, in D. Gambetta (ed.) *Trust.* Cambridge: Cambridge University Press

Helman, Sarit (1993) Conscientious Objection to Military Service as an Attempt to Redefine the Content of Citizenship. PhD dissertation, Hebrew University, Jerusalem

Henslin, J. (1972) What Makes for Trust?, in *Down to Earth Sociology.* New York: Free Press

Herzfeld, Michael (1993) *The Social Production of Indifference.* Chicago: University of Chicago Press

Heyman, M. (1970) (ed.) *The Uganda Controversy.* Jerusalem: The Institute for Zionist Research at Tel-Aviv University

Holzner, B. (1973) Sociological Reflections on Trust. *Humanities* vol. 9:333–45

Horowitz, Dan and Moshe Lissak, (1990) *Trouble in Utopia.* Tel-Aviv: Am Oved (in Hebrew)

Horowitz, Dan, and Baruch Kimmerling (1974) Some Social Implications of Military Service and Reserve System in Israel. *European Journal of Sociology* vol. 15 no. 2:262–76

Hotam (Weekly supplement of *Al Hamishmar*) (1982) 'Arabs Want to Takeover Natzerat Illit', by Omri Mishor. December 3:20–1 (in Hebrew)

(1984) Reuven Amiel Against MENA. 27 January:8–9 (in Hebrew)

Hughes, Everet C. (1945) Dilemmas and Contradictions of Status. *The American Journal of Sociology* vol. 50: 353–9

Illich, I. (1970) Schooling: the Ritual of Progress. *New York Review of Books* vol. 15 no. 10, 3 December:20–6

Jiryas, Sabri (1966) *The Arabs in Israel.* Haifa: Al-Itihad (in Hebrew)

Kana'na, Sharif (1976) *Socio-Cultural and Psychological Adjustment of the Arab Minority in Israel.* San Francisco: R. and E. Research Associates

Kapferer, J.L. (1981) Socialization and the Symbolic Order of the School. *Anthropology and Educational Quarterly* vol. 12, no. 4:258–74

Kapferer, Bruce (1988) *Legends of People, Myths of States: Violence, Intolerance, and Political Culture in Sri Lanka and Australia.* Washington, DC and London: Smithsonian Institute Press

Kaplan, Martha and John D. Kelly (1994) Rethinking Resistance: Dialogics of 'Disaffection' in Colonial Fiji. *American Ethnologist* vol. 21(1):123–51

Karilowsky, J. (1982) Two Types of Altruistic Behaviour: Doing Good to Feel Good or to Make the Other Feel Good, in V. Derlega and J. Grzelak (eds.) *Cooperation and Helping Behavior.* New York, Academic Press

Katriel, Tamar (1986) *Dugri.* Cambridge: Cambridge University Press

Katriel, Tamar and Aliza Shenhar (1990) Tower and Stockade: Dialogic Narration in Israeli Settlement Ethos. *The Quarterly Journal of Speech* vol. 76 no. 4:359–80

Kelly, John (1991) *A Politics of Virtue: Hinduism, Sexuality and Counter-Colonial Discourse in Fiji.* Chicago: Chicago University Press

Kerzer, David (1988) *Ritual, Politics, and Power.* New Haven, CT: Yale University Press

Khamaisi, Rasem (1989) *The Establishment of Strategic Planning Units in the Arab Towns of Nazareth and Um-al Fahim: A Feasibility Study.* Mimeographed report, submitted to Israel Joint Distribution Commitee, Jerusalem (in Hebrew)

Kimmerling Baruch (1977) Sovereignty, Ownership and Presence in the Israeli-Palestinian Territorial Conflict. The Case of Ikrit and Bir'im. *Comparative Political Studies* vol. 10 no. 2:155–76

(1983) *Zionism and Territory.* Berkeley: Institute of International Studies

(1992) Sociology, Ideology, and Nation-Building: the Palestinians and Their Meaning in Israeli Sociology. *American Sociological Review* vol. 57, August:1–15

(1993) Militarism in Israeli Society. *Teorya Uvikoret* 4:123–40

Kimmerling, Baruch and Yoel Migdal (1993) *Palestinians – the Making of a People.* New York: Free Press

Kipnis, Baruch, (1983) The Development of the Jewish Settlement in the Galilee, 1948–1980 in A. Shmueli, A. Sofer, and N. Keliot (eds.) *The Lands of Galilee.* Haifa: The Society for Applied Social Research, University of Haifa (in Hebrew)

Koenig, Israel (1976) Koenig Memorandum. Translated from *Al Hamishmar* in SWASIA vol. 3, no. 41, October 1976:1–8

Kressel, Gideon (1976) *Individuality and Tribalism: the Dynamics of an Israeli Bedouin Community in the Process of Urbanization.* Tel-Aviv: Hakibbutz Hameuchad (in Hebrew)

Kretzmer, David (1990) *The Legal Status of the Arabs in Israel.* Boulder, CO: Westview.

Kugelmass, Jack (1993) Surviving Poland: The Split Self. Paper presented at the American Ethnological invited session on Twice Strangers: Jewish Fieldworkers in the Christian West. American Anthropological Association annual meeting, Washington DC 20 November 1993

Kunda, Gideon (1992) The Test of Criticism: Ethnography and Cultural Critique in Israel. *Teorya Uvikoret* no. 2:7–24 (in Hebrew)

Lamdan, Mordechai and Avraham Ronen, (1983) Prehistory, in Galilee in A. Shmueli, N. Keliot and A. Sofer (eds.) *The Lands of Galilee* vol. 1. Haifa: Haifa University Press

Landau, Jacob (1969) *The Arabs in Israel: A Political Study.* New York: Oxford Universiy Press

  (1971) *The Arabs in Israel.* Tel-Aviv: Ministry of Defence Publishing

  (1993) *The Arab Minority in Israel,* 1969–1993. Tel-Aviv: Am oved (in Hebrew)

Lavie, Smadar (1990) *The Poetics of Military Occupation.* Berkeley: University of California Press

Layish, Aharon (1989) The Arabs of Israel – A Crisis of Identity. *Hamizrah Hahadash* vol. 23:1–9 (in Hebrew)

Layne, Linda (1987) Tribesmen as Citizens: 'Primordial Ties' and Democracy in Rural Jordan, in Linda Layne (ed.) *Elections in the Middle East.* Boulder, CO: Westview

Levy, S. and L. Guttmann (1976) *Values and Attitudes of Israeli Youth.* Jerusalem: Institute of Applied Social Research (in Hebrew)

Lewis, J.D. and A.J. Weigart (1985a) Trust as Social Reality. *Social Forces* vol. 63:967–85

  (1985b) Social Atomism, Holism, and Trust. *Sociological Quarterly* vol 26, no. 4:455–71

Lieblich, Amia (1987) *The Spring of Their Years.* Tel-Aviv: Schocken

Lijphardt, Arend (1977) *Democracy in Plural Societies.* New Haven, CT: Yale University Press

Lissak, Moshe and Baruch Kimmerling (1984) (eds.) *Military and Security.* Jerusalem: Hebrew University

Littlewood, P. (1981) Patrons or Bigshots? Paternalism and Clientile Welfare in Southern Italy. *Sociologica Ruralis* vol. 21,1:1– 18

Lorenz, E. (1988) Neither friends nor strangers: informal networks of subcontracting in French industry, in D. Gambetta (ed.) *Trust.* Cambridge: Cambridge University Press

Luhmann, N. (1979) *Trust and Power.* Chichester: Wiley.

  (1988) Familiarity, Confidence, Trust in Gambetta, D. (ed.) *Trust.* Cambridge: Cambridge University Press

Lustick, Ian (1980) *Arabs in the Jewish State.* Austin: University of Texas Press

  (1989) *The Political Road to Binationalism: Arabs in Jewish Politics,* in Peleg, Ilan, and Ofira Seliktar (eds.) *The Emergence of a Binational Israel: The Second Republic in the Making.* Boulder: Westview.

Maariv (Daily paper) (1983) We are not Wanted in Natzerat Illit. By Tehila Ofer. 18 November:26 (in Hebrew)

Malkki, Lisa (1992) National Geographic: The Rooting of Peoples and the Territorialization of National Identity Among Scholars and Refugees. *Cultural Anthropology* vol. 7, no. 1:24– 44

Mann, Michael (1970) The Social Cohesion of Liberal Democracy. *American Sociological Review* vol. 35 no. 3:423–39

(1973) *Consciousness and Action Among the Western Working Class.* London: Macmillan

Marcus, George E. and Michael M.J. Fisher (1986) *Anthropology as Cultural Critique: An Experimental Moment in the Human Sciences.* Chicago: University of Chicago Press

Mar'i, Sammy (1978) *Arab Education in Israel.* Syracuse, NY: Syracuse University Press

(1985) Arab Education in Israel: Pupils as Educators and Educators as Pupils. *Politika* 4:34–6. (in Hebrew).

Marx, Emmanuel (1967) *Bedouin of the Negev.* Manchester: Manchester University Press

Matras, J. (1973) Israel's New Front: The Urban Periphery, in M. Curtis and M.S. Chertoff (eds.) *Israel: Social Structure and Change* vol. 3, no.14. New Brunswick, NJ: Transaction

McLaren P. (1986) *Schooling as a Ritual Performance.* London: Routledge & Kegan Paul

Morris, Benny (1987) *The Birth of the Palestinian Refugee Problem, 1947–1949.* Cambridge: Cambridge University Press

(1994) *1948 And After.* Oxford: Oxford University Press

Nakhleh, Khalil (1973) Shifting Patterns of Conflict in Selected Arab Villages in Israel. PhD Dissertation, Bloomington, IN

Natzerat Illit (1980) *Department of Education – Facts and Figures 1979/1980.* Natzerat Illit: Municipality of Natzerat Illit (mimeographed report, in Hebrew)

(1987) *Sheloshim Shana Lenatzerat Illit.* (Booklet commemorating thirty years of Natzerat Illit.) Natzerat Illit: Municipality of Natzerat Illit (in Hebrew)

(1989) *Department of Education – Facts and Figures 1988/1989.* Natzerat Illit: Municipality of Natzerat Illit (mimeographed report, in Hebrew)

Oiliavin, J.A. and H.W. Charng (1990) Altruism: a Review of Recent Theory and Research. *Annual Review of Sociology,* vol. 16:27–65

Oppenheimer, F. (1913) *Die Siedlungsgenossenschaft.* Jena: Gustav Fischer

Oppenheimer Jonathan (1979) The Druze in Israel as Arabs and as Non-Arabs. *Mahbarot Lemehkar Ulvikoret* no.3:41–58

Orlove, Benjamin (1993) *Familiarization: Making Myself of Home, Making Myself in Peru.* Paper presented at the American Ethnological invited session on Twice Strangers: Jewish Fieldworkers in the Christian West. American Anthropological Association annual meeting, Washington DC 20 November 1993

Oz, Amos (1984) *My Michael.* London: Fontana. Original version (in Hebrew), 1968. Tel-Aviv: Am oved)

Palestinian Encyclopaedia (1980). Beirut: Centre of Palestine Studies (in Arabic)

Pappe, Ilan (1988) *Britain and the Arab-Israeli Conflict, 1948–51.* New York: St Martin's Press

(1994) *The Making of the Arab-Israeli Conflict.* London: Tauris

Parsons, Talcot (1939) The Professional and the Social Structure. *Social Forces,* vol. 17:457–67

(1969) *Politics and Social Structure.* New York: Free Press

Peled, Yoav (1992) Ethnic Democracy and the Legal Construction of Citizenship:

Arab Citizens of the Jewish State. *American Political Science Review* vol. 86, no. 2:432–43

Peled, Yoav and Yagil Levy (1993) The Break that Never Was: Israeli Sociology Reflected Through the Six-Day War. *Teorya Uvikoret* vol.1, no. 3:115–28 (in Hebrew)

Peres, Yochanan (1970) Modernization and Nationalism in the Identity of the Israeli Arabs. *Middle East Journal* vol. 24, no. 4:479–92

(1971) Ethnic Relations in Israel. *American Journal of Sociology* vol. 76, no 6:1021–47

Peres, Yochanan and Zipora Levy (1969) Jews and Arabs: ethnic group stereotypes in Israel. *Race* vol. 10, no. 4:479–92

Peteet, Julie (1991) *Gender In Crisis: Women and the Palestinian Resistance Movement.* New York: Columbia University Press

(1994) Male Gender and Rituals of Resistance in the Palestinian *Intifada*; a Cultural Politics of Violence. *American Ethnologist* vol. 21 (1):31–49

Peters, E. (1968) The Tied and the Free in J. Peristiany (ed.) *Contributions to Mediterranean Sociology.* The Hague

Portugali, Juval (1993) *Implicated Relations.* Dordrecht: Kluwer Academic Publishers

Rabinow, Paul (1977) *Reflections on Fieldwork in Morocco.* Berkeley: University of California Press

Rabinowitz, Dan (1988) Interview with 'Abd 'al-Wahab Darawsha, *Sevivot* vol. 21:125–155 (in Hebrew)

(1990) Relations Between Arabs and Jews in the Mixed Town of Natzerat Illit, Northern Israel. PhD Dissertation, Cambridge University

(1992a) In Favour of Semantics. *Haaretz* 12.5.1992 (op-ed) (in Hebrew)

(1992b) An Acre is an Acre is an Acre? Differentiated Attitudes to Social Space and Territory on the Jewish-Arab Urban Frontier in Israel. *Urban Anthropology* vol. 21, no. 1:67–89

(1992c) Trust and the Attribution of Rationality: Inverted Roles Amongst Palestinian Arabs and Jews in Israel. *Man* vol. 27, no. 3:517–37

(1993) Oriental Nostalgia: How the Palestinians Became 'Israel's Arabs'. *Teorya Uvikoret* no. 4:141– 52 (in Hebrew)

Rassam, A. (1977) Al Tabaiy'a – Power Patronage and Marginal Groups in Northern Iraq, in E. Gellner and J. Waterbury (eds.) *Patrons and Clients.* London: Duckworth

Raz-Krakotzkin, Amnon (1993) Exile within Sovereignty: Toward a Critique of the 'Negation of the Exile' in Israeli Culture. *Teorya Uvikoret* no. 4:23–55 (in Hebrew)

Regev, Motti (1993) *'Oud and Guitar: The Musical Culture of the Arabs in Israel.* Beit Berl: The Institute for Israeli Arab Studies (in Hebrew)

Reichman, S. and Shlomo Hasson (1984) A Cross-Cultural Diffusion of Colonization: From Posen to Palestine. *Annals of the Association of American Geographers* vol. 74, no. 1

Reiter, Yitzhak and Reuven Aharoni (1992) *The Political Life of Arabs in Israel.* Beit Berl: The Institute for Israeli Arab studies (in Hebrew)

Rekhes, Eli (1976) *Israel's Arabs after 1967: Accentuation of the Orientation*

Problem. Tel-Aviv: Shiloah Centre. Sekirot publications no. 45. Tel-Aviv: Shiloah Centre (in Hebrew)

(1979) The Israeli Arab Intelligentsia. *The Jerusalem Quarterly* vol. 11:51–69

(1986) Between Communism and Arab Nationalism: Rakah and the Arab Minority in Israel, 1965–1977. PhD dissertation, Tel-Aviv University (in Hebrew)

(1989) Israeli Arabs and the Arabs of the West Bank and Gaza Strip: Political Ties and National Identification. *Hamizraḥ Haḥadash* vol. 23:165–91 (in Hebrew)

(1993) *The Arab Minority in Israel: Between Communism and Arab Nationalism 1965–1991.* Tel-Aviv: Hakibbutz Hameukhad (in Hebrew)

Ricoeur, Paul (1969) *Le Conflit des Interpretations.* Paris: Editions du Seuil.

Ringel-Hofman, A. (1989) Adnan Comes to Live in Carmiel. *Yediot Aharonot* October 8. (in Hebrew)

Robin, E. (1972) Attitudes, Stereotypes and Prejudice Among Arabs and Jews in Israel. *New Outlook* vol. 15, no.9:3– 17

Rodman, Margaret (1992) Empowering Place: Multilocality and Multivocality. *American Anthropologist* vol. 94 no. 3:640–56

Roniger, Luis (1990) *Hierarchy and Trust in Modern Mexico and Brazil.* New York: Praeger

Roniger, Luis and Michael Feige (1992) From Pioneer to Freier: the Changing Models of Generalized Exchange in Israel. *Archives Européenes de Sociologie* vol. 23, no.2

Rosaldo, Renato (1988) Ideology, Place and People Without Culture. *Cultural Anthropology* vol. 3 no. 1:77–87

(1989) Imperialist Nostalgia. *Representations* vol. 26, (spring):107–22

Rosenfeld, Henry (1958) Processes of Structural Change Within the Arab Village Family. *American Anthropologist* vol. 60 no. 6:1127–39

(1964) From Peasantry to Wage Labour and Residual Peasantry: The Transformation of an Arab Village, in Manners, R. (ed.) *Process and Pattern in Culture.* Chicago: Aldine

(1968) The Contradictions Between Property, Kinship and Power, as Reflected in the Marriage System of an Arab village, in J.G. Peristiany (ed.) *Contributions to Mediterranean Sociology*

(1988) Nazareth and Upper Nazareth in the Political Economy of Israel, in J. Hofman (ed.) *Arab Jewish Relations in Israel.* Bristol, Indiana: Wyndham Hall Press

Rosenhak, Zeev (1993) New Developments in the Sociology of the Palestinian Citizens of Israel: An Analytical Review. Unpublished Manuscript (in Hebrew)

Roth, P.A. (1989) Ethnography Without Tears. *Current Anthropology* vol. 30, no. 5:555–69

Sa'adi, Ahmad (1992) Between State Ideology and Minority National Identity: Palestinians in Israel and in Israeli Social Science Research. *Review of Middle East Studies* vol. 5

Said, Edward (1978) *Orientalism.* New York: Pantheon

(1980) *The Question of Palestine.* London: Routledge & Kegan Paul

Sangren, P.S. (1988) Rhetoric and the Authority of Anthropology. *Current Anthropology* vol. 29, No.3:405–35

Sarsur, Sa'ad (1988) Development of the Arab Education System in Israel in *The Arab Citizens of Israel*. Jerusalem: Ministry of Education and the Van Leer Jerusalem Foundation (in Hebrew)

Schiefellin, Edward (1985) Performance and the Cultural Construction of Reality. *American Ethnologist* vol. 12:707–24

Schuman, H. (1982) Free Will and Determinism in Public Belief about Race, in N.R. Yetman and C.H Steele (eds.) *Majority and Minority – the Dynamics of Race and Ethnicity in American Life*. Boston: Allyn and Acon

Scott, James C. (1990) *Domination and the Arts of Resistance: Hidden Transcripts*. New Haven, CT: Yale University Press

Segev, Tom (1984) *1949 – The First Israelis*. Jerusalem: Domino Press (in Hebrew)

Semyonov, Moshe and Noah Lewin-Epstein (1987) *Hewers of Wood and Drawers of Water: Noncitizen Arabs in the Israeli Labour Market*. New York: ILR Press, Cornell Univeristy

Shafir, Gershon (1989) *Land, Labour, and the Israeli Palestinian Conflict, 1882–1920*. Cambridge: Cambridge University Press

Shalev, Michael (1992) *Labour and the Political Economy in Israel*. Oxford: Oxford University Press

Shapiro, S.P (1987) The social control of impersonal trust. *American Journal of Sociology* vol. 93, no. 3:623–58

Shemueli, Avshalom, Arnon Sofer and Nurit Keliot (1983) *The Lands of Galilee* vol.I Haifa: Haifa University (in Hebrew)

Shim'oni, Y. (1947) *The Arabs of The Land of Israel*. Tel Aviv: Am-Oved (in Hebrew)

Shipler, David (1987) *Arab and Jew*. New York: Times Books

Shlaim, Avi (1990) *The Politics of Partition*. Oxford: Oxford University Press

Shohat, Ella (1988) Sepharadim in Israel: Zionism from the Viewpoint of its Jewish Victims. *Social Text* nos. 19–20:1–35

  (1989) *Israeli Cinema: East/West and the Politics of Representation*. Austin: University of Texas Press

Shokeid Moshe (1982) The Ordeal of Honour: Local Politics Among Urban Palestinians, in M. Shoked and S. Deshen *Distant Relations*. New York: Praeger

  (1992) Exceptional Experiences in Everyday Life. *Cultural Anthropology* vol. 7, no. 2:232–43

Sibley, A. (1987) Racism and Settlement Policy: the State's Response to a Semi-Nomadic Minority, in P. Jackson (ed.) *Race and Racism* London: Allen & Unwin

Singer, M. (1971) *Shlomo Kaplansky: His Life and Work* vol. 1. Jerusalem: Zionist Library (in Hebrew)

Slater, P. (1976) Social Bases of Personality in L. Coser, and B. Rosenberg (eds.) *Sociological Theory*. New York: Macmillan

Smith, A. (1981) *The Ethnic Revival*. Cambridge: Cambridge University Press

Smith, Anthony D. (1988) The Myth of the 'Modern Nation' *Ethnic and Racial Studies* vol. 11, no. 1:1–26

Smooha, Sammy (1988) Jewish and Arab Ethnocentricism in Israel in J. Hofman (ed.) *Arab-Jewish Relations in Israel.* Bristol, IN: Wyndham Hall Press

(1989a) *Arabs and Jews in Israel* vol. 1. Boulder, CO: Westview

(1989b) The Arab Minority in Israel: Radicalization or Politicization? *Studies in Contemporary Jewry* vol. 5:59–88

(1990) Minority Status in an Ethnic Democracy: the Status of the Arab Minority in Israel. *Ethnic and Racial Studies* vol. 13, no. 3:389–413

(1992) *Arabs and Jews in Israel* vol. II: *Conflict and Change in a Mutual Intolerance.* Boulder, CO: Westview Press

Sofer, A. (1989) The Arabs in Israel: from Village to Metropolis, and What Next? *Hamizraḥ Heḥadash* vol. 32:97–105 (in Hebrew)

Spencer-Brown, G. (1971) *Laws of Form.* London: George Allen and Unwin

State of Israel (1984) *The 1983 Population and Housing Census.* Jerusalem: Central Bureau of Statistics

(1985) *The 1983 Population and Housing Census* vol. 5. Jerusalem: Central Bureau of Statistics

(1988) *Statistical Abstract of Israel.* Jerusalem: Central Bureau of Statistics

(1989) Voters roll (Natzerat Illit). Jerusalem: Central Elections Committee

(1990) *Statistical Abstract of Israel.* Jerusalem: Central Bureau of Statistics

(1993) *Statistical Abstract of Israel.* Jerusalem: Central Bureau of Statistics

Stendel, Ori (1982) Nazareth Past and Present. *Kardom* vol. 19:44–52 (in Hebrew)

(1992) *The Arabs in Israel. Between Hammer and Anvil.* Jerusalem: Academon (in Hebrew)

Stewart, Frank (1994) *Honor.* Chicago: University of Chicago Press

Swedenburg, Ted (1989) Occupational Hazards: Palestine Ethnography. *Cultural Anthropolog* vol. 4(3):265–72

(1990) The Palestinian Peasant as National Signifier. *Anthropological Quarterly* vol. 63, no. 1:18–30

(1991) Popular Memory and the Palestinian National Past, in Joy O'Brien and William Rosebury (eds.) *Golden Ages, Dark Ages: Imagining the Past in History and Anthropology* Berkeley: University of California Press

Swirski, Shlomo (1985) *The Development Towns of Israel.* Haifa: Breirot (in Hebrew)

(1989) *Israel – The Oriental Majority.* London and New Jersey: Zed Books

Tambiah, Stanley (1990) *Magic, Science, Religion and the Scope of Rationality.* Cambridge: Cambridge University Press

Taussig, Michael (1987) *Shamanism, Colonialism and the Wild Man: A Study in Terror and Healing.* Chicago: University of Chicago Press

(1990) Violence and Resistance in the Americas: The Legacy of Conquest. *Journal of Historical Sociology* vol. 3:209–24

Tedlock, B. (1991) From Participant Observation to Observations of Participants: The Emergence of Narrative Anthropology. *Journal of Anthropological Research* vol. 47, no. 1:69–94

Thompson, J.B (1984) *Studies in the Theory of Ideology.* Cambridge: Polity Press

Trope, Y. (1989) Stereotypes and Dispositional Judgement, in D. Bar-Tal et al. (eds.) *Stereotyping and Prejudices.* New York: Pringer Verlag

Tsimhoni, Daphna (1989) The Political Configuration of the Christians in the State of Israel. *Hamizrah Hahadash* vol. 32 (128–5):139–64

Weber, E. (1976) *Peasants into Frenchmen*. Oxford: Oxford University Press

Weil, Shalva (1986) The Language and Rituals of Socialization: Birthday Parties in a Kindergarten Context. *Man* vol. 21, no. 2:329–41

Weintraub, D. and V. Kraus (1982) Spatial Differentiation and Place of Residence: Spatial Dispersion and Composition of Population and Stratification in Israel *Megamot* vol. 27(4):367–81 (in Hebrew)

Willensky, H.L. (1964) The Professionalization of Everyone. *American Journal of Sociology* vol. 70:135–58

Williams, C.H. and A.D. Smith (1983) The National Construction of Social Space. *Progress in Human Geography* vol. 7:502–18

Yediot Aharonot (daily paper) (1983) Zionism Natzerat Style. By Asher Meniv. 15 December 25 (in Hebrew)

Yiftachel, Oren (1994) Regional Mix and Ethnic Relations: Evidence from Israel. *Geoforum* vol. 25, no. 1:41–55

Zemach, Mina (1980) *Attitudes of the Jewish Majority in Israel Towards the Arab Minority*. Jerusalem: The Van-Leer Foundation (in Hebrew)

Zonabend, Francoise (1993). *Nuclear Peninsula*. Cambridge: Cambridge University Press

Zucker, L.G. (1986) Production of Trust: Institutional Sources of Economic Structure, 1840–1920, in B.M.Staw and L.L. Cummings (eds.) *Research in Organizational Behaviour* vol. VIII. Greenwich, CT: JAI

Zuckerman, A. (1977) Clientilist Politics in Italy, in E. Gellner and Waterbury (eds.) *Patrons and Clients*. London: Duckworth

Zureik, Elia (1979) *The Palestinians in Israel: A Study in Internal Colonialism*. London: Routledge & Kegan Paul

Index

Cambridge Studies in
Social and Cultural Anthropolgy

*available in paperback